Successful Dissertations

Second Edition

ALSO AVAILABLE FROM BLOOMSBURY

Educational Research, Jerry Wellington

Philosophy of Educational Research, Richard Pring

Research Methods for Pedagogy, Melanie Nind, Kathy Hall and Alicia Curtin

Taking Control of Writing Your Thesis, Kay Guccione and Jerry Wellington

Successful Dissertations

The Complete Guide for Education, Childhood and Early Childhood Studies Students

Second Edition

Edited by Caron Carter

Bloomsbury Academic
An imprint of Bloomsbury Publishing Plc

B L O O M S B U R Y
LONDON · OXFORD · NEW YORK · NEW DELHI · SYDNEY

Bloomsbury Academic

An imprint of Bloomsbury Publishing Plc

50 Bedford Square   1385 Broadway
London   New York
WC1B 3DP   NY 10018
UK   USA

www.bloomsbury.com

BLOOMSBURY and the Diana logo are trademarks of Bloomsbury Publishing Plc

First edition published 2011
Second edition published 2018

British Library Cataloguing-in-Publication Data

A catalogue record for this book is available from the British Library.

ISBN: HB: 978-1-3500-0487-0
PB: 978-1-3500-0486-3
ePDF: 978-1-3500-0489-4
ePub: 978-1-3500-0488-7

Library of Congress Cataloging-in-Publication Data

Names: Carter, Caron, editor. Title: Successful dissertations :
the complete guide for education, childhood and early childhood studies students /
edited by Caron Carter. Description: Second Edition. | New York :
Bloomsbury Academic, An imprint of Bloomsbury Publishing Plc, 2018. |
Mark O'Hara appears as principal author on the first edition's published title page. |
"First edition published 2011"–T.p. verso. | Includes bibliographical references
and index. Identifiers: LCCN 2017049000 (print) | LCCN 2017050931 (ebook) |
ISBN 9781350004894 (PDF eBook) | ISBN 9781350004887 (EPUB eBook) |
ISBN 9781350004870 (Hardback : alk. paper) | ISBN 9781350004863
(Paperback : alk. paper) Subjects: LCSH: Dissertations, Academic–Research–
Methodology. | Academic writing. | Education–Research–Methodology. |
Early childhood education–Research–Methodology. Classification: LCC LB2369
(ebook) | LCC LB2369 .O4 2018 (print) | DDC 808.02–dc23
LC record available at https://lccn.loc.gov/2017049000

Cover image © izusek / iStock

Typeset by Deanta Global Publishing Services, Chennai, India
Printed and bound in Great Britain

To find out more about our authors and books visit www.bloomsbury.com. Here you will find extracts, author interviews, details of forthcoming events and the option to sign up for our newsletters.

Contents

Notes on Contributors

Caron Carter is Senior Lecturer in Early Childhood Education at the Sheffield Institute of Education, Sheffield Hallam University, UK. She has taught on the BA (Hons) Early Childhood Degree at Hallam since 2007. Before this, she taught children in the 3–11 age range for ten years and served as Assistant Headteacher, Deputy Headteacher and Acting Headteacher, achieving NPQH. Her practice in school was informed by research. This included being awarded an MA in Early Childhood Education in 2005 and a PhD focused on 'Children's Friendship Experiences' from the University of Sheffield in 2013. Caron's recent publications include:

Carter, C. and Bath, C. (2016). 'The Pirate in the Pump: Children's Views of Objects as Imaginary Friends at the Start of School', *Education* 3–13.
Carter, C. and Nutbrown, C. (2016). 'A Pedagogy of Friendship: Young Children's Friendships and how Schools can Support them', *The International Journal of Early Years Education*.

Pam Dewis (SFHEA; MSc Health Promotion; HV Dip; RM; RGN) is Principal Lecturer at Sheffield Hallam University, UK. She has taught on the BA (Hons) Early Childhood Degree at Hallam since 2005. A nurse, midwife and health visitor by professional background, her specialist teaching areas are children's public health and medical conditions. She also supervises undergraduate students doing their research dissertations and is module leader for a final year undergraduate research project module.

Janet Kay is a retired Principal Lecturer in children and childhood who also previously worked as a social worker with children and families. Her teaching and research interests are in the field of children's social and emotional development, safeguarding and adoption. She has published a number of texts for students and practitioners in these areas and also has a PhD in parenting in sibling adoption. She has extensive experience of supporting the development of students' academic and research skills and supervising dissertations at the UG and PG levels. Janet is currently involved in voluntary work with adoption agencies to increase adopter feedback and to develop better post-adoption support.

Mark O'Hara is National Teaching Fellow and Principal Fellow of the UK's Higher Education Academy and a Professor of Learning and Teaching at Birmingham City University, UK. He works as Associate Dean (Student Learning Experience and Quality) for the Faculty of Health, Education and Life Sciences. The overarching narrative underpinning his practice in Higher Education (HE) is one of widening participation and inclusion, whether pushing for enhanced engagement and inclusivity among students or developing imaginative opportunities to empower staff. A major part of his work over the past decade has included providing strategic leadership in relation to employability, high achievers recognition, inclusive educational practices and the development of systems to support disabled learners. He chairs the UK RAISE Network's Special Interest Group on Inclusive Practice and sits on the Department for Education's Disabled Students' Sector Leadership Group (DSSLG). Alongside these student engagement interests he has led numerous staff development initiatives in HE focusing on teaching observations, programme leadership and personal tuition. Mark is an active member of the European Association of Institutional Research (EAIR) and was Conference Chair for its 38th Annual Forum in 2016 on the theme of Partnerships in Higher Education.

Jonathan Wainwright is Principal Lecturer in the Sheffield Institute of Education at Sheffield Hallam University, UK. He teaches and supervises across a number of courses in the institute, ranging from childhood and early childhood undergraduate degrees through to the doctorate in education. His doctorate is in leadership in children's centres, an interest which stemmed from a deep involvement with the National Professional Qualification in Integrated Centre Leadership. His current interests lie in narrative research, school governance and stories of leadership in specialist schools.

1

An Introduction to the Process of Enquiry and Research

Mark O'Hara

Chapter Outline

Chapter Aims

By the end of this chapter you will

- know what makes a dissertation distinct from other essays and assignments that you have completed in the past;
- have an overview of the process involved in planning, researching and writing an undergraduate dissertation in education;
- be ready to make the best possible use of the support available to you.

This chapter introduces you to the purposes and benefits of dissertations for students and offers an outline of the process to set the scene for the subsequent chapters. It sets out some of the key features that make the dissertation qualitatively different from most of the essays and assignments that you will have tackled previously. To do this it provides you with a brief overview of some of the salient features of undergraduate dissertations and directs you to relevant chapters later in the book that discuss these issues in more depth. The chapter also offers some general advice on good practice for students wishing to do well with their dissertation and, not least, on making effective use of your research supervisor(s). While the chapter may present the various components of dissertations in a somewhat discrete and linear fashion, it is important to remember that the reality is likely to be much more connected, iterative and, frankly, on occasions untidy. As a former British prime minister famously noted, 'events' have a habit of happening and you need to be flexible and responsive enough to take them in your stride.

What's so different about a dissertation?

Dissertations examine topics at length, with substantial reference to the relevant literature and other published materials in the field, and are characterized by an extended discussion of the evidence and arguments involved. In some ways the dissertation is the pinnacle of your undergraduate studies and represents a pulling together of all your earlier efforts during your degree to master your subject (Walliman, 2014). For those of you planning further postgraduate study it can provide valuable research training and for everyone it should provide fascinating, stimulating and sometimes infuriating opportunities to wrestle with intellectual and practical challenges as you

- grapple with the philosophical basis of differing methodologies;
- formulate, reformulate and refine your research question(s);
- struggle with some of the ethical dilemmas that research in education and social science disciplines can throw up;
- find and seek access to potential sources and/or participants;
- gather and try to make sense of your data;
- rise to the challenge of being a self-directed, self-motivating, proactive, well-organized, autonomous learner.

For some the dissertation may be philosophical, theoretical or be largely based on archive or documentary data of various kinds. However, for many students on degrees focusing on education, childhood, young people and families, the dissertation may also include a strong practical dimension involving experiments or primary data collection in the field (Davies and Hughes, 2014). It is important to stress straight away that it would be a mistake to see any one model as inherently easier or superior to the other, as each has its advantages and disadvantages. Irrespective of whether you are concentrating on analysing secondary data already in existence or are planning to base your work on the collection of your own primary data all dissertations are synonymous with intellectual enquiry and research activity. The following examples illustrate the almost unlimited nature of the topics, themes and questions open to you when planning your dissertation:

- Evaluating a Community-based Approach for Managing Juvenile Delinquency
- Conflicts in the Lives of a Group of Children with EAL and their Families
- Cognition in Children with ADHD
- Young Children's Imaginary Friends
- Violence on Television and its Effects on Key Stage 3 and 4 Students
- Gender, Self-concepts and Eating Behaviour in Young People
- The Inclusion of Children with Special Educational Needs in Primary School Lessons: A Case Study
- Mystery and Magic in Young Children's Literature
- Encouraging Physical Development among Babies in a Day Care Setting
- Multidisciplinary, Multi-professional Working in a Secondary School
- Enhancing Role Play in a Children's Centre: Practitioners' and Children's Perspectives
- After- and Out-of-School Provision for Children and Young People: A Case Study

An overview of the process

Deciding on your question

Although the heading above uses the term 'question', some dissertations will set out to test a proposition, to prove or disprove a hypothesis or to evaluate a set of interventions (Walliman, 2014). Many people will know even before they start their dissertation what the topic is that they wish to pursue. For others it takes a little longer to focus down on something that is of interest. From gestation to completion most undergraduate dissertations will take up the best part of an academic year, so it is a good idea to select a topic that will keep you interested and engaged over that time. Selecting a topic that has 'relevance' is a good way to ensure that this is the case. Relevance may be defined in a number of ways; for example, a topic may be professionally relevant in that it may be helpful in terms of your future career aspirations. Alternatively, a topic may have a relevance arising from its connection with the rest of your studies such as previous or parallel assignments. Equally a topic may simply have a personal relevance in that you have a keen interest in or passion for it, although if this is the case you need to be careful not to select something too unusual. Picking a topic in which little or no previous work exists may sound very groundbreaking but you could be making life very difficult for yourself not least when it comes to completing your literature review. There is a good chance that a dissertation topic could be relevant on more than one level simultaneously. The box below contains some brief examples of relevance and you are also advised to follow up on this section by examining Chapter 2 in which the business of choosing your topic and refining your question are dealt with in more detail.

Points to Think About – Selecting a Topic That is Relevant

Selecting a dissertation topic that is relevant in some way will help you to maintain the momentum over an extended period of time.

- Imran was studying to become a primary teacher. He opted to focus his dissertation on children who have English as an additional language (EAL). The choice was professionally relevant as it linked in well with ongoing national educational debates and as it might prove useful when applying for jobs.
- Mark's education studies dissertation focused on adult education in Sheffield since 1945. One of his mandatory education studies modules that year was titled 'History of Education'. His choice of dissertation had relevance in that it would allow him to make some connections between the two assignments and benefit from a potential overlap of academic sources and ideas.
- Helen's choice of dissertation theme as part of her childhood studies degree centred on the experiences of two families with children with special educational needs in mainstream schools. This was a topic dear to Helen's heart as she was the parent of a child with Down's Syndrome and had considerable first-hand experience of some of the issues that the move towards greater inclusion could throw up for children, their parents and schools.

Whatever topic you eventually settle on, the next stage is to refine and clarify the exact focus or question (see Chapter 2). While framing the exact question may sound like a relatively simple task it most certainly is not; in fact, for many people it can be one of the most intellectually demanding aspects of the process of completing a dissertation. Your dissertation may seek to forecast, to explain causes and consequences, to critique and evaluate, to describe, to develop good practice to empower any participants or be a combination of two or more of these types (Creswell, 2009). Not only does the act of refining your question help to keep your intentions realistic but it can also help you to clarify your own understanding and thinking about the topic, and this increase in your own clarity and sharpness of focus will greatly aid your attempts to work out what needs to be done and to plan a schedule for your research. Being more focused on your research question(s) helps you to organize and direct your work, provides boundaries, creates a framework around which to write and helps to signpost the data that you will need (Punch, 2005, p. 37).

As a rule of thumb the more convoluted and complicated your question the more confused you are likely to become. Try to capture your intentions in twelve words or less. Manageability is crucial and it is all too easy to start out with a question that is far too global in its scope, one that you could not possibly hope to do justice to within the time available and using the resources at your disposal (Greetham, 2009). Your supervisor will play an invaluable role in helping you to dodge this particular pitfall and early reading too can help you to become more precise about what it is that you wish to find out. It seems highly unlikely, for example, that you would be able to generate large-scale data. Equally the timescale involved in undergraduate dissertations may make 'before and after' studies difficult while the number of variables associated with some education and social science endeavour can make 'cause and effect' claims difficult to prove.

Case Study – Refining Your Question

Sandra, an education studies and psychology undergraduate, completed her research proposal form and took it to her dissertation supervisor for discussion. The form stated that the theme of Sandra's dissertation would be children with special educational needs (SEN). Sandra's supervisor pointed out that this was a truly colossal area of enquiry and that Sandra would need to sharpen her focus in order to develop a project that would be achievable given the time and resources at her disposal. After further discussion over the subsequent fortnight Sandra eventually decided on the following, much more specific and manageable title, 'ADHD: A case of atypical child development'.

Chapter 2 offers more detailed guidance on choosing a feasible research question, producing a research proposal, and thinking about your positionality and its implications for your methodology and methods.

Reviewing the literature

Looking at what has already been written on a topic will form a substantial part of your dissertation, and it is hard to underestimate the importance of reading in improving your academic performance. Being able to locate and access a range of relevant and reputable sources is a vital first step in broadening your knowledge of a topic and in helping you to think more analytically about things. The following sections offer a quick guide to searching and reading, although you are advised to read Chapter 4 for a more comprehensive review of reading for your dissertation.

When tackling a dissertation, you will need to read widely and often, not just about your chosen topic but also about methods and methodology. For many undergraduate dissertations, the reading starts early as it helps you in setting the stage for what follows (Cresswell, 2009) and may well assist you in identifying and refining your research question (Booth et al., 2013). However, there may be some instances – for example, if you are engaged in grounded theory (see Chapter 4) – where some of the reading at least may not start until later in the process (Punch, 2005). This section sets out some of the key things to think about in relation to the reading and literature reviews that are part of most undergraduate education and social science dissertations. Whenever and wherever your reading occurs, developing a thorough knowledge of the literature can help you to

- identify key features, themes, concepts and ideas associated with your chosen topic;
- position your enquiry within a wider context;
- refine your research question and design;
- make more informed decisions on the most appropriate approach(es) and method(s) to adopt;
- analyse your data more thoroughly;
- support your conclusions.

It is worth mentioning straight away that not all sources are equally regarded and you need to be sensitive to the different status that can be attached to these different sources. Official reports, papers in refereed journals and books by acknowledged experts are likely to carry greater authority in academic terms than opinion pieces in the press or internet encyclopedias. However, irrespective of the perceived status of your sources, you need to be ready to question and challenge some of the material and ideas you encounter. Reading widely will make it much easier for you to spot unreliable propositions and ideas as it will enable you to draw on, compare and contrast a much wider range of views on a particular topic.

Ideas to Use – Using Concept Mapping for Initial Searching

Concept mapping keywords, names and concepts can help you to search electronic databases and/or the internet.

Searching for material on the Early Years curriculum

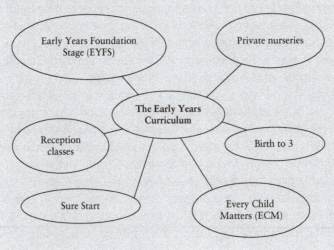

Ideas to Use – Cont'd

Searching for material on body image and eating disorders

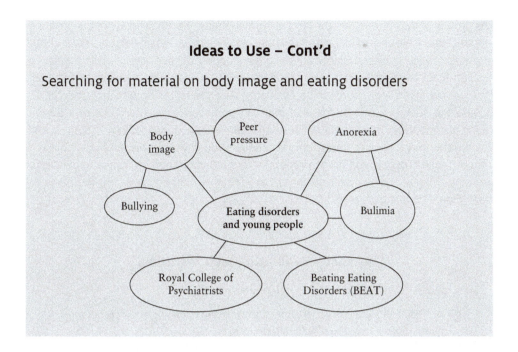

Having located likely sources, you are then faced with the task of reading them all. The classic mistake is to sit down and do an in-depth read straight away making copious notes as you go. Not only is this very time-consuming, it may also result in you simply copying out large chunks of text. In any literature search, you will undoubtedly come across material that is at best peripheral to your topic and which, in some cases, may not be of any use at all. It is much better to reach this conclusion early on rather than spending hours ploughing laboriously through the material line by line before reluctantly conceding that you have just wasted a whole evening. There are techniques that you can adopt once you have identified your sources to make you more efficient at reading and note-taking (Grix and Watkins, 2010). For example, if you are looking at papers in refereed journals the abstracts at the beginning of each paper can be very helpful in working out which papers are worth reading and which ones are not. Where the document you are looking at does not have an abstract or an executive summary try scanning the material fairly quickly to begin with and 'speed reading' to get the 'gist'. You may decide at this point that

- it does not contain anything of any use to you and you can move onto the next source without wasting any more time on it;
- certain sections look promising and these are worth looking at in more detail, even though you do not wish or need to read everything in detail;
- this is a key text with a great deal to say on your topic and is therefore worthy of extended study.

The growth of the internet and the increasing availability of a whole range of publications electronically have greatly increased the opportunities for accessing a truly vast number of resources very quickly. However, these developments have also created their own problems not least by placing temptation in people's way. Some web-based sources, for example, need their worth to be evaluated (see the following box and Chapter 4). Equally the sheer volume of material that can be accessed at the touch of a button can make stopping the search hard. At the same time downloading or cutting and pasting chunks of text from electronic sources as you draft your dissertation is playing with fire, particularly if you fail to properly reference your sources. You are advised to examine Chapter 9 closely for advice on academic writing and avoiding the perils of plagiarism (Pears and Shields, 2016).

Checklist – Evaluating Web Materials

Look for clues to the worth or relevance of web materials:

- Are you looking at personal web pages offering opinion pieces? A person's name/nickname in the URL could be a clue.
- Are you looking at a commercial site? Could they be trying to sell you something and might this affect the content of the site?
- Is the author/organization identified and contactable?
- Has the author/organization produced other materials in this or other media?
- Are you looking at material from recognized and generally more respected domains? Codes such as gov, org and edu in the URL could be a clue.
- Are the country codes in the URL appropriate for your purposes?
- When was the site/material last updated?
- Are there any links to other sites or corroborating materials?

Thinking about methodology and ethics

When considering your methodological standpoint, you will be influenced by your way of looking at the world and your views on the nature and limits of knowledge itself (Davies and Hughes, 2014). Not surprisingly there are differing philosophical positions on this matter. For some researchers, the social world should be treated in the same way as the natural world; in other words, the researcher's task is to develop theories of human behaviour and to discover universal, natural laws governing human activity based on measurable patterns and phenomena. In this world view, reality and knowledge are objective and human beings react in certain ways as a result of the environment they find themselves in (Cohen et al., 2007). This tradition is variously described as normative, positivist or objectivist, and researchers that are rooted in this tradition tend to adopt particular methodological approaches or styles characterized by predominantly quantitative methods of data collection, including questionnaires, surveys and experiments.

Others reject the idea of any absolute truths arguing instead that people are different from inanimate materials and from each other and that we all construct meaning from our interactions with people and events and that consequently our perceptions will differ and be unique. This alternative to the positivist tradition is often referred to as the subjectivist, anti-positivist or interpretivist tradition (Denzin and Lincoln, 2011). In this world view, human beings do not just respond to their environment, instead they are active participants in that environment and their actions have meaning. Interpretivist researchers tend to adopt methodological approaches and styles characterized by predominantly qualitative data-collection methods, which include interviewing and observation (Cohen et al., 2007).

It may seem as though researchers are rooted firmly in one research tradition or another, with, for example, one group using mathematical models, statistics, graphs, charts and third person aloofness while another relies on ethnographic prose, historical narrative, images, biography and first-person accounts (Denzin and Lincoln, 2011). Often, however, researchers adopt a more down-to-earth and pragmatic approach to their work seeing that the different traditions have different strengths and that all academic disciplines benefit from research using a range of approaches (Davies and Hughes, 2014; Punch, 2005). You may decide that your dissertation sits neatly and wholly in one tradition or another however it is just as likely that you will decide to adopt a more pragmatic and mixed-method approach (Cresswell, 2009).

In addition to the methodological considerations, as a researcher you must also approach every aspect of your dissertation in an ethical fashion. Searching and reviewing the literature must be unbiased and any quotes or ideas have to be put in context and be properly referenced to avoid charges of plagiarism. Similarly, when it comes to analysing your data and drawing conclusions the analysis should accurately reflect the views or expressions of any participants and any intentionally misleading or downright false conclusions must be avoided at all costs. You should expect ethical considerations to *pervade the whole process of research* (Cohen et al., 2007, p. 57). Chapter 4 offers a more detailed appraisal of the different methodological perspectives that you may need to consider and Chapter 5 deals with the ethical considerations involved in undergraduate dissertations.

Collecting your data

If a methodology is derived from your philosophical and epistemological approach to enquiry and study then your method or methods are much more operational in nature and are basically your answer to the question 'How will I find out?' All dissertations draw on some secondary data (e.g. documents, second-hand accounts and interpretations, official statistics), even if only in the literature review section. For literature-based dissertations the existing documentation and secondary sources of data will provide all of the data used in the dissertation. The list of potential secondary sources is considerable and could include books and articles written by other authors on a particular topic, publicly available official statistics, contemporary images, artefacts, eyewitness accounts and other archives, manuscripts or publications. Students engaged in these types of dissertations may need, therefore, to gauge the authenticity of these data sources as well as their worth on occasion (Cohen et al., 2007, p. 162).

However, some of you will also wish to seek primary data about people's ideas and perceptions and/or some of the events and activities involving those people (Walliman, 2014). Chapters 6 and 7 contain a wealth of advice and guidance on different methods and the box below lists a few of the most common. Seeking and gaining access to your sources can take time and while methods of enquiry are not necessarily the preserve of one methodological tradition or another it is certainly the case that some methods sit more comfortably within broadly interpretivist/qualitative approaches while others appear more frequently in positivist/quantitative approaches (Denzin and Lincoln, 2011). When you are planning an empirical study featuring primary data collection of some kind your methods are likely to involve one or more of the following activities:

- watching
- listening
- reading
- asking questions (in writing/verbally)
- setting structured activities/tests/making planned interventions.

Points to Think About – Research Methods

Examples of research methods often used in undergraduate dissertations include

- questionnaires (featuring a wide range of question types including closed, open-ended, multiple choice and scaled);
- interviews (including structured, semi-structured, formal, informal, individual and group approaches);
- observations (participant and non-participant, natural and formal);
- document/content analysis.

Many dissertations seek to acquire data using more than one method as a means of strengthening the reliability and validity of the work. Validity refers to the accuracy of your findings. Reliability meanwhile refers to the dependability and reproducibility of your findings; in other words, how confident you are that if your work was repeated it would throw up the same sorts of results all over again. Needless to say, the validity and reliability of any dissertation can be influenced by your methodology, methods, sample selection or data interpretation and data analysis techniques. Validity and reliability can also be problematic concepts for small-scale qualitative research projects of the kind that most undergraduate education students are engaged in. An alternative way of thinking about validity and reliability therefore is to ask yourself whether your findings are 'sound' or 'trustworthy' in the sense that they are the product of a rigorous approach to enquiry and constitute an accurate reflection of reality as you experienced it (Marshall and Rossman, 2006).

Every data-collection method has its champions and strengths as well as its detractors and weaknesses. There will not necessarily be one 'right' answer to the question of what method or methods to select. Instead in your dissertation you will need to set out your reasoning for choosing the methods that you have (see Chapters 6 and 7). The final decision is bound to be influenced by your assessment of what would best suit your research question and methodological standpoint as well as the nature of the data you are seeking, the options open to you for capturing and recording data and any ethical considerations. It is also advisable if you are planning to collect primary data with human participants to pilot your proposed method(s) to make sure that they do actually provide the sort of information that you are seeking and in a way that is manageable. Apparently simple methods can actually prove to be quite complex to carry out in practice. Piloting your methods can even feed back into your research question itself, helping to either confirm or clarify your purpose.

Analysing your data and reaching your conclusions

Analysing your findings is an intellectually demanding and organizational challenge, as Chapter 8 makes clear. Rather than analysing once you have done your reading and collected your data, in reality, the activities can often run in parallel for a time (Cresswell, 2009). The data may take many forms – all needing analysis and interpretation – including

- interview tapes/transcripts;
- questionnaire/survey responses;
- documentation/papers/correspondence;
- observational notes and accounts;
- audio/video recordings;
- photographs and other visual images.

For those of you opting for a qualitative project, data must be selected, collated, organized, categorized and possibly coded as it comes in to facilitate your attempts to make sense of it all (Denzin and Lincoln, 2011). This kind of data can be very complex and rich in character – for example, interview transcripts. Dealing with the written and spoken word will mean getting to grips with genres, styles and conventions as well as different registers and the specialized use of language in order to analyse the content (King and Horrocks, 2010). There may be critical incidents that need highlighting, there may be emerging themes, patterns, similarities and differences that recur across the data sets and at all points you are constantly having to question, test and challenge your interpretation and conclusions (Cresswell, 2009). This means acknowledging any data that is discrepant as well as that which supports your case. It also means checking to see if your interpretation is supported by any other sources. You are trying to put together a coherent story based on the evidence at your disposal, one which avoids unsubstantiated assumptions and conclusions, and a story which acknowledges the possibility of alternative interpretations of qualitative data.

Alternatively, you may be dealing with quantitative data which will also require manipulation to ensure that the information is accessible and clear to the reader (Punch, 2005). Quantitative data can have a certain cache attached to it – after all, tables, graphs, percentages and numbers look very 'scientific', objective, robust and highly trustworthy (Denscombe, 2007). However you do need to exercise care over claims of significance particularly with small datasets; remember the expression 'Lies, damn lies, and statistics'. Eighty per cent may sound significant but if your sample size was five it may be highly misleading. Similarly, if research does not involve random sampling then attempting to measure probability through the application of statistical significance tests may prove a meaningless exercise (Gorard, 2003). You should exercise caution about the application of statistical tools to small datasets, particularly where the data has been generated from convenience or snowball samples. Statistical tools only work properly when the sample is truly random, when there is a full response, no dropout rate and no measurement error (Gorard, 2003). With many undergraduate dissertations involving small-scale primary data collection, the data gathered will fall well short of these criteria and so the application of statistical tools risks generating invalid and spurious claims.

Data analysis is not necessarily about demonstrating or illuminating the undisputed truth of something, it is about summarizing and interpreting your findings and presenting trustworthy conclusions. This does not mean that your work will lack intellectual rigour as your analysis will need to be systematic and the data must be portrayed accurately and honestly, 'warts and all', including clear reporting of and reflection on any discrepant data. You also need to be careful about any claims made. Most dissertations – apart from those drawing on publicly available surveys – at the undergraduate level are unlikely to involve large data sets, and you should therefore avoid making generalized claims that cannot be supported by the evidence (see Chapter 8). In some ways, almost all empirical undergraduate dissertations have to be case studies of one kind or another and any claims you make therefore are likely to relate to that case alone.

Writing up your work

It is not enough to do some interesting research for your dissertation; you also need to communicate that fact effectively and Chapter 9 offers guidance on all aspects of writing up your project. Poor writing can seriously undermine all your other efforts and will affect your marks. A good clear logical structure to your account is crucial, as the reader needs to know what your dissertation is about and should be able to follow your thinking. In part you will need to pay careful attention to certain practical and technical matters such as spelling, punctuation, grammar and adherence to the conventions associated with academic writing. However, you will also need to demonstrate critical thinking by adopting a thoughtful and reflective approach to the literature, offering an intelligent response to methodological issues and analysing as well as reporting on data.

Far from being a summative activity once all your other work is complete, writing up your dissertation is actually a continuous activity that ought to start early on in the process. Nor will your writing follow an entirely linear, sequential pattern. It is better to see the process as iterative, as you will often find yourself drafting the various sections out of sequence as well as returning to them at different times to edit the text. Your course documentation will set out certain requirements relating to the presentation of your dissertation which you must follow if you are not to lose marks unnecessarily. For example, it is important to pay attention to the word limit and referencing conventions (Kirton and McMillan, 2007; Pears and Shields, 2016). It is not unusual for institutions to operate a system of plus or minus 10 per cent of the word limit before marking penalties are incurred. Adopting some simple writing strategies early on can pay dividends in the longer term, as the box below indicates.

Ideas to Use – Simple Strategies to Make Your Dissertation Project Easier

1. Use a word processor from the outset rather than typing up lots of handwritten notes.
2. Save your work regularly and back up your files.
3. Create a 'spare parts' file to store ideas, phrases, vocabulary and text for future use.
4. Be prepared to draft, redraft and edit; the best written dissertations have been worked on over time, crafted, amended and tinkered with.

Get into good habits, work hard but work smart too

Make the most of the support available to you

A key relationship during your completion of a dissertation will be between you and your research supervisor or dissertation tutor. The role of the supervisor is usually set out in course and module documentation and it is important to familiarize yourself with this so that you know what you can and cannot expect. Such documentation will often specify how much time your supervisor is supposed to give you, what the pattern of contact and supervision will involve, whether and how you can contact your supervisor outside of any face-to-face sessions and whether or not you are entitled to formative feedback on draft materials. Remember dissertations place a high value on learner autonomy and independence, so make sure you are proactive not passive in this relationship (see Chapter 2).

Your supervisor may or may not have an expertise that is an exact match for your chosen topic but she/he should have experience of research in general and will be able to guide you in managing this extended study. Their support may take a variety of forms ranging from leading group seminars, offering one-to-one tutorial support, providing advice and guidance via email and telephone and, in some cases, providing formative feedback on draft material. Your supervisor can

- advise you on your choice of topic;
- help you to refine your question;
- suggest useful sources and contacts;
- counsel you over methodology, methods and research ethics;
- check and approve any correspondence or data-collection tools prior to use;
- help you to plan and sequence what needs to be done to organize and manage your time effectively;
- help you to think critically about your reading and to interpret and analyse your findings;
- make sure that you adhere to your institution's administrative procedures and presentation protocols related to dissertations.

Supervisors will have limited time to work with you on your dissertation so it is important to make the best possible use of that time. Ideally your face-to-face meetings should be planned for so that you can get the most out of them. Do not just arrive without any thought of what needs to be discussed, be prepared to give a progress report and list any queries and questions that you wish to ask beforehand. It is also a good idea to clear some time in your diary following these meetings so that you can follow up on any of your supervisor's suggestions while they are still fresh in your mind. Having an outline plan or timeline for your dissertation will help you to synchronize some of these meetings with important milestones in your work, such as gaining ethical approval. Remember that at the end of each meeting if you have not already arranged the next meeting then agree a date and time as well as a schedule of what you will do in between. The final deadline also needs to be brought into your plans and you need work backwards to allow sufficient time for supervisor feedback on any penultimate draft followed by your amendments, corrections and additions; you may need to allow as much as a month for this to happen properly.

If your supervisor is expected to offer formative feedback on draft material then there are three important points to bear in mind before asking her/him to do so. First there will be a strong correlation between the scope of what you give your supervisor and what he/she can give back to you in terms of its usefulness. Supervisors are highly unlikely to look at endless iterations of your dissertation so make sure you do not squander this chance, give your supervisor things that are sufficiently advanced or substantial enough to make good quality feedback possible. For example, if you give your supervisor an A4 sheet of rough notes then the feedback he/she will be able to offer is unlikely to be as comprehensive as it would have been if you had provided a full draft chapter or two. Secondly try not to leave things until the last minute. Your supervisor will need time to respond to you; she/he will almost certainly have many other items on her/his 'to do' list including, probably, supervising some of your peers. Put another way, emailing a 4,000 word document as an attachment to your supervisor late on a Sunday night and expecting a detailed response by Monday lunchtime is at best a little unrealistic. Thirdly your supervisor can provide feedback and guidance but she/he is not there to write your dissertation for you nor does the feedback given constitute a guarantee of the eventual outcome. Supervisors cannot fully assess a dissertation in bits. Dissertations are marked in the round and so your supervisor will not be in a position to say to you that you will achieve a particular grade in advance of the final submission date.

Your supervisor is there in part to challenge you; hopefully she/he will do this constructively and sensitively but you must prepare yourself emotionally to take criticism in the spirit in which it was given. At times you will be asked to justify your decisions, to explain your thinking and to demonstrate your understanding and this may not always be a comfortable experience for you, particularly if you have invested large amounts of time and energy in a particular line of enquiry that your supervisor seems to want you to move away from. Remember though that being challenged in this way is good for you. If you can engage positively with the process and recognize that your supervisor's critique of your work is aimed at improving your understanding and does not constitute a personal attack on you then you will benefit greatly from the exchange.

In addition to your supervisors, universities have librarians and/or learning support advisers whose job it is to support students in upgrading their skills. These services should not been seen as solely for students who are struggling to pass; everyone can benefit from advice and guidance in this area and anyone looking to improve their grades including those seeking to achieve first class awards should make a point of seeking advice, particularly in relation to literature searches (Booth et al., 2013; Grix and Watkins, 2010). Library staff should be able to offer you additional guidance on ways in which you can get to the right sources and will be well placed to offer suggestions on possible alternative keywords as well as search tools and techniques. They can also help you to narrow down searches where the number of potential sources is simply too big to handle. Take the time early on to find out what your library and librarians can do to assist you in finding sources and putting together a literature review (see Chapter 3). Here are just a few of the activities they may be able to help you with:

- using information databases;
- searching the internet;
- guidance on referencing;
- interlibrary loans;
- gaining access to archives and other collections.

Keep an eye on the little things: Record your sources

Although you will be used to accessing a range of academic, professional and other sources during your earlier studies the order of magnitude and the level of material involved in completing your dissertation may represent a *step change* for you in comparison to previous, possibly less substantial, pieces of work. It is impossible to quantify exactly what this might look like in terms of the number of sources cited in your final submission as every dissertation is unique but certainly reference lists with 50-plus sources cited are not unusual and these are just those sources that are referred to in the final text, there may well be other sources that were consulted during the process of completing the dissertation that did not make it into the final list of references. Clearly then this is a lot of work both in terms of locating the sources in the first place and then gleaning useful information from them. Where you already know of particular authors, organizations and titles it is possible to get access to further sources as a result of looking at the links and references they themselves cite. However you may decide that you also want to do more open-ended keyword searches using electronic catalogues and databases.

One of the simplest yet most effective good habits to get into right from the start is to record, in full, all your reading/sources as you go along. This is vital, as you do not want to have to spend huge amounts of time going back to texts looking for page numbers or publishers' details. Keep your records in alphabetical order as you go and use this record as an opportunity to practice using the referencing system that is required by your course. Remember that when using material gleaned from the internet you need to note down when you accessed the material. Once again you may decide to opt for an electronic component to your record and there is software available such as Refworks (www.refworks.com) that will help you to organize your references. Chapter 4 contains more detailed guidance on using these kinds of packages. Your reading record may also contain more than just references and accompanying notes; on occasion it may also include handouts, print outs or photocopied materials. These sources can be bulky and get very messy, very quickly so make sure you keep them filed carefully and that you write the full reference on each of them at the time of filing as you will need this information later if you decide to refer to the material at any point in your dissertation.

Keep yourself safe

If your dissertation will involve gathering data from human participants then you ought to give some thought to whether your own well-being might be an issue at any point in the process and particularly during data collection. For the overwhelming majority of undergraduate education students personal safety and well-being will not be major considerations during the completion of their dissertations. However some research proposals may require a risk assessment. For example if you were planning to engage in some home-visiting as part of your field work you ought to contemplate any potential hazards and identify measures or safety precautions that would need to be put into place to avoid any harm coming either to participants or to yourself.

If your dissertation relies on data from human participants then it is safest for you to carry out your field work in public places such as schools or offices and your dissertation supervisor(s) may well prefer you to choose one of these safer options. However, if the nature of your research proposal means that you have no choice but to carry out some of your research in more private locations, then there are some simple security measures that you should take (UCL, 2017). To begin with write down the details of where you are going and who you are going to see and place this information in a sealed envelope to preserve confidentiality and anonymity. On the front of this envelope jot down your intended arrival time, your estimated completion time and the time that you expect to arrive back at your home or university. Give the envelope to a trusted and reliable person, either a fellow student or your supervisor. Arrange with your contact to call her/him at or around the prearranged times on the envelope to confirm your safety and agree what she/he will do in the event that you fail to make contact at the appropriate time. Leave your mobile phone switched on during any such meetings/visits so that your contact person can attempt to phone you if you they have not heard from you. In the event that you have not made contact and your trusted contact has been unable to contact you on your mobile phone the envelope can then be opened in an emergency. You should take precautions even if you feel the participant(s) you are visiting could not possibly present any sort of threat to you whatsoever. You might be right and your participant(s) might not pose any threat to you but you do not know who else might be present or arrive later. Below is a checklist for use if your dissertation will require you to gather data from people off-campus or in private locations.

Checklist – Research Risk Assessment/Safety Check

1. Will your data collection take place on campus?
    ☐ Yes (*Answer question 5 only*)
    ☐ No (*Complete all questions*)

2. Where will the data collection take place? (*Tick as many as apply if data collection will take place in multiple venues*)
    ☐ Own house/flat
    ☐ Residence of participant
    ☐ School
    ☐ Business/voluntary organization
    ☐ Public venue (e.g. youth club, church)
    ☐ Other (please specify) _____

3. How will you travel to and from the data collection venue?
    ☐ On foot
    ☐ By car
    ☐ Public transport
    ☐ Other (Please specify) _____

3a. If appropriate, outline how you will ensure your personal safety when travelling to and from the data-collection venue:
    _____
    _____

4. If you are carrying out research off-campus, you must ensure that each time you go out to collect data you ensure that someone you trust knows where you are going (without breaching the confidentiality of your participants), how you are getting there (preferably including your travel route), when you expect to get back and what to do should you not return at the specified time. Please outline below the procedure you propose to use to do this:
    _____
    _____

5. Are there any potential risks to your health and well-being associated with either (a) the venue where the research will take place and/or (b) the research topic itself?
    ☐ None that I am aware of
    ☐ Yes (*Outline nature of potential risks below*)
    _____
    _____

Source: Adapted from SHU, 2009a.

Summary of key points

- Dissertations are characterized by extended study and high levels of student autonomy.
- Getting your research question right is vital and it can take time to refine your original ideas down to something that is focused and manageable enough to be feasible.
- Every dissertation is unique but all will require the ability to engage in extensive reading, to deal with methodological considerations, to carry out data collection and analysis as well as drafting and editing throughout the process.
- Your dissertation supervisor is your most valuable resource, use her/him wisely.
- If you are planning fieldwork with human participants you may need to carry out a risk assessment and to take steps to ensure your safety.

Reflective task

As a result of reading and/or experience, what broad research themes are you considering?

For each of these what sub-themes emerge?

What is interesting or intriguing about any of these sub-themes? What questions could be asked?

Why would answering any of these questions be of interest or use? What might be learnt/gained either by you or by others? For example:

- Is it a chance to test a theory in a real-world setting?
- Is it an area where not much research been carried out previously?
- Is it a chance to try out a particular methodology or data-collection methods?
- Will it repeat a previous piece of research but in a new/different context?

How realistic / manageable / practicable /
feasible are your ideas? (10 = very;
1 = not very)

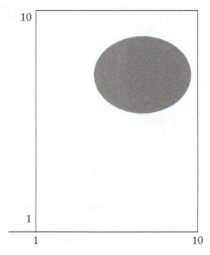

How knowledgeable about / interested in
them are you? (10 = very; 1 = not very)

Plot your ideas for research questions in the box
(Those that fall in the top right quadrant may offer you a better chance of success)

Link to companion website

https://bloomsbury.com/cw/successful-dissertations-second-edition/student-resources/
chapter-1/

Recommended reading and further sources of information

Bell, J. (2014, 6th edition), *Doing Your Research Project: A Guide for First-time Researchers in Education, Health and Social Science*. Maidenhead: Open University Press.

Denzin, N. K. and Lincoln, Y. S. (2011, 4th edition), *The Sage Handbook of Qualitative Research*. London: Sage.

Greetham, B. (2009), *How to Write your Undergraduate Dissertation*. Basingstoke: Palgrave Macmillan.

Guide to Undergraduate Dissertations in the Social Sciences. http://www.socscidiss.bham.ac.uk/research-question.html

Smith, K., Todd, M. and Waldman, J. (2009), *Doing Your Undergraduate Social Science Dissertation*. Abingdon: Routledge.

Thomas, G. (2009), *How to do Your Research Project: A Guide for Students in Education and Applied Social Sciences*. London: Sage.

Walliman, N. (2014, 2nd edition), *Your Undergraduate Dissertation: The Essential Guide for Success*. London: Sage.

2

Choosing Your Research Question and Getting Organized

Caron Carter

Chapter Aims

By the end of this chapter you will

- know how to plan and prepare for the various stages of your dissertation;
- know how to manage your time effectively in order to complete your dissertation;
- know how to identify a research topic or area of interest;
- know how to turn an area of interest into a feasible research question;
- be aware of the potential impact of your own positionality/personal story.

This chapter will focus on formulating a research question and explaining the concept of positionality. It will guide you through the several stages of identifying a feasible question, starting from broad areas of interest and help you to arrive at the final point of having a refined and polished question. In the process the chapter will offer some advice and guidance on time management and work planning which will be essential if you are to maintain the momentum of your research over an extended period of time and meet the deadlines involved. The chapter will conclude with an introduction to the concept of positionality which will be illustrated using two short case studies. By the end of this chapter you should feel more confident to begin your own journey towards a viable research question and to contemplate your own positionality in relation to that question.

Planning, and getting started

Just before you are about to embark on the final year of your degree course, you will almost certainly be asked to begin the process of identifying possible themes or areas of interest that might form the starting point for your eventual dissertation. The majority of undergraduate students will experience a degree of anxiety and even intimidation at the prospect of undertaking dissertation study. For some it is the sheer volume that has to be written that is so overwhelming; for others the concerns centre on the nature of the research, such as the challenges associated with data collection involving people. However, it is probably best to try and view it as several small assignments that will come together upon completion. If you keep an overview in the back of your mind but focus upon a specific section at a time, for example the literature review chapter, then this should help.

A key message to get across straight away is that before you do anything relating to your dissertation you ought to familiarize yourself with the documentation provided by your university. Courses vary from institution to institution but most will have some sort of written guidance in relation to dissertation study such as a course or module handbook or an online resource which provides detailed information and advice (Mukherji and Albon, 2015). This guidance will set out the arrangements, expectations and protocols associated with successfully completing a dissertation in your institution and it is essential that you follow it (Walliman, 2014). Such documents are carefully and meticulously written and should be referred to throughout your work. Check back regularly to ensure that you are keeping to course/module requirements. Expectations and requirements in relation to referencing are a good example of the need to pay attention to the guidance. Any dissertation must be clearly and properly referenced, but there are differing conventions and systems – some, for example, use footnotes, others do not. It is essential therefore that you follow the guidelines for your course; otherwise, you risk losing marks unnecessarily. Your dissertation supervisor will help you to stick to the arrangements for your course, but if you have specific questions you should refer to your handbook or online resource first before contacting your supervisor. It is a waste of their time if they have to repeat what is already in the handbook. The box below sets out some simple but very important questions you should know the answers to before you do anything else.

Points to Think About – Before You Start

Use your course documentation to find the answers to the following questions:

How much work will the dissertation involve?

- What is the word count and does it include your references and/or any appendices?
- Are there a recommended number of hours per week that you are expected to devote to your dissertation?
- What is the academic credit weighting of the dissertation in relation to the rest of your studies?

* Remember the individual nature of dissertation study can be highly motivating for many students and there may be a temptation to invest a disproportionate amount of time on the project at the expense of your other studies.

How long do you have to complete the work?

- When is the final deadline for submission?
- Are there any other/interim deadlines associated with the dissertation?

* Remember everything will take longer than you think so working back from the deadline can help you to plan your time more effectively. For example, you may be required to submit a research proposal before being allowed to proceed with the dissertation proper and if you are planning primary data collection with human participants then you will need ethical approval before any field work starts.

In addition to any written guidance, your institution may provide taught sessions on particular aspects of the dissertation, such as ethical issues, how to carry out a literature review or how to go about analysing your data (see the bulleted list below). Attendance at these sessions is vital as there is a strong correspondence between attendance at taught sessions and success in assessments, including dissertations. Tutors sometimes retain copies of successful dissertations that have been submitted in previous years and will on occasion use their taught sessions to give students sight of these. Although this might seem a little off-putting, particularly at an early stage of the process, it can actually provide a very valuable shortcut to enable you to comprehend what is being asked of you. As the saying goes, 'A picture paints a thousand words' and certainly an opportunity to look at how others have approached the task of writing a dissertation can be a very powerful learning experience to get a feel for the range of topics tackled, the diversity of methodologies and approaches used, as well as the layout, structure and protocols employed. Some university libraries also stock undergraduate dissertations from previous years that you can access; so, if your taught sessions do not include an opportunity to look at past examples, it is worth investigating your library catalogue to see what might be available elsewhere in your institution.

Points to Think About – Guidance and Support

What support and guidance are you entitled to?

- Are there any lectures and seminars accompanying the dissertation?
- Who is your supervisor?
- What are the arrangements for consulting and meeting with your supervisor?
- What other support and guidance – for example, library staff – is available?

*Remember dissertations emphasize student autonomy, so you have to be proactive; do not expect your supervisor to be chasing you, you will be expected to be able to take the initiative.

Student/Supervisor Relationships

It is important to develop a positive working relationship with your supervisor (Bell and Waters, 2014; Cryer, 2006). It might be useful to start the supervision journey by asking the questions.

1) What do you expect from your student?
   - To be prepared for your meetings (email prior to the meeting what you would like to focus on. Some bullet points will suffice.)
   - To agree a date to send drafts if you would like a draft read prior to your meeting, as supervisors will be very busy and will not be able to look at things at short notice
   - To engage and participate in sessions
   - To keep to deadlines and maintain contact with your supervisor (let them know if you are having any difficulties that may affect your work)
   - To keep a brief summary of your supervision meeting, including targets to work (Bell and Waters, 2014)
2) What do you expect from your supervisor?
   - To inspire and motivate students
   - To respond to emails within the specified timeframe
   - To read and constructively respond to students, work
   - To demonstrate equitable practice with all students

Talking with your supervisor about expectations can avoid any misunderstanding further down the line.

A third option when trying to get started is to talk to other students who have successfully completed a dissertation (Mukherji and Albon, 2015). The authors of this book can all recall being given useful tips by previous students – such as making sure to keep an up-to-date reference list as you go along in order to avoid having to scramble around hours before the deadline trying to locate references for sources that you have used. These were wise words, and it is something we still try to do to this day. However, although such conversations might provide you with valuable insights into the pitfalls and challenges associated with completing a dissertation we need to insert a word of caution here. It is possible that you might come away from such a conversation feeling more anxious rather than empowered particularly if the person you spoke to tended to overemphasize the negative or more problematic aspects of their experiences. This said though, drawing on the experiences of someone who has been through the process can result in some very useful advice on how to manage your workload effectively and how to avoid potential problems.

Choosing a research topic or broad area of interest

The first stage of a dissertation module is often to complete a preliminary research proposal form. This is often used to allocate you to a tutor/supervisor. The tutor will usually be someone with expertise within the field you have chosen to research. The purposes of a dissertation proposal include the need to provide a scaffold or framework on which you can build your understanding and refine your thinking. Such a proposal stage also gives dissertation supervisors an opportunity to spot problems at an early point so that they can intervene before it is too late to assist students whose projects are unmanageable, unclear or unethical (see Chapter 5). A research proposal outlines your work and is the study in a summary format. See Roberts-Holmes (2014: 89–93) for more detail. The proforma for such proposals may vary from institution to institution; however, the following elements will figure:

- often around 2,000 words in total;
- a title or theme, albeit a working title at this stage;
- the aims and objectives of the project;
- an overview of the question, problem, key ideas, concepts, debates and/or issues involved;
- some discussion of the proposed methodology and methods, including an acknowledgement of any potential ethical dimensions to the study;
- an outline of the anticipated outcomes;
- a schedule, programme or timetable for the project.

Checklist – Research Proposal Form

Topic: Outline the topic you are interested in studying and how you decided on this. Is this a personal/professional interest? Does it result from previous course work? Has a particular experience led you here?

Title: Do you have a provisional title in mind?

Objectives/Aims: By conducting your research what do you aim to find out?

Question: Do you have a potential question?

Background and Context: Why is this subject area important? What is the problem you wish to investigate? What is the issue?

Literature Review: How does this fit in with other research?

Methodology and Methods: Will your work be qualitative or quantitative? How will you collect your data? What methods will you use, for example interviews, questionnaires, observations, literature searches, content analysis?

Ethical Issues: How will you gain informed consent, if necessary, from your participants and/or gatekeepers? What are the potential risks, if any? How will you ensure that no harm comes to your participants?

Timetable: List the months you have up until your work needs to be submitted and set out what you propose to be doing in each to ensure that you complete your dissertation on time.

Conclusion: What will be the research outcomes? What will be the benefits of the research?

References: What literature will you be reviewing? Provide six to ten examples as a starting point.

Before you can submit your research proposal therefore, you will need to spend time selecting the area you wish to focus upon. Bell and Waters (2014) recommends that you select two areas of interest. The first, the main area, is covered in your proposal and the second is a reserve or fallback in case the first throws up too many difficulties and cannot be pursued for any reason. It is worth giving this part of the process a decent amount of time and attention because you will be devoting a substantial part of your final year to this study. Clough and Nutbrown (2012) stress how important it is to select something that you are personally interested in and that has some relevance for you as this will help you to retain your motivation throughout the project. Realizing midway through the year that you wish that you had selected something else when it is too late to change will make the remainder of your study a depressing and probably tedious experience.

In situations where you find yourself struggling to identify or settle on a topic and are faced with having to search more systematically for your theme there are a number of things that you can do to assist you in the task. Discussing the matter with your tutor or supervisor (where that person has already been identified) can be a good place to start. She/he will be well placed to talk about current issues in your discipline with you and to help you to gauge the relative pros and cons of any competing topics that you have in mind. Some courses will start the dissertation off with a programme of seminars and group tutorials which provide opportunities to compare notes with your peers too and this can be another useful means of triggering ideas. It may also be helpful to make a few notes on your previous experiences and learning to see whether your topic can be found there.

If you are going to start your project in September or October you could begin to think through possible topics of interest over the summer months while you have more time to mull things over (see the box below). Smith, Todd and Waldman (2009) use the analogy of deciding where to go for an annual holiday to explain the thought and consideration that is necessary when deciding on your broad topic, theme or area of interest. You need to ask yourself several questions and to read through the brochures before you eventually decide on a destination. This stage of the dissertation is actually quite an exciting prospect, particularly if previously your course has tended to prescribe quite tightly the scope and focus of your work. In contrast this will be an opportunity for you to select the topic or area of interest and it should be viewed as a *unique opportunity to explore in depth a subject in which you have a personal interest or to further develop an interest from previous study* (Smith, Todd and Waldman, 2009, p. 24). One of the joys of your dissertation will be the significant amount of freedom to go in the direction of your choice, allowing you to extend your knowledge in a particular field, to develop your passion for a subject and/or to make a contribution to your future career aspirations.

Points to Think About – Your Dissertation Theme

Consider the following points when thinking about the broad theme of your dissertation:

- think back to an incident on a work placement that would suggest a theme;
- consider aspects of your life outside of university that relate to your course – for example, voluntary activity, previous work or family experiences and responsibilities;
- reflect on earlier course work and/or reading during your degree threw up themes, issues or questions that you could now follow up;
- consider current events in the world around you could form a starting point; maybe recent reports in the press and other media have a bearing on your chosen discipline;
- chatting with tutors, colleagues, peers, family and friends might suggest a topic of interest that would sustain your interest over the year;
- do a key word search and a bit of background reading in your library to help you identify a likely looking topic.

Narrowing down the focus and sharpening up your 'question'

Deciding on your broad theme will often prove harder to do than you might at first think; however, an equally challenging task now lies ahead of you and that involves distilling this broad area of interest down into a viable and manageable research question. For example, you could have decided that you would like to focus your dissertation on the theme of disability and inclusion in education, but this is simply too broad and vague a description to be useful. Without further thought and consideration your dissertation would lack a clear focus and sense of direction and purpose (Punch, 2014). You must be more precise and identify with much greater clarity what it is exactly that you wish to learn or explore. There are a number of techniques that you can draw on for inspiration when attempting to clarify the precise focus for your dissertation. The following paragraphs set out four alternative approaches using the theme of educational transitions to illustrate the differences.

One approach is to create what is sometimes referred to as a concept map or spider diagram (Bell, 2005). These are visual representations of your thinking, question what you mean and ultimately assist in narrowing down your focus area (see examples below). These visual representations should be working documents. They do not need to be neat as the purpose is to get your ideas to flow. You can use concept maps and spider diagrams to record and group what you already know or think you know about your chosen theme; you can also note down any questions, thoughts, ideas, as they occur to you often in a fairly random order before attempting to introduce a degree of order, focus and coherence afterwards (Bell and Waters, 2014). Not everyone finds this visual approach to clarifying your thoughts easy or helpful though and if this is true for you a second alternative is to opt for a 'list' approach instead (Mukherji and Albon, 2015). A diagram or list can also be recorded electronically using apps such as OneNote or Notepad to use on your tablet or phone (Bell and Waters, 2014).

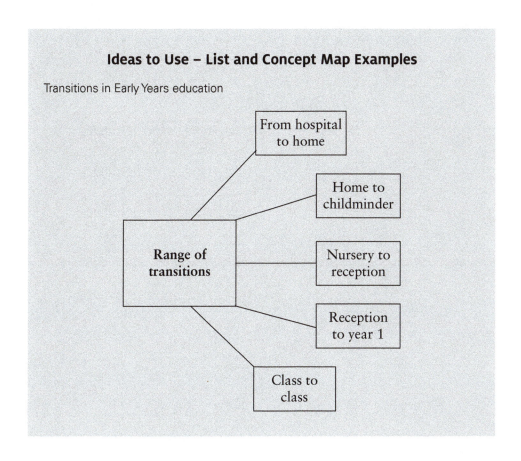

Ideas to Use – List and Concept Map Examples

Transitions in Early Years education

From hospital to home

Home to childminder

Range of transitions

Nursery to reception

Reception to year 1

Class to class

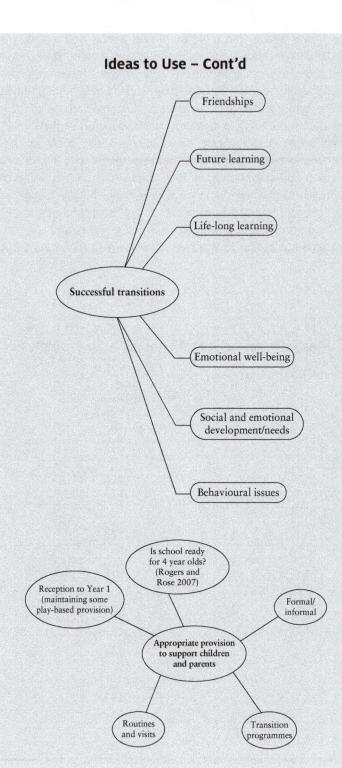

Ideas to Use – Cont'd

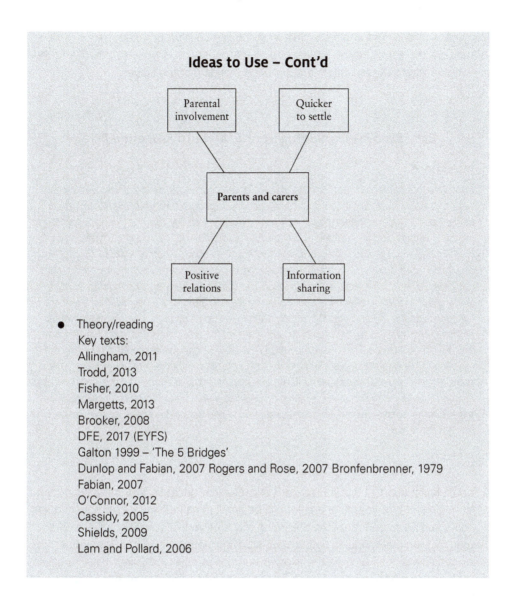

Ideas to Use – Cont'd

- Theory/reading
  Key texts:
  Allingham, 2011
  Trodd, 2013
  Fisher, 2010
  Margetts, 2013
  Brooker, 2008
  DFE, 2017 (EYFS)
  Galton 1999 – 'The 5 Bridges'
  Dunlop and Fabian, 2007 Rogers and Rose, 2007 Bronfenbrenner, 1979
  Fabian, 2007
  O'Connor, 2012
  Cassidy, 2005
  Shields, 2009
  Lam and Pollard, 2006

A third technique that you can try is to draft a paragraph for someone else to give them a clear picture of the issues (Smith, Todd and Waldman, 2009, p. 27). This would identify where your interest in the theme or topic originated from, it would summarize any relevant experiences and outline what links there might be to other academic or professional studies (see the box below). Cresswell (2012) suggests a similar strategy with the emphasis on identifying potential issues and problems and/or the need for study in your chosen area. Once you have drafted your paragraph you should ask someone else to read through it and to question you about it. This process will offer you some insight into how clear and concise your written summary has been. In addition, the act of having to respond to the questions is likely to provoke further thinking on your part resulting in greater understanding of the issues.

Case Study – Explaining Your Project to Someone Else

Transitions

I am a mature student in the final year of my degree course. I started the course after ten years working in industry. I had a company car and a good salary. I left this to embark on degree study. I had a partner and a mortgage to pay so I really felt that I was taking the plunge. I remember my first day at University. There were lots of younger students and I was worried that I would not fit in. I also had anxieties about whether I would be capable of degree level study. This personal experience is where my interest in transitions first originated. Even at 30 years of age I found the transition from employment to studying challenging. Managing this huge change in my life was not easy. I was able to relate my experience to the children starting school when I was on placement. My final placement is currently in a Year 3 class in a junior school. I am interested in how the transition process was for these children. They have moved from a small village infant school. There is lots of research in the field that focuses on the transition process for nursery to reception and also more recently on reception to Year 1. There is less on the transition to junior school. For this reason I would like to focus my research around this area. I intend to focus in particular on the children's perspectives. My initial question is: What do children think of the transition process from Year 2 to Year 3?

A fourth technique to help you to get your research question into perspective is to remind yourself that your final project will be small in nature. You will almost certainly be restricted by factors such as the word count of your dissertation, the work load created by the other modules that you are studying alongside your dissertation as well other considerations, such as the allotted number of days you might have to collect any primary data (see the box below). Taking these and other factors into consideration will help you to visualize the optimum scale for your project (Smith, Todd and Waldman, 2009). It is something that many students find challenging, but your supervisor will be able to offer you realistic advice and guidance on what is and is not achievable given the time and resources at your disposal.

Example – Understanding the Scale of the Project and Planning Accordingly

Question: How do children cope with the transition from Year 6 to Year 7? Approach: Case study approach focusing on three or four children involving:

- an individual interview to be conducted with each child (discussion focused around a drawing to illustrate their feelings/thoughts on the move);
- individual interviews with the two class teachers;
- a questionnaire to parents;
- asking the children to keep a journal/diary where they can write or draw as much or as little as they like.

Having brainstormed your theme using a concept map, jotted down your ideas and prompts, asked and answered questions or talked through the issues with a critical friend you will then need to formulate possible research questions to arrive, eventually, at your central researchable question (Bell and Waters, 2014). One issue that will face you is how to avoid simply repeating work that others have already done by injecting a degree of creativity and originality into the mix (Fabb and Durant, 1993). Nobody will expect you to come up with something completely new that no one in your discipline has ever thought of before; however, you must do more than simply repeat or copy previous research (Denscombe, 2009). There are a number of ways you might seek to give your work a degree of originality that do not rely on you being able to identify a completely new topic. You could, for example, examine well-known ideas but in a new context or setting; alternatively, you might find a way of using an interesting methodology or some novel data-collection methods. You might even seek to offer a new analysis of something whereby your originality is derived from the way(s) in which you compare, contrast and evaluate the strengths and weaknesses of different arguments.

As Smith, Todd and Waldman (2009) state, good research questions are *formed, shaped and worked on and are very rarely simply found* (Smith, Todd and Waldman, 2009, p. 28). You will probably need to keep coming back to your question repeatedly tweaking and fine-tuning it before you settle on the final version. In some cases, you may find yourself agonizing for days over a single word. Green and Stoneman (2015) calls this stage *step 1 go large*. 'Going large' involves writing down your broad topic area in the middle of a sheet of paper and then around the outside noting down as many potential research questions relating to that theme that you can think of (see the box below). You need to 'go large' first, and think about the bigger picture, before you can refine and go small.

Example – 'Going Large' on Outdoor Play

- What are children's/parents'/practitioners' views and perceptions of their outdoor play provision?
- How is the outdoor space used?
- How could the outdoor space be adapted to help develop children's literacy/language/mathematical skills/knowledge and understanding of the world/well-being?
- What is the adult role in children's outdoor learning?
- How does the outdoor area provide children with natural learning experiences?
- What areas of the outdoor space are utilized the most? Why is this?
- How are resources used to develop learning in the outdoor area?
- How can children participate in the development of an outdoor space?
- What learning opportunities are provided in the outdoor space?
- Does the setting have an outdoor play policy and how effective is this?
- Do all children in the setting have access to outdoor learning opportunities?
- Does the outdoor area provide opportunities for sustained shared thinking?

Once you have a list of potential questions you can then begin to assess them to see which ones have the potential to become *the* question. While there are unlikely to be many perfect research questions there can be *bad research questions* and you need to avoid opting for a question that is in some way inappropriate, unsuitable or unmanageable (Smith, Todd and Waldman, 2009, p. 29). There are a variety of criteria available in the literature on this subject that can be applied during this assessment process. For some a research question could be judged good because it is *relevant, interesting, feasible, concise, ethical* and *answerable* (Green and Stoneman, 2015). For others, the definition of a good research question is one that is *relevant, interesting, manageable, clear and simple, consistent* and *substantial* (Smith, Todd and Waldman, 2009).

Other strategies for determining whether your questions are worthwhile or not include applying the *Russian doll principle* or administering the *Goldilocks test* (Clough and Nutbrown, 2012, pp. 41–5). The Russian doll principle is shorthand for stripping back your question until you have a focused and more defined final product a bit like the tiny doll at the centre of the Russian doll. The Goldilocks test, meanwhile, is a metaphor for getting you to think about the suitability of your question by asking yourself whether a particular question is too large, too small or too 'hot'. For the purposes of this text there are four questions that you can ask to gauge the worth or otherwise of your potential questions: Is your question relevant? Is your question intriguing? Is your question realistic? And, is your question ethical?

Points to Think About – Your Question

Is your question relevant?

Your question needs to be clear and concise and relevant to your chosen field of study. It should arise from the literature and/or from your professional practice and should hold out the prospect of contributing to the existing knowledge and research in the field. Ultimately the question you have formulated must be researchable and answerable (Laws et al., 2003). This may sound ridiculous, but it is all too easy to get carried away and become distracted or sidetracked, only to realize too late that you have not answered your question.

Is your question intriguing?

The question you have selected should allow you to maintain your interest and enthusiasm for the duration of your study. Your *passion* for your chosen focus will see you through those challenging, depressing days when you find yourself struggling to write a section, or when your interviewees have failed to turn up or when things in general just seem to be going wrong (Game and Metcalfe, 1996).

Is your question realistic?

This is where you need to be sensible and to reflect on the time and resources that you have at your disposal. You need to be confident that you will have sufficient time to collect the data you would need to answer the question, that any costs that might be involved are tolerable and that you have the necessary skills.

Is your question ethical?

An ethical approach will need to characterize your dissertation from start to finish (see Chapter 5). You have a duty to abide by ethical principles such as doing good, avoiding harm and ensuring informed consent, participant autonomy, confidentiality and anonymity. When weighing up your alternative research questions therefore you will need to reject any that would put these principles at risk.

At this stage you may have more than one question with the potential to become the focus of your dissertation and so you will need to eliminate some and refine others (Green and Stoneman, 2012). This may involve ranking your questions, deciding which could be main questions and which could be sub-questions. You will have to think carefully about the wording of each question too, and it is highly likely that you will find yourself returning to the questions regularly in this early stage to reword and amend them. Keep a record of your thinking so that you can show the development and evolution of your question(s); this may prove useful in discussions with your supervisor. It is possible that you may end up with a single, overarching question accompanied by a small number of sub-questions, as in the example given below (Cresswell, 2012, p. 140).

Example – Breaking Your Question Down

Main question:
What are parents' perspectives on the transition process from primary to secondary school?

Sub-questions:
What support is available for children and parents?
What information do children and parents receive?
Can Galton et al.'s (1999) five bridges of transition (bureaucratic, social, curriculum, pedagogic, management of learning) be used to assess the strengths and weaknesses of current practice in the two schools concerned?

Additional research questions can be found on the companion website (see the end of this chapter).

Managing the tasks and your time: Get organized

Completing a dissertation is a challenge and your ability to do so successfully is greatly increased by thinking ahead and acting systematically. This is sometimes referred to as 'The 5 Ps'; planning and preparation prevent poor performance. With a project as large as a dissertation, attempting to keep everything in your head is likely to prove impossible and so mapping out a schedule or timeline of what needs doing and by when will greatly improve your chances of successfully answering your research question. It may feel a bit like the project management associated with construction sites rather than education or social sciences, but these timelines are invaluable in helping you to monitor your progress as you go. It is worth noting straight away that these schedules are 'live' documents and are highly likely to need a certain amount of updating and revision as you go along (Smith, 2002). You need to respond to changing circumstances to keep on track and on target in order to complete the work by the given date. Actually, the process of completing any dissertation will be much more iterative and complicated than any of the examples below suggest, but here are some of the things that you will need to plan for once you have decided on the exact focus of your research:

- getting institutional ethical approval (particularly for dissertations involving primary data collection with human subjects);
- reading for the literature review;
- reading for the methodology and methods section(s);
- data collection;
- data analysis; developing your arguments, theories and/or hypotheses;
- drawing your conclusions and completing the final written dissertation.

Ideas to Use – Sample Dissertation Schedules

Dissertation involving human subjects and the collection of primary data in the field

	September	October	November	December	January	February	March	April	May	June
Identify questions/aims/objectives	■	■	■							
Review the literature	■		■					■		
Decide on the most appropriate methodology/methods			■							
Consider any ethical issues or dilemmas	■									
Design data-collection tools	■									
Recruit research participants	■	■								
Pilot data-collection tools				■						
Initial analysis and refinement of data-collection tools				■						
Data collection	■									
Analysis and reflection	■							■		
Making links between analysis and the literature. Drawing conclusions	■					■		■		
Draft chapters/Writing up			■		■			■		■

Dissertation involving library/archive-based data collection

	September	October	November	December	January	February	March	April	May	June
Clarify research question(s)	■	■								
Develop a manageable proposal		■	■							
Select appropriate method(s) of enquiry		■								
Review others' research and other literature	■	■								
Secure access/permissions to data			■	■						
Collect and evaluate data			■	■						
Analyse, reflect on and discuss findings					■	■	■	■		
Draft chapters/Writing up			■					■		

Any dissertation likely to involve primary data collection with human participants will make additional organizational demands on you as it can be a particularly time-consuming and sometimes frustrating process. For example, drafting an interview schedule takes time and is likely to involve a number of versions; similarly, your research participants may not be available at the times of your choice, and if you are planning to transcribe interview data you may need to allow as much as four or five hours for the transcription of just one hour of conversation. As a result of these and other difficulties it is a good idea to build in more time than you think you will need (*slippage time*) to give yourself a cushion that will protect you against the inevitable complications that arise from time to time (Smith, Todd and Waldman, 2009). Those of you planning dissertations involving primary data collection will therefore also need to think ahead about when you are going to

- secure permissions and access to your sample population(s), setting(s) or data sources;
- pilot any draft data-collection tools;
- record, code, transcribe and organize your data.

If at any point in your study you find that you are going off track then talk to your supervisor straight away. She/he will be able to help you to refocus and get back on schedule. Do not leave it until you are so far behind that you cannot hope to catch up in the time remaining.

Journaling

As part of your efforts to get organized you might wish to consider keeping a research diary or journal and this is the time to begin doing so (Moon, 2006; Clough and Nutbrown, 2012). It is difficult to retain information along the research journey and a journal of this sort which is a live document offers a good way of capturing your ideas, evaluations and reflections as they happen. It can be a good idea therefore to create a log, diary or notebook of some kind (possibly in electronic form) where you can store your thoughts, jottings, prompts, questions, factual information, plans and timetables as you go along (Creme and Lea, 2008). Bell and Waters (2014: 40) state the merits of keeping a journal and view this as 'writing as you go along'. If your preference is for an electronic form of research journal that can be carried around with you, Bell and Waters (2014) advise the use of a note-taking app or an audio-recording facility on your mobile phone. The list below highlights some of the material that might be included into a journal/log of this sort.

Ideas to Use – Write a Dissertation Journal

What could go into your journal?

- Ideas, thoughts, questions, reflections, concept maps on interest areas
- Notes on what you have read
- References for future reading
- Relevant discussions with tutors, colleagues, peers, friends, family
- Notes on the problem/need for study
- Notes on related materials from newspapers, radio, internet
- Questions around your selected area
- Potential main questions and sub-questions
- Notes/thoughts on possible methods and methodology
- Comments on your own positionality and any implications for your research
- Notes on data-collection sessions

Source: Adapted from Roberts-Holmes, 2005 and Smith, Todd and Waldman, 2009.

As you write up your dissertation you may find that your journal proves to be invaluable and should help you in the task of reflecting critically upon everything from the literature, to the data, to the process of the research itself (see the example below). Having a repository for these things helps you to marshal your ideas and organize your time more efficiently, it will also help you to be accountable – something that is equally important for you as a researcher (Denscombe, 2009). Start the diary as soon as you start your dissertation journey and get into the habit of writing little and often (Bell and Waters, 2014).

Example – Extracts from a Research Journal

Entry 1

Child behaving badly? It's permissive parents' fault
This article reports on a small minority of children who are allegedly throwing tantrums in class because they cannot get their own way. It says that research indicates that parents are indulging children and not saying 'no' to them. Refer back to this article. Where was the research conducted? How many schools were involved in the study? (Curtis, 2008)

Entry 2

Had a discussion with Rachel (work colleague) about ASBOs. She mentioned a recent incident where a 19-year-old male had committed suicide. He had an ASBO and a photograph was put up in the street naming and shaming him. Consequently, he ended his life. His mother felt that this public humiliation was what caused him to commit suicide. Must look for the newspaper articles about this story as it portrays the negative side of the utilization of ASBOs.

Example – Cont'd

Entry 3

Spoke to Eric, who owns a small business in the village. He was adjusting some tarpaulin, and I asked if he was replacing a pane of glass. Eric said that he did not replace broken glass anymore as young kids just break them again. He said since the garage next to his business had started to sell alcohol, young folks had started to hang around and cause problems. He went on to say that 12–16-year-olds were drinking alcohol, taking drugs and were not interested in going to college or University. Eric felt that this did not bode well for the future and questioned what future these young people would have. I thought this rant was interesting seeing as this week the media has been full of reports about children who binge drink. An Ofsted report discussed a poll that had been conducted. It discusses the levels of smoking, drinking and drug abuse among children. This is all part of a drive to listen to children. See newspaper clippings below.

Entry 4

Useful quote from Maybin and Woodhead (2003, p. 56)
   'Childhood is a social phenomenon … socially constructed. … These are human creations that regulate children's lives.'
   Need to refer back to this – could support the argument that society needs to take some responsibility. Could link to work by Sue Palmer on Toxic Childhood.

Your journal will be personal to you and the layout and format that you use will be of your own choice. If you decide to opt for an electronic approach to a research log/journal then make sure you back up all your files as insurance against any technical problems and take care with 'version control' to avoid overwriting important information or replacing updated text with out-of-date versions. Some courses/modules require students to submit a separate piece of work focused on the critical reflection of their dissertation journey; for others, it is integrated into the rest of the finished thesis and forms part of the process of writing up the dissertation. Either way keeping a diary/journal can be a very effective way of improving your organization and management of your research.

Positionality and reflexivity

Your positionality and the need to be reflexive are key elements to consider when selecting a dissertation topic and question that will involve empirical data collection and human participants, will concern positionality and reflexivity (library- and archive-based dissertations are not immune from the need to think about these things either).

The terms positionality and reflexivity refer to the fact that who you are and what you believe in will influence how you view the world and events in it; how you behave in certain contexts and how other people may behave towards you.

Reflexivity is the term sometimes used in relation to the first of these issues, that is the need to remain aware of how your views, beliefs, biases and assumptions might influence your research (Roberts-Holmes, 2014; Mukherji and Albon, 2015). For example, you may be conscious that you feel very strongly about your area of interest and that this needs to be acknowledged in your work. If you do not acknowledge and reflect on your ideas, expectations and beliefs during the research process it is possible that these strongly held views could lead you to dismiss certain alternative viewpoints without sufficient consideration when in fact you ought to *remain open to others' viewpoints and perspectives* even if you choose not to agree with them (Roberts-Holmes, 2014, p. 17). Just as importantly the failure to conduct your work in a suitably reflexive fashion could result in you missing things, ignoring key data that do not fit your world view or acting in a manner that does not fully take into consideration the needs and rights of any research participants.

Case Study – Being Reflexive

Jenny's research focused on the experience of mothers returning to work after having a child/children. She was interested in mothers' views and perceptions on the return to work process and the challenges and difficulties that some mothers face during this time. When Jenny had her first child she had not anticipated how challenging she would find it to return to work. She initially planned to take nine months maternity leave and then her son would go to a local nursery near to her workplace. All the arrangements were put in place while Jenny was still pregnant. She visited several nurseries in the run-up to giving birth and decided on a particular nursery which had been recommended to her by a colleague. However, when Oliver was 4 months old Jenny went for a second visit to the nursery. This time she felt quite different than when she had been pregnant. As she walked around the setting she had a lump in her throat and was not sure why. The nursery was lovely and the practitioners were kind and gentle. Jenny then spent two weeks feeling very anxious about what to do and could not think about returning to work. As the nine-months period started to draw to an end she spoke to her line manager. Luckily, they had a very good relationship and she also had three children of her own so could identify and empathize with how Jenny was feeling. After this discussion and chatting with her partner, Jenny decided to take a further three months off work. While she was on this extended maternity leave, a friend phoned her to say that a mutual friend of theirs had started to childmind. This was an option that Jenny had not considered before. She decided to meet this friend for a coffee and as a result Oliver went to the childminder and Jenny returned to work after her 12 months leave.

Case Study – Cont'd

Jenny realized that she had never really appreciated how challenging it is for some mothers to return to work. Before she had Oliver she had sometimes been quite dismissive when on placement and had often felt that some mothers were just fussing. Similarly, she now recognized the significance of parents feeling confident and contented with their choice of childcare provision. Jenny hoped that listening to other mothers and researching their stories would help to inform and improve her future work as an Early Years practitioner.

As an example of the second element, that is how your positionality might affect the behaviour of others, imagine yourself in the position of being a male student interested in researching young children's experiences of music in nursery settings. In this case people's perceptions of men wanting to work with young children are something that you would have to consider (Sumsion, 2002). These perceptions might impact adversely on your ability to gain access to some nurseries and to find willing participants due to suspicions or concerns about child protection. Paradoxically, in other situations being male might actually make access easier as some Early Years settings might be very keen for children to see positive male role models. Being aware of your positionality can therefore be an important first step in sensitizing you to potential problems before they happen and you need to plan ahead by thinking about how it might affect your ability to gain access, carry out and complete your chosen research. Below are some of the characteristics and factors that might generate issues associated with positionality.

Points to Think About – Positionality

The positionality criteria below could all impact on your ability to conduct research for your dissertation:

- Sex/gender
- Class/social status
- Race
- Age
- Disability
- Culture
- Religion
- Political allegiances/beliefs

Isobel's and Handa's stories, see below, help to illustrate the issues surrounding reflexivity and positionality. Both students were inspired by personal experience to pursue particular themes in their dissertations and therefore they both had to be careful not to assume that they knew the answers to their questions before they had started. At the same time, their positionality meant that they had to give careful consideration to how others might behave towards them.

Case Study – Isobel's Story

Isobel was an Early Years practitioner studying on a part-time BA Early Childhood Studies degree. When she was a young child she had found it difficult to make friends and fit in. Over the years the situation got progressively worse and she felt isolated from many of her peers. As she entered her teenage years she became more and more withdrawn and spent lunchtimes and break-times alone. She was bullied by certain individuals, where objects were thrown at her and verbally abusive comments were made. Several years later Isobel became a nursery nurse in a Foundation Stage 1 class. She was able to identify with certain individuals in her setting who, like herself previously, were finding it challenging to achieve socially and fit in with the group. Isobel felt particular empathy for a girl who was always left out of play activities. As a professional, she now understood the impact on children's health and well-being and also how this could impact on their learning. When she started to study for a part-time degree her interest in this area deepened. When Isobel started her dissertation module she knew that this was the area she wanted to focus upon. Her dissertation proposal set out an ethnographic, case study approach drawing on her day-to-day interactions with the children in her setting.

Observing and talking to the children would be Isobel's primary data-collection method. Interviews with fellow practitioners and parents would also be used to give a fuller picture. Her initial research questions were:

- How do practitioners identify children who are struggling to make friends?
- Can children be helped to learn strategies for accessing play?
- What intervention programmes are available and how effective are they?

Her own personal experience impacted positively on her professional practice. Isobel was able to turn her negative experience around for the benefit of the children she worked with. She sought to develop her own knowledge around children's friendships, through academic reading, researching and writing for her dissertation. Not only would this fulfil the requirements for her degree course, it would also enable her to develop practical strategies to help children's personal, social and emotional development and learning in her setting. However, as a practitioner in the setting Isobel also had to think carefully about how others might react to her – for example parents and children might feel unable to say 'no' if invited to take part in Isobel's research.

Case Study – Handa's Story

Handa was a student on PGCE secondary course and her first language was Urdu. As a child she had started school with some English, which developed well during her primary school years. Despite her positive experience, though, Handa had a close friend who had struggled much more to settle and fit in during her own school years. Handa's friend felt that she had not been supported enough in school as a learner with English as an additional language (EAL) and that consequently she had not achieved her full academic potential. Handa had also discussed the issue with members of her family and in seeking to find out about their experiences she also received very mixed views. Handa could not recall how she became fluent in English herself and really wanted to investigate the strategies that schools employed to support children with EAL. Her placement school was culturally diverse and she had recently attended an EAL training course that the school ran that sparked her enthusiasm still further. Handa's research proposal set out a phenomenological and child-centred approach in which she planned to conduct individual interviews with Key Stage 2 pupils in her class and use drawings and circle time sessions to help corroborate her findings. Handa's initial research questions were:

- Did the school have a policy for EAL learners and how effective was it?
- What strategies/pedagogies were used in class to support children with EAL?

Handa was using personal experience to inform her research. While her own experience was very positive she acknowledged that this was not the case for everyone. She needed to be reflexive and to bear in mind therefore that her own fairly positive experience could cloud her judgement; there could be many reasons why someone has a positive or negative experience. Handa's positionality also had implications for access and informed consent (see Chapter 3). Questions such as 'Does the school have a policy for EAL learners and how effective is this in practice?' could easily leave the school feeling that its practice was about to be openly criticized which would make approval and access much harder to secure. In the end Handa opted to merge her questions into one which would enable her to get at the issues she was interested in without antagonizing the school. Handa's final question was 'What policies and pedagogies support the learning of children with EAL?'

Summary of key points

- Use lists and visual representations to help generate your ideas for areas of interest and potential questions – for example, concept maps, spider diagrams.
- 'Go large' to help generate potential questions.
- Write a paragraph about your area of interest and the relevant issues. This will help you to clarify your thinking.

- Make sure your eventual question is 'appropriate, intriguing, realistic and ethical'.
- Keep a journal so that you can critically reflect on your study as you go along and at the writing-up stage.
- Remember to adopt a reflexive approach to your work and to be aware of your own positionality. What has influenced you and how have you got to this point? What are the alternative viewpoints? How might your positionality affect how others behave?

Reflective task

1 Start to make notes on your research. Use the subheadings: topic, problem/ issue, title, question, what will you read?

2 Here are some example research questions. Apply the Goldilocks test and the Russian Doll approach to the questions to evaluate how suitable they are (Clough and Nutbrown, 2012: 41–5).

Goldilocks test: Asks the questions – is it too hot, too big, too small, just right. Russian Doll Approach: Requires the student to strip back any unnecessary layers to get to arrive at a focused and clear question.

- Are primary schools meeting the needs of the children?
- Is TV impacting on children's learning?
- Can outdoor play improve children's behaviour in the classroom?
- What are children's views and perceptions of the transition process from year six to secondary school?
- How are EAL learners supported in the primary classroom?
- How is the key person approach implemented in an Early Years setting?
- How is breastfeeding promoted to mothers to be?
- Is social class linked to antisocial youth behaviour?
- How do international approaches impact on childhood education?
- Can under threes form relationships with adults and their peers?

Link to companion website

https://bloomsbury.com/cw/successful-dissertations-second-edition/student-resources/chapter-2/

Recommended reading and further sources of information

Alderson, P. and Morrow, V. (2011), *The Ethics of Research with Children and Young People*. London: Sage.

Ali, S. and Kelly, M. (2012), 'Ethics and social research', in Seale, C. (ed.), *Researching Society and Culture*. London: Sage.

Clough, P. and Nutbrown, C. (2012, 3rd edition), *A Student's Guide to Methodology*. London: Sage.

Kodish, E. (ed.) (2005), *Ethics and Research with Children*. Oxford: Oxford University Press.

Oliver, P. (2010, 2nd edition), *The Student's Guide to Research Ethics*. Maidenhead: Open University Press.

Smith, K., Todd, M. and Waldman, J. (2009), *Doing Your Undergraduate Social Science Dissertation*. Abingdon: Routledge.

3

Adopting an Ethical Approach to Your Research

Caron Carter

Chapter Outline

Chapter Aims

By the end of this chapter you will

- know what is meant by the term ethics;
- understand why ethical considerations are so important when planning and conducting your dissertation;
- appreciate the need for ethical judgements throughout the research process;
- understand the meaning of ethical terms such as informed consent, confidentiality and anonymity;
- be able to outline some of the ethical issues associated with internet research methods.

This chapter will introduce the concept of ethics and explain why ethics are so important by discussing some of the key underlying principles such as doing no harm, obtaining informed consent and guaranteeing participant autonomy. Examples will be given of past cases of unethical research which have helped to lead to the development of ethical codes of conduct for those proposing to conduct research in disciplines such as education, healthcare and the social sciences. The chapter will also discuss the necessity for ethical considerations to be contemplated throughout the whole research process. In addition, the chapter will explore ways in which undergraduate student researchers can seek access to research subjects and will offer an overview of some of the ethical issues surrounding research with vulnerable groups and individuals including children. The chapter concludes with a consideration of the potential ethical dimensions to document-based research projects and dissertations that do not involve any first-hand direct contact with young research participants, their carers or their teachers, including guidance on the use of internet sources.

The what, why and when of ethics

What are ethics?

Ethics is the term used to sum up the rules that govern a researcher's conduct when planning and carrying out her/his research (Walliman, 2015, p. 148). Ethics are in effect *a set of moral principles that aim to prevent researchers from harming those they research* (Dickson-Swift, in Liamputtong, 2007, p. 21). As such they are akin to the types of code of conduct that students and practitioners are often already subject to in professions linked to academic disciplines such as education, health or social-care services. In many cases you will not be allowed to proceed with your dissertation until you have been granted ethical approval either by your course tutor(s) or in some cases by an ethics committee. Ethically your project should be worthwhile in that it should be of interest and/or serve to inform. At the same time you must ensure that your desire to contribute something to your discipline does not overwhelm your ethical responsibilities to any individuals or groups involved or affected (Walliman, 2013). In short you will be expected to treat any participants with respect through the way in which your research is conducted and through the way in which the outcomes are communicated (Denscombe, 2009). As you read through the rest of this chapter you might wish to consider the two short scenarios below. They are two possible research dissertation topics each with ethical implications attached to them. Try noting down a list of the ethical issues that you think could arise for each scenario and what measures you could take to address them. The scenarios are revisited at the end of the chapter where you will find the authors' suggestions.

Points to Think About – Different Scenarios

Scenario A

You are interested in the issues facing education, health and social-care practitioners involved in multidisciplinary working and the implementation of inclusion policies and practices. You are focusing on the experiences of staff located in an emotional and behavioural difficulties (EBD) unit within a primary school. You want to interview the staff to get their impressions and opinions.

Scenario B

You want to find out about the opportunities for, and the incidence of, outdoor play for nursery and reception children in your placement school. You decide you want to interview the children to get their perspectives.

Why do ethics matter?

Following a code of ethics ensures that your research will have integrity and credibility (Walliman, 2016; Bryman, 2015). It is also a safeguard for you as a researcher in case anything goes wrong. The drive to develop ethical codes of conduct to guide research developed rapidly in the latter part of the twentieth century. It was lent impetus by numerous cases of research practice in medicine, education and the social sciences that at best might be deemed ethically dubious and in the worst cases have been judged crimes against humanity. During the Second World War millions of innocent civilians and captured soldiers were held in prisoner of war and concentration camps by both Nazi Germany and the Empire of Japan. Some of those incarcerated in German concentration camps including many children were subjected to Nazi medical experiments and many died as a result. None gave their consent. In Japanese prisoner of war camps meanwhile, scientists used captured allied prisoners of war for similarly lethal medical experimentation as part of their investigations into potential biological weapons. The post-war Nuremberg trials in Germany and their equivalent war crimes trials in Asia exposed this infamous practice in which people had been forced on pain of death to participate in experiments against their will. Not surprisingly there were calls for a universal code of ethics for medicine and science. These events led initially to the Nuremberg Code and then later, in the 1960s, to the Declaration of Helsinki, which aimed to ensure that such atrocities could never happen again (Ali and Kelly, 2011; Greig et al., 2012).

In addition to global outrages such as the wartime concentration camps of Nazi Germany, much smaller but equally worrying events in medicine came to light as the twentieth century progressed. The Tuskegee syphillis experiment in the United States between 1932 and 1972 also highlighted the necessity for ethical codes. In this example, 399 African American men were not informed by medical professionals that they had the disease syphilis. Consequently they did not receive any medical treatment for the disease which increased their suffering, caused unnecessary fatalities and placed others (i.e. wives and partners) at risk of also contracting the condition. The rationale behind this decision was that it would inform research into the disease because when these men died their bodies could be compared at postmortem to white sufferers of the disease who had been treated (Ali and Kelly, 2011; Marvasti, 2004).

The unethical excesses in research during the twentieth century were not confined to wartime situations or the medical profession; the social sciences were not without their problems. In 1971, the Stanford prison experiment (SPE) recruited a number of volunteer undergraduate students to participate in a simulation prison scenario. Some students took on the role of prisoners and the remainder became the prison officers. All the participants were made aware that this was an imitational experiment; yet, despite this the consequences were alarming. Those adopting the role of prison officers quickly became cruel and in some cases sadistic and violent in their role, while the prisoners became increasingly distressed and ultimately rebelled against the oppressive conditions they were being subjected to. The situation became so charged and dangerous that the experiment had to be brought to an early conclusion (Burkeman, 2007).

Clearly, the examples given above are extreme and may seem a million miles from the sort of research project most undergraduate students in education and related disciplines might undertake. However, even small ethical oversights can cause considerable distress to research participants and could undermine or even derail your attempts to conduct your research. For example, those of you planning a dissertation that will involve children in schools will need to consider whose consent you will need. Alternatively your work might propose observations and discussions with young people under the age of 18 in an out-of-school environment such as a youth or sports club of some kind and once again you will be faced with questions about whose consent you need and in what order. In many of these types of situations where potentially vulnerable participants such as children are involved it is quite likely that obtaining informed consent from practitioners without any corresponding consent from the parents or the children could well render your data collection unethical (Kodish, 2005). A more detailed discussion of the implications of conducting your research with potentially vulnerable participants can be found on pp. 126–32.

The fact that your dissertation may not involve data collection with live participants does not necessarily mean that ethical considerations are something that you do not need to worry about. Considerable sensitivity can still be required when basing your dissertation on other forms of data. For students pursuing literature- or document-based dissertations some archives have codicils relating to certain collections which place restrictions on their use. In circumstances where such a dissertation is about named individuals, a government agency or other organization the custodians of their papers or other archive material may wish or be entitled to review draft material. It is possible that they may even have the right to veto the inclusion of certain material in your final dissertation. Imagine for a moment the interesting ethical dilemma not to mention the need for diplomatic skills created in a situation where your dissertation, based on access to personal papers, minutes from meetings or policy documents granted by the custodians of those documents, had resulted in you reaching some less-than-flattering conclusions. Below are some more examples which might also require sensitive handling.

Points to Think About – Ethical Issues in Literature-based Dissertations

Even document- and literature-based dissertations can have an ethical dimension:

- 'Portrayals and accounts of child abuse in popular literature'
- 'Clause 28 and the treatment of gay and lesbian teachers in the British education system'
- 'Representations of black and Asian peoples in education'

When should you think about ethics?

Your dissertation tutor will provide you with guidance on underlying ethical principles as well as advising you about any administrative requirements. There may be forms that you will need to complete or checklists that you will have to go through in order to demonstrate that you have considered any ethical dimensions to your work. In addition, there are a number of organizations, societies and professional associations that provide freely available ethical practice guidelines covering a range of disciplines some of which are identified in the recommended reading section at the end of this chapter. You should also find that course and module handbooks often contain instructions about what is expected of you and if your dissertation involves human participants you are unlikely to be allowed to proceed with the dissertation until you have secured ethical approval in some way. These processes show that you have had to think your research through carefully at the start and that you are following ethical codes of conduct. Some courses require students to submit an ethical approval or research ethics proposal form before any field work can begin. In many institutions low-risk undergraduate research projects are often reviewed for their ethical robustness using a process of local self-regulation and your dissertation supervisors will be the people who give ethical approval for you to proceed, or not. However, in cases where the ethical considerations are particularly complex or challenging the decision might have to be taken by a more formal ethics committee within your department, faculty or university. Such a process is more likely if you are engaged in postgraduate research nevertheless if you do find that your research proposal needs to go through a committee of this sort it can be a time-consuming process so start early to avoid any unnecessary delays. If you are intending to work with children your project may be reviewed as high-risk research and will be reviewed intensively by your university. Again, this may take longer. Be careful not to underestimate the fact that this stage of your research will be time-consuming. Make sure that you leave sufficient time to put in your application and then to address any requested revisions. One way to make sure that you achieve this is to start thinking about a potential research topic and question at the end of your second year and certainly over the summer break. Usually, you will be expected to complete your dissertation in just two semesters so time management and getting ahead are crucial. When working with children, you will also need to consider how you will develop a rapport with them so they feel at ease (Coady, 2010). Your methods will need to be appropriate for the age and/or stage of the children and you will need to reflect on how you will sustain their interest. Children may not be as interested as you are and you will need to respect this where necessary. As Roberts-Holmes (2014: 57) states '*Very young children may indicate that they like or dislike taking part in a research study in a number of different ways'*. Be prepared for some honest and '*unflattering feedback*' (Sargeant and Harcourt, 2012: 18). The researcher's role is to listen to children's viewpoints. This could mean bringing a session to end prematurely.

Checklist – Ethical Approval Questionnaire

1. Describe your arrangements for selecting/sampling and briefing potential participants. This should include copies of any advertisements for volunteers or letters to individuals/organizations inviting participation.

2. Describe any possible negative consequences of participation in the research along with the ways in which these consequences will be limited. This should include details, where appropriate, of any withholding of information or misleading of participants along with a justification of why this is necessary.

3. Describe how participants will be made aware of their right to withdraw from the research. This should also include information about participants' right to withhold information.

4. Describe the arrangements for obtaining participants' consent. This should include copies of the information that they will receive and written consent forms where appropriate. If children or vulnerable people are to be participants in the study, details of the arrangements for obtaining consent from those acting in loco parentis or as advocates should be provided.

5. If you intend to undertake research with children or other vulnerable participants does the data collection involve you being alone with the participant(s)? Please provide details.

6. If your data collection requires that you work alone with children or other vulnerable participants, have you undergone Criminal Records Bureau screening? Please supply details.

7. Describe the arrangements for debriefing the participants. This should include copies of information that participants will receive where appropriate.

8. Describe the arrangements for ensuring participant confidentiality. This should include details of how data will be stored and how results will be presented.

9. Are there any conflicts of interest in you undertaking this research; for example, are you undertaking research on work colleagues? Please supply details.

Source: SHU, 2009b

A common misconception is that ethical issues only need to be considered at the planning and designing stage of a research project or dissertation. Instead in many cases ethical considerations will often be a recurring theme that crops up during the process at a number of points (Roberts-Holmes, 2014). For example, the data-collection stage of your research is likely to throw up numerous ethical issues such as ensuring that even contradictory or discrepant data is not destroyed or ignored but is recorded and considered alongside everything else. Nor will these ongoing ethical considerations be restricted to data collection. Keeping a research diary or log can be an effective way of keeping an *ethics checklist* and monitoring and recording your ethical decisions and thoughts as you go along (Walliman, 2015, p. 147). Such a record can be very useful when the time comes to write up your dissertation (see Chapter 9). Your supervisor(s) will be able to offer advice on the areas that you will need to contemplate before you start, such as:

- your research question(s);
- the rationale for your research;
- your methodological/theoretical standpoint and any ethical considerations relating to activities such as sample selection, securing informed consent, data collection and/or data analysis;
- any steps that you will need to take to avoid or minimize any potential harm or distress to participants;
- whether there are any issues of personal safety for you as the researcher and if so how you propose to reduce those risks to acceptable levels.

Key underlying ethical principles

Irrespective of your chosen topic or question there are a number of core ethical principles that any research must address. These principles are variously described in the literature; however, the core elements focus on the need for research:

- to do some good (*beneficence*);
- to do no harm (*non-malfeasance*);
- to be based on informed consent and participant autonomy (i.e. participants can change their minds and withdraw from your research whenever they choose);
- to assure participant confidentiality and anonymity (unless this places participants or others at risk).

Your tutors will be looking for evidence that you understand and can apply your understanding of the need for your research to be conducted ethically.

The following sections of the chapter discuss some of the issues raised for undergraduate students writing dissertations and offer some suggestions on what these principles might look like in educational and related contexts.

Seeking to do good not harm

Doing good is sometimes referred to in the literature as *beneficence*, a term which refers to the need for your research to be worthwhile in some way and to have a valid purpose. When trying to ascertain whether your research proposal is beneficent you can ask yourself who or what will benefit from it? There are many ways in which your work might be regarded as beneficial, if your research was into teaching and learning your results might be used by a school to inform future policy or practice in a particular classroom or even across the whole school. Alternatively your work might explore a familiar theme but in a new and different context or in a new way thereby making a small contribution to the body of knowledge in that area. For example, giving young children cameras and asking them to photograph people and places that are most important to them around their schools has been used before as a research method. However, if you were to take this method and use it to explore an aspect of the school environment or the curriculum where the technique had never been used before, you would be doing something original and the results would, therefore, be worthwhile as they might offer new insights into learning and teaching.

Accompanying the requirement that you do some good is the requirement that you do no harm; this is sometimes referred to as *non-malfeasance*. As an undergraduate student you are unlikely to be proposing projects that might deliberately put participants at physical or emotional risk although you still need to be careful that your ideas do not put people at risk inadvertently and this includes yourself as the researcher (see Chapter 1). As you begin to plan and design your research and then as you carry out that work you must continue to consider your participants' rights and dignity and the risk of any potential harm arising from your actions or inaction. The Universal Declaration of Human Rights and the Convention on the Rights of the Child outline basic human rights to which everyone is entitled (Greig et al., 2012). You will need to exercise judgement, in consultation with your supervisor(s), about what are and are not ethical and acceptable risks. To do this you will need to weigh up the costs/benefits ratio and try to balance any of the potential benefits of your study against the potential costs, including the costs to your participants. Collecting data and advancing knowledge should not be at the expense of those involved and ensuring that participants are respected and not harmed in any way should be paramount for the researcher during the design process.

At the very least those involved in your dissertation should be *no worse off at the end of their participation* (Denscombe, 2014, p. 143). This balancing act can often present you with some complicated issues in which clear and obviously 'right' answers are sometimes hard to come by; *the process of balancing benefits against possible costs is chiefly a subjective one and not at all easy* (Cohen et al., 2011, p. 52). Ultimately, the decisions that you make will be personal and reflect your own morals and code of conduct and when considering harm it is worth noting that it may take a number of different forms, as shown in Table 3.1, of which physical harm is only one kind (Denscombe, 2014).

A key consideration in relation to beneficence and non-malfeasance is the issue of deception and you will be expected to act with honesty and integrity at all times (Denscombe, 2012). With the development of internationally recognized ethical codes of conduct and guidance for researchers, occurrences of deliberate deception are greatly reduced. Where it does occur it usually involves participants being deceived as to the identity of the researcher, or about the true purpose of the research or that data is collected without the knowledge and therefore consent of either participants or gatekeepers (Cresswell, 2012). It is worth nothing though that the potential for deception is not just restricted to the planning and execution phases of data collection. For instance, if you have previously explained and agreed the purposes for the use of data you cannot then decide at a later date to use it without permission for another purpose that you did not originally specify (Denscombe, 2014). You are expected to keep your word even if that is at the expense of your findings. Ultimately *deception lies in not telling the whole truth* (Cohen et al., 2011,

Table 3.1 Types of harm with examples

Types of harm	Examples
Physical	A participant is injured during an observation when the researcher failed to intervene to stop the behaviour that resulted in the injury. An interviewee is assaulted by her partner when he learns that she has been talking to a researcher.
Psychological	Participants experience anxiety and emotional turmoil before, during and/or after taking part in the research due either to the traumatic, controversial or embarrassing nature of the topic being investigated or as a result of an insensitive, invasive or deceptive approach adopted by the researcher.
Personal	A participant finds themselves financially disadvantaged as a result of revealing certain information to the researcher. A participant faces legal/disciplinary action as a result of revealing certain information to a researcher.

p. 66) and you would be well-advised therefore to avoid using covert research methods as they

- ignore the concept of informed consent;
- may be an infringement of human rights;
- damage the reputation and integrity of social research in general and your thesis in particular;
- may result in personal and emotional harm to participants;
- may break the law (Homan, 1992).

Case Study – Deceiving Participants in the Name of Research

In 1963 an American social scientist, Milgram, wanted to discover how obedient people were to authority. Participants were asked to deliver a series of electric shocks to 'volunteers' out of sight in an adjacent room whenever they answered a question incorrectly. Those on the receiving end of the shocks were in fact role playing and were only pretending to feel the intense pain. However, the research participants did not know that these people were acting. Milgram encouraged the participants to administer increasingly powerful shocks despite the ever more agonized cries coming from the other room. Milgram's work certainly demonstrated how a high proportion of otherwise mild-mannered and decent people could be induced to behave in cruel and inhuman ways by authority figures. He had clearly deceived the participants because he wanted them to behave naturally and had he informed them about what was really going on the validity of the investigation would have been completely undermined. He also felt that by creating these conditions he would be setting up a mirror reflection of the kinds of practices that had produced the concentration camps of the 1930s and 1940s. However, it could be argued that the benefits of the work did not outweigh the costs because the participants were subjected to acute anxiety and stress by having to administer these shocks and were therefore harmed psychologically by the process (Silverman, 2014; Bryman, 2015).

Although outright deception is ethically questionable, the issue of honesty, openness and disclosure can be more complicated than it first appears. As Bryman points out, it can sometimes be difficult to know where to draw the line (Bryman, 2015). Although information collected covertly would likely be an infringement of people's human rights and could even be illegal in some circumstances (Liamputtong, 2007) providing too much information to participants and/or using inappropriate and overly academic terminology could compromise the collection of data. For example, long, jargon-filled explanations to young children might worry them or result in uncharacteristic, unusual or exaggerated behaviour. Some children might seek to play to the gallery or to second guess what they think you want them to say; other children meanwhile might become shy, withdrawn, intimidated or monosyllabic (Tizard and Hughes, 1984 in Clark et al., 2003). If you are concerned about how much information to share or the methods that you are employing you should discuss these issues with your supervisor(s).

Informed consent, participant autonomy and securing access

Before any empirical research involving human participants can begin those participants and/or their guardians need to have made an informed decision about whether they want to be involved or not and if so to grant their permission. Gaining access to potential participants is dependent on you convincing those in charge of your *integrity and the worth of your research* (Bell, 2007, p. 43). Informed consent is *the condition in which participants understand and agree to their participation without duress* (BERA, 2004, p. 6). Seeking consent by whatever means provides potential participants and gatekeepers with

- information about the researcher;
- an outline explanation of the research, including its main purpose;
- clarification as to what the level and nature of involvement would be for participants, including their right to withdraw their consent at any point;
- confirmation of the arrangements concerning confidentiality and anonymity;
- a summary of any anticipated benefits of the research including those for the setting or the participants (Roberts-Holmes, 2011).

As a researcher you will be expected to provide potential participants with *full and open information* (Denzin and Lincoln, 2011, p. 65). Not only is this in the interest of participants, it is also in the researcher's interests. If a research topic is not explained sufficiently and there is no time for reflection then this amounts to gaining only assent, that is passive acceptance or non-refusal (Alderson and Morrow, 2011). This could mean that in the short term your research subjects go ahead with the fieldwork partially unaware of both their potential involvement and the purpose of the project and that once they become more aware they elect to withdraw (Heath et al., 2007).

Case Study – The Absence of Informed Consent and Participant Autonomy

The case of 'Little Albert' in the 1920s demonstrates unethical practice in relation to an absence of informed consent and harm to a research participant, although research 'subject' might be a more appropriate description of Albert's status. John Watson was the researcher leading an investigation into how *early experiences affect the kinds of people we become* (Burkeman, 2007, p. 30). Albert was nine months old and the investigation involved him being introduced to furry animals and objects accompanied by loud noises which caused him, by association, to become afraid. Albert's mother, as the obvious gatekeeper in this particular case had not given her consent for him to take part. The experiment was conducted in a hospital environment without his mother's knowledge and Albert left without these newly acquired fears being addressed. Clearly, he had been emotionally and psychologically harmed and an informed decision by his gatekeeper had been neither sought nor secured (Burkeman, 2007).

Securing informed consent with adult research participants or gatekeepers often starts with a discussion, supplemented with written information possibly in the form of a letter or even a card or flyer (Oliver, 2010). The written information helps to ensure that all the participants have received the same core information. Once potential participants have had the information there should then be a period for reflection to enable people to arrive at their decisions about whether to decline or to participate. It is better to give a potential participant time to *read and reread the protocol for himself or herself at his or her own pace, and to negotiate any additions or changes to it* (Hart and Bond, 1995, p. 199). Not only will this approach help you to avoid any suggestion that participants have been pressured into taking part but it also improves the chances that people will make the right decision for them and that those who say 'yes' to you will be more likely to stay the course rather than changing their minds and dropping out part way through the process.

Ideas to Use – Sample Consent Letter

Dear Parent/Guardian,

A final year student from _____ University will be carrying out observations in school during the winter and spring terms as part of her studies. Her research is on boys and girls play in the outdoor area. The student will be working with Mrs Jones, the nursery teacher.

The student will make notes during her observations in the same way that nursery staff normally use for recording children's learning. In addition, some of the activities may be recorded using photographs, audio tape or video recording. All such images will be kept confidential and will not be used for any purposes other than the student's research. The university's ethical guidelines forbid any photograph to be taken of a child without parental permission. We would be grateful, therefore, if you could complete the reply slip below and return it to your child's class teacher. If we do not receive a reply we will assume that you do not wish to give your consent and no picture or video footage will be taken in which your child appears.

Thank you for your help and cooperation.

_____

_____

_____

Child's name _____ (*Please write full name*)

(*Please tick the appropriate box below*)

   I am willing to give consent   ☐

   I am not willing to give consent   ☐

Signature _____ (*Parent/Guardian*)

Date __ / __ / _____

It is important to make sure that your participants understand exactly what they have agreed to and that there is no confusion; *clarity, brevity and frankness are key attributes in providing information on which consent is based* (Walliman, 2015, p. 155). It is also a good idea not to make assumptions and to check in case of possible misunderstandings (Silverman, 2013; Bell and Waters, 2014). Drafting a letter that provides sufficient information in a succinct and readable form can be a challenge:

- Letters need to be clear and well written, show your supervisor before sending one.
- Make it clear that the research is linked to part of your university studies.
- State clearly what you are proposing to do and why.
- State clearly what you are asking people to consent to.
- Give a clear explanation of any time commitment that will be required.
- Tell people what will happen to the data that will be collected.
- Provide an opportunity for potential participants to ask for further details.

However, as the exercise below shows, although talk of informed consent may sound relatively straightforward, in many cases it will not be; seeking informed consent from research subjects can be problematic (Miller and Bell, 2002).

Points to Think About – Seeking Informed Consent Is not Always Straightforward

Imagine you want to conduct a series of observations of teachers in the classroom followed up by some short interviews:

- How could you communicate your intentions to prospective participants so that they are clear what they would be consenting to?
- How could consent be given and recorded?
- How could you ensure that the teachers feel able to withdraw at any time?
- It's clear what you get out of this process but what would the teachers get out of it?

Now imagine that the participants you wish to observe are not adult teachers but are instead 4-year-old children. How would this change your answers to the questions above?

Intertwined with the need for informed consent and autonomy, therefore, is the issue of how to gain access to your chosen setting or sample in order to carry out your research when this access cannot be taken for granted. You will need to demonstrate that you have given sufficient thought and planning to the study, including the purpose for your investigation. As Roberts-Holmes explains, gatekeepers of institutions are *doing you a favour by allowing you access to carry out your research* (Roberts-Holmes, 2014, p. 63). Gatekeepers such as nursery managers, company directors, local government officers or head teachers have it in their gift to grant permission or deny access to researchers to enter a setting and carry out their work. Access via these gatekeepers needs to be carefully negotiated both in writing and in person. Having something in writing provides an important safeguard and record for you in the event that there is any subsequent dispute about what was agreed in the initial stages. It is also the researchers, responsibility to make sure that 'participants understand what they are consenting to' (Robson and McCartan, 2013, p. 215). Ideally, a draft letter taken in person to an appointment will help you to properly outline the research and respond to any questions. This needs to happen at an early stage in the process of completing your dissertation bearing in mind that your request for access may be rejected leaving you with the need to seek alternative partners.

Ideas to Use – Consent Request Letter

Dear _____,

I am currently on the final year of my degree in education studies at _____ University and I am carrying out research into the transition between Key Stage 1 and Key Stage 2. As part of my research I would like to gather data from some of the practitioners and parents at your school using questionnaires and some follow-up interviews.

I would like to emphasize that

    any participation by practitioners or parents would be entirely voluntary;
    participants would be free to refuse to answer any questions;
    participants would be free to withdraw at any time.

In addition, I would like to assure you that any data gathered would only be used for this project and would be kept confidential throughout, unless information was disclosed which would impact on child safety and welfare in which case I would inform you immediately.

Yours sincerely,

_____

If you are willing to allow me to carry out my research in your school I would be grateful if you could sign below.

_____ (Signed)

_____ (Printed)

_____ (Date)

One way of encouraging gatekeepers to grant you access is to consider whether there are potential benefits to their institution or organization arising out of your work. Your dissertation could be an opportunity for an organization to learn valuable information that might result in improved practice in the future; both parties, therefore, could have *a great deal to gain* from a positive researcher and gatekeeper relationship (Oliver, 2010, p. 40). You may be able to adapt your study to incorporate areas that would be of benefit to a particular setting (Robson, 2002). Clearly, this would be welcomed in many instances; however, it is important to exercise a degree of caution in case you find that a gatekeeper tries to modify or influence your study unduly. In extreme instances, someone might seek to veto your findings (Bryman, 2008). Understandably, gatekeepers may feel uneasy about the effects that your research could have on their institution.

Ideas to Think About – Seeking Consent to Use Audio-visual Materials

If you plan to use digital images and/or audio-visual materials (e.g. photographs, video cameras, Dictaphones) as part of your research project, you should discuss this intention with the setting where you intend to collect your data. They may already have a policy or set of guidelines that relate to this. If they do, you must respect this and follow their advice. Usually, you would be asked to obtain consent to use such materials. If you are working with children who are under 16 years, then consent also needs to be obtained from gatekeepers/legal guardians. Written consent should be obtained from legal guardians, inviting them to return the form with or without their signed consent. Only when you have this specific written permission should you use any audio-visual materials. If you do not have this then you should not use the material. Any letter that you write to children's legal guardians should be checked with your supervisor(s) and your setting before it is sent out. It would also be good practice to discuss who the letters will be sent to because there may be some individuals that could be put at risk if you were to use materials that included them.

Even once you have managed to gain access to a setting you may still need to gain access to your participants within that location (Bryman, 2016). This could mean that securing access to research participants ends up involving a series of negotiations. Any student wishing to conduct research with young children, for example, must consider a number of constituencies from whom consent must be sought. To begin with the setting or school will need to agree; if you are also planning to observe or talk to children then parents will need to give their permission and the children too must have a means of agreeing to be involved or not. Access to a setting or school, to carry out your research, is not automatic. You will need to make an appointment to see the head teacher or manager. Even if you are already on placement in a setting, it is appropriate and courteous to share your research intentions to get permission to go ahead. Be prepared to take your research proposal, consent letters, interview schedules etc., and be ready to answer any questions about your research. Nor can it be assumed that consent once given is given for all time and in all circumstances. Children, for example, may be happy to participate one day but could have no interest the next and it is possible that informed consent has be checked, reconfirmed and continuously negotiated at various points throughout your fieldwork (Roberts-Holmes, 2014). When initial consent has been granted some participants still need to be asked again, perhaps at the beginning of each session, if they want to take part. Heath et al. refer to this as *process consent* (2004, p. 409). Your participants also need to feel secure in the knowledge that at any point they can terminate a session or withdraw from the whole process, knowing any data will be destroyed. A participant's decision to withdraw temporarily or completely needs to be respected, however challenging this may be for the researcher (Lancaster and Broadbent, 2003). A decision to withdraw either temporarily or permanently should not be questioned and any data gained up to that point about or from that participant must be destroyed and cannot be used (Fine and Sandstrom, 1988).

Checklist – Informed Consent

- Provide sufficient details of the research (verbal and written)
- Participation must be voluntary
- Check understanding and do not make assumptions
- Allow time for reflection
- Ensure no element of coercion is present
- Obtain written permission from participants or gatekeepers
- Submit an ethical approval form to the relevant ethics committee or supervising tutor
- Remind participants that they can withdraw at any point during the research process and the data will be destroyed.

Source: Adapted from Bryman, 2008.

Defending confidentiality and anonymity

Confidentiality and anonymity are often talked of in the same breath and are sometimes used interchangeably when completing a dissertation or final project; although as you will see below they mean different things. The terms serve as a prompt though to remind you that when planning to carry out research you will need to think through a number of issues, such as:

- whether and how confidentiality and/or anonymity will be ensured?
- how will your data be stored and accessed and for how long?
- what arrangements have been made for the destruction of data where participants have withdrawn from your study?

When you give an undertaking of confidentiality it means that you have promised not to disclose certain information arising from your research to anyone other than authorized persons such as your dissertation supervisor or examiner (Cohen et al., 2011). Guaranteeing anonymity however means that you have promised not to name or identify the sources of your information. You can have anonymity without confidentiality, but it is hard to see how you could have confidentiality without anonymity; so, for example, you might promise to keep your participant's names out of the final dissertation yet make what they have told you available to anyone who reads the work.

When participants agree to take part in research they may need to be reassured that their identity will remain hidden. Even when participants tell you that they want to use their own name at that point in time, it is a decision they could come to regret at some point in the future and so it is usually safer just to maintain anonymity as standard practice. In general, therefore, when data is disseminated to the public in anyway it is best done *behind a shield of anonymity* (Denzin and Lincoln, 2005, p. 78). It is also the case that assurances about anonymity may well improve the numbers of participants who agree to take part in your research as well as making those participants feel more confident and comfortable about being open and honest in expressing their true views and attitudes (Oliver, 2010, p. 78).

When writing up your research the issue of anonymity is normally dealt with either by using pseudonyms, for example altering *Mrs Smith* to *Mrs Jones*, or by using numbers and letters such as *Parent A* or *School 1* (Frankfort-Nachmias and Nachmias, 1992). Using pseudonyms is usually recommended rather than the use of numbers or letters as this allows the personal element to be maintained. This said if you are going to use a pseudonym then you need to do so carefully and characteristics such as the gender or ethnic group of the real participants should remain the same or similar, for example altering *Mrs Khan* to *Mr Jones* could be highly misleading and affect the authenticity of the research (Oliver, 2010). It is important to note though that there may well be circumstances in which confidentiality and anonymity are either hard to maintain or impossible to guarantee. For example, in an organization where there were two health visitors and one was involved in your research project, it would mean that the identity of your participant would be quite easy to uncover. Even in situations and settings where the number of possibilities is greater than two it is still the case that *pseudonyms and disguised locations are often recognized by insiders* (Denzin and Lincoln, 2005, p. 145). In these situations, therefore, you may need to discuss with your supervisor about how best and to what extent you can realistically maintain the privacy of your participants.

As a researcher, therefore, you have certain responsibilities to ensure that the rights of participants to privacy are adhered to (Ali and Kelly, 2012; Walliman, 2015). You might find it useful to refer to the 1998 Data Protection Act when thinking through your approach to confidentiality and anonymity to make certain that personal information remains private during collection and later upon dissemination. The act sets out a number of principles of good practice, relating to these aspects of research including advice upon keeping data secure including data stored electronically (https://www.gov.uk/data-protection?).

Research with children and other potentially vulnerable groups

When working with potentially vulnerable individuals or groups, following an ethical code of conduct is even more essential. The term vulnerable usually refers to those who are less able to make choices and decisions and in effect therefore to say 'no'. Potentially vulnerable people may be vulnerable because they are disadvantaged or marginalized within society. This could include ethic minority groups, old-age pensioners, those living in poverty, single parents or the mentally disabled/disordered (Liamputtong, 2007). The term vulnerable participants may also cover participants with learning or communication difficulties, patients in hospital or under the care of social services, people in custody or on probation, persons practising illegal activities such as drug abusers and/or people with a condition or illness that is being researched such as cancer patients (British Psychological Society, 2004).

Researchers may experience a degree of anxiety about carrying out research with potentially vulnerable groups or individuals for fear of being accused of exploiting people. However, provided ethical guidelines are followed, many vulnerable people may be keen to participate in research and to exclude them would be inappropriate and potentially discriminatory (Beauchamp et al., 2002). For example, a teenage research participant with an eating disorder could be entirely competent and wish to be involved in research and this could be made possible by carefully considering access via gatekeepers and the procedures adopted to secure informed consent. Less powerful groups or individuals in society should have the same rights as anyone else to have their voices heard on matters that affect or interest them. In addition, it is important to guard against making patronizing, sometimes stereotypical, assumptions about groups and individuals. Researchers working with apparently similar individuals, such as lone parents living in poverty, need to bear in mind that although a group may share some characteristics there will still be many differences within and between individual members of that group.

This said, the sensitivities and risks associated with research involving potentially vulnerable groups are considerable and your supervisor may well advise you that a particular line of enquiry is too intrusive, too ambitious or too risky for you to undertake as an undergraduate student. For example, the sample dissertation titles below might well be deemed too challenging ethically for an undergraduate dissertation involving primary data collection:

- 'How supportive is the adoption process for new parents?'
- 'Teacher's perceptions on children's bereavement experiences'
- 'Young people's views and opinions on being homeless'

Although many potentially vulnerable groups would probably be 'off limits' to most undergraduate education students, projects involving children and/or young people would not be. Most publications on research that make mention of children under the age of 18 tend to treat them in a similar fashion to other groups that might feature under the 'vulnerable participants' category. You must give some thought to the impact that their potential vulnerability might have on your ethical considerations. For example, there may be some instances where confidentiality and anonymity cannot be guaranteed because as a researcher you have to play your part in safeguarding potential vulnerable participants. Complete confidentiality cannot be promised in research relating to or involving these groups. If, for example, a child were to make a disclosure in an interview that implied that he/she was being maltreated by someone you must not keep that confidential due to the potential risk to the safety of your participant (Liamputtong, 2007, p. 36). In a child-protection scenario such as this you would need to halt the research process and tell the child that it was necessary to inform someone else. In consultation and discussion with the child this information would need to be passed on to the appropriate person and the relevant action taken and support put into place (Roberts-Holmes, 2014). Researchers are required by law to report any allegation of abuse.

The participants and gatekeepers such as parents and practitioners who control access to potentially vulnerable participants such as children need to be informed in advance about the conditions on which confidentiality might be breached (Oliver, 2010; Liamputtong, 2007). Research plans need to make mention of the limits of confidentiality and anonymity in respect of the possible disclosure or identification of suspected abuse or similarly illegal or unethical conduct during the research process. Your research does not have to be about abuse or illegality of any kind for information about these sorts of things to come to light. Nor are children and other vulnerable groups the only participants who may make disclosures, information about inappropriate conduct may come from adults too. This may arise where adults give information or behave in a way that you feel might constitute a risk; for example,

- neglectful behaviour, such as leaving a young child unattended;
- revealing personal information in conversation that suggests they themselves pose a risk to a child, or that another adult does.

Clearly then the limits of confidentiality and anonymity need to be set out unambiguously. The guidelines below offer an example of how you might handle a scenario, where a safeguarding issue of some kind had emerged during your research, but if you have any concerns about any of your participants you should seek advice from your supervisor in the setting, the designated person for child protection in your setting if appropriate and/or your research supervisor(s).

Points to Think About – Safeguarding Children and/or Vulnerable Groups

Issues relating to the safety and well-being of vulnerable groups and individuals (safeguarding) may arise in any research context, not just when working with children. This may involve reporting harm or the risk of harm to other professionals which raises issues of the limits of confidentiality in research. These limits should be agreed by you with participants and gatekeepers before embarking on any research. Before starting the research it is good practice to explain to the participant that should you become aware of the risk of harm to a child you will need to pass on relevant information.

The main categories of abuse are physical injury, sexual abuse and exploitation, emotional abuse and neglect. If you see or hear anything that worries you in relation to these categories while conducting your research you should follow the procedures below.

Research with children or young people in a formal setting, for example nursery, school or college

Follow the safeguarding child-protection procedures for that setting.

If you have any concerns speak to the setting's designated person for child protection.

If you need advice or support or in the absence of a designated person for the setting then contact the relevant Child Protection Group via your research supervisor(s).

Research with children or young people outside of an educational or related setting: for example family home; sports or youth club

Do not ask leading questions but allow the child to tell you their concerns and to talk freely.

Do not promise confidentiality as you may need to pass on the information.

Contact the relevant Child Protection Group via your research supervisor(s) (Kay et al., 2009).

Not only are confidentiality and anonymity affected by the potential vulnerability of children and young people, securing informed consent is also affected. In the case of schools, for example, you will need the permission of key gatekeepers such as parents or head teachers before you can proceed. In addition, childhood is often regarded as a period of time that is distinct and unique during which children are 'becoming' and so are not yet fully able to give informed consent. Researchers need to take great care over adult–child relationships in which adults know best and are therefore in a position to ignore children's feelings or wishes; it is important not to make it difficult for children to deny consent (Robinson and Kellet, 2004; Hill, 2005). The means of gaining informed consent from children within a setting in which adults may be associated with authority is far from straightforward and those without power apparently consenting to the requests of those with power, does not necessarily equate with autonomy. Asking a child if you can watch or join in an activity may not constitute seeking consent without interference. The child might feel as though no real choice is possible given adult–child power relationships. Children who are accustomed to having to do as they are told by adults may not feel that they have an option to say 'no'. Younger children in particular often want to please adults and this should be borne in mind when seeking informed consent.

The term 'informed' also has to be carefully thought through given the developmental stage of younger participants. While obtaining informed consent in writing using documentation is common in research involving adults it is difficult to see how preliterate children or emergent writers would cope with this requirement. What is more, seeking written consent from 3- and 4-year-olds might actually cause more harm in terms of children's anxiety than not seeking it. Rigorous application of the two principles of informed consent and autonomy appear to require the researcher to ensure that the children know what the research is about; they know what their role is; they know that they have a choice about whether to participate or not and they know that they can change their minds and withdraw at any point. However, Donaldson's work on language and communication suggests that this will be far from unproblematic in situations where researchers have to try to explain the purpose of their research and seek consent from 3- or 4-year-olds who may well be *differently* articulate (Donaldson, 1978). An explanation involving a lot of adult talk and ill-matched vocabulary could bore or even intimidate children. There is a balance to be achieved when giving information to potential child participants. The children need to have the basic facts without being overwhelmed with information in such a way as to adversely influence data collection or skew the outcomes of the study (Oliver, 2003, p. 30; Cohen et al., 2011).

None of this means that children's informed consent should not be sought, far from it. If we choose to deny children the opportunity to decide we are assuming consent (Heath et al., 2007). Children need to be told as much as possible, even if they do not always understand the full explanation. Age does not diminish their rights, although any explanations offered must take account of children's age and comprehension (Fine and Sandstrom, 1988). One option would be to use 'witnessed consent' where the researcher explains what is proposed to the children in the presence of another adult, perhaps a practitioner, perhaps a parent. One difficulty with this approach, according to Spencer and Flin (1993), is that adults may be less likely to respond sensitively to the needs, experiences and perceptions of children. Whatever approach is adopted, such conversations and any accompanying documentation need to be phrased in developmentally appropriate language.

Example – Children's Consent Leaflet for Year 2 Pupils

A project about the school day:

My name is Claire Jones.

I am doing a project about the school day and I would like to know if you can help? I am asking if you would like to take part in this project because you are a school representative. Some of the adults will also be asked if they would like to talk about the school day.

- Mrs Smith the head teacher
- Your teachers and parents

I am interested in the things that you enjoy doing when you are at school.

I will ask a few questions about what you like to do.

We will draw pictures and then talk about them.

I will tape record the things we talk about, to help me remember the important things you say.

I will not tell other people what we talk about unless I think you are in any danger.

I will see you about six times.

You can decide if you would like to take part. No one will be cross or upset if you say no. You can change your mind at any time.

If you want to talk about what you enjoy doing at school, please write your name and then tick the box so that I know if you want to take part.

_____   ☐   yes please

_____   ☐   no thank you

However, the notion of children as uniquely vulnerable and incompetent has been challenged in a number of quarters as views of childhood have changed and evolved through research in recent years (Brooker, 2001; Christiansen and Prout, 2002). There has been a shift in emphasis away from models of childhood in which children were seen as socially incompetent needing adults to speak for them and away from *research on children* towards *research with them* (Ali and Kelly, 2012, p. 69). Young children, for example, can actually be very powerful in some research contexts (Aubrey et al., 2000). They are quite likely to vote with their feet if an activity bores them, or will change a topic of conversation in order to discuss matters of significance to them rather than those of significance to the researcher.

The introduction of the United Nations Convention on the Rights of the Child (1989, Article 12) and The Children Act (DCSF, 2004) both support the notion that *children have the right to be consulted and taken account of, to have access to information, to freedom of speech and opinion and to challenge decisions made on their behalf* (Morrow and Richards, 1996, p. 91). This shift it is argued is characterized by a more respectful appreciation of this distinct phase in life coupled with an acknowledgement that it is vital to listen to children who are in fact experts within this phase (Lancaster and Broadbent, 2003). Consequently, the expectations and perceptions of children as competent beings, rather than *human becomings* are being recognized more and more (Quortrup, 1987). Researchers may well need to recast children as potentially powerful players in research by consciously transferring some control at least of the research to the child (Ring, 2000).

Checklist – Ethical Issues to Consider When Researching with Children and/or Potentially Vulnerable Groups

1. Provide a clear explanation of the research at an appropriate level/using appropriate language.
2. Check participants' understanding of your research and their involvement in it.
3. Make certain you have permission/informed consent to carry out your research from any gatekeepers involved, for example parents and guardians both verbally and (where appropriate) in writing.
4. Remember that informed consent may well need to be renegotiated at various points throughout the process of research.
5. Carry out a pilot investigation.
6. Arrange appropriate times to interview, observe or visit your participants.
7. Consider the health and safety of those involved including yourself.
8. Be considerate of your participants' needs to stop and take a break, for example if a child is fidgety and restless; young children's attention spans can vary.
9. Conduct your research in an appropriate, familiar or otherwise safe environment so that participants feel more comfortable and at ease.
10. Look for ways to overcome or at least diminish the concept of the researcher being in a position of power, for example getting down to children's height when talking to them.
11. Find ways to reduce the likelihood that participants are simply saying what they think you want them to say, rather than what they truly feel.
12. Use appropriate language that participants will understand.
13. Use open-ended questions to encourage participants to express themselves.
14. Use projection techniques where appropriate, for example pictures, dolls, photographs or puppets to encourage participants to talk/open up.

Source: Adapted from Liamputtong, 2007 and Cohen et al., 2007.

Ethics and the internet

Using the internet to carry out research is becoming more commonplace within education and the social sciences partly, though not exclusively, due to the reduced cost and time that it requires. What is being discussed here is not the day-to-day online literature searches that all undergraduate students will do as part of their research but the development and use of data-collection tools such as questionnaires (see Chapters 6 and 7) via the internet. In terms of ethics, the usual practices associated with research are necessary but there are also particular considerations that are pertinent to this approach.

To begin with Denscombe points out that particular attention needs to be paid to *informed consent, privacy, deception and confidentiality* (Denscombe, 2007, p. 148). Informed consent can become even more complicated when it is not possible to have a face-to-face meeting with potential participants. One response is to have a consent form online (either to email or on a website page), which includes a tick box (yes/no) which respondents tick and return (Denscombe, 2014). This would indicate that a participant is willing to take part; however, it does not incorporate a formal signature. The second option would be to include a form that can be printed, signed by the potential participant and returned via fax or post. This would be more rigorous and would consequently provide an additional safeguard for the researcher but it requires greater effort and participation from potential participants which might affect uptake and reduce the number of people choosing to participate. As part of this process it must be made clear to participants that they can withdraw at anytime and Cohen et al. suggest using a 'withdraw' button at the bottom of the screen so that this is an integral part of the research and is available as an option throughout (Cohen et al., 2007, p. 231).

If the research involves children then, the usual practice referred to earlier in the chapter needs to be adhered to. In addition you must check that any respondent is over 18 years of age. Where children are underage gatekeeper permission needs to be obtained. Equally, even if your research investigation does not involve children, you may need to make an effort to check the age of respondents, particularly if topics of a sensitive or adult nature are being examined (Denscombe, 2014). However, proving the age of participants is likely to be very difficult or even impossible and this could lead to the ethics of a dissertation being questioned. Normally, you should also make it clear who you are and the purposes of your research investigation. There are, in spite of this advice, instances where researchers may feel that it is necessary to keep their own identity hidden; perhaps when working with a particular sample. These instances would be unusual and would need to be discussed with your supervisor and would most probably have to be sanctioned by an ethics committee. It should also be made clear to respondents who will be able to access their contributions. For instance, will all participants in the project be able to view entries within a chatroom context? Will the researcher log into a chatroom and be able to exist unobserved? Will only one researcher have access to their postings? In most instances, it would be good practice to make this clear during the initial stages, when information is being supplied so that an informed decision can be made about whether to take part or not (Denscombe, 2014).

In spite of the concerns expressed above there are nevertheless ethical advantages to internet research including the fact that participation and consent will certainly be voluntary as there is a greatly reduced possibility of any coercion. Some respondents will also feel more comfortable about getting involved behind the shield of their computer. This is likely to be the case with sensitive topics such as substance abuse or domestic violence, where the prospect of divulging experiences and feelings without being directly confronted in person may be welcomed (Cohen et al., 2007). Having the screen of anonymity and knowing that information can be given and be non-traceable with internet research can be comforting to those who contribute. Nevertheless, one difference with internet information and privacy is the possibility that responses could be traced by those with sufficient technical expertise to particular IP addresses. How real a threat this is in most undergraduate education dissertations is, however, very questionable. You must state clearly at the initial stages that every reasonable effort will be made to ensure that information given remains confidential but in the light of these facts (Denscombe, 2014). This is not dissimilar to face-to-face research where participants are informed that confidentiality will be broken in rare instances, such as a child-protection issue coming to light during the research process.

Social media and research

The place of social media has become popular in academic research. This is for many reasons including reaching research participants, being part of an online research community where you can develop your ideas and research questions in the same way you might talk to a colleague in the office and increasing the impact of your research by reaching a wider audience (Beth and Waters, 2014). Using LinkedIn, Twitter, Facebook, blogs and Youtube are probably the most popular ways to network in the world of research. You may be familiar with using something like Facebook on a personal level, but it is worth considering how you might use this in a more professional format. Using these forms of networking does come with a word of caution. Start by asking yourself three questions:

1 How will this help you with your research? (keep a focus in mind)

2 How much time do I have to spare for this? (you may find you start to overuse this)

3 How will I give a professional impression online? (keep profiles and talking to online researchers professional at all times) (Bell and Waters, 2014). Keeping these three questions in mind will help you make the best of using social media in your research if you feel this works for you. Your university will probably give you specific advice on using social networking sites such as LinkedIn and Twitter. See Bell and Waters (2014: 148-153) for specific advice on specific networking sites.

Applying your understanding of ethical research

At the start of the chapter you were asked to consider two scenarios from an ethical perspective. As you have read through this chapter you will have had the opportunity to consider what the ethical issues might be for each of the scenarios and to give some thought to how you might respond to them.

Points to Think About – Ethical Issues and Putting Appropriate Measures into Action

Scenario A

You are interested in the issues facing education, health and social-care practitioners involved in multidisciplinary working and the implementation of inclusion policies and practices. You are focusing on the experiences of staff located in an emotional and behavioural difficulties (EBD) unit within a primary school. You want to interview the staff to get their impressions and opinions.

Ethical issue	Measures
Gaining access to the primary school	Discussion with the head teacher accompanied by a written letter to be signed
Gaining informed consent from the participants	Explanation accompanied by a written letter to be signed
Making sure that the school and participants remain anonymous	Use of pseudonyms
Making sure that the information given remains confidential	Keep data secure and destroy on completion of the project
Think carefully about how to report back to the school (some material could be sensitive)	Decide before the project how you will report back, for example an A4 sized report and select just two or three areas for comment that will not threaten the anonymity of participants

Points to Think About – Cont'd

Scenario B

You want to find out about the opportunities for, and the incidence of, outdoor play for nursery and reception children in your placement school. You decide you want to interview the children to get their perspectives.

Ethical issue	Measures
Gaining access and permission from gatekeepers	Discussion with the head teacher/parents/carers accompanied by a written letters to be signed
Gaining informed consent from the children	Discussion with the children at their level and use a pictorial leaflet to accompany this. Ask the children each time you work with them if they still want to participate
Making sure that the school and participants remain anonymous	Use of pseudonyms
Making sure that the information given remains confidential	Keep data secure and destroy on completion of the project
Allow children to stop at any point during the interview	Tune into the children during the interview. Note non-verbal cues and signals, for example their body language
Think about how you will feed back to the children	Perhaps photographs could be used to summarize what they have said and check that is what they meant
Dealing with possible disclosures from children	Make it clear to gatekeepers that if safeguarding issues are raised during data collection then these will need to be shared with the relevant staff

Summary of key points

- Ethical issues need to be considered throughout your research project, not just initially at the design stage.
- Familiarize yourself with the relevant ethical guidelines for your discipline/course.
- Submit a research proposal to your supervisor or ethical committee to safeguard yourself and your participants.
- If your research involves human participants do not approach people or begin to collect data until your work has been given ethical approval.
- Gatekeeper permission is required when working with children and other potentially vulnerable participants.

- Treat all participants in your research with respect and honesty.
- When ensuring anonymity and confidentiality make sure that you have a clear and shared understanding about what has been agreed. Summarize what has been said and do not take anything for granted.
- Make sure that no element of your practice could be seen as deceptive.
- Conducting internet research needs particular consideration in relation to informed consent, privacy, deception and confidentiality.

Reflective task

- Think about your own potential research project and what ethical issues may arise?
- Consider the following questions and write down your thoughts to share with your tutor.
- Who will be your participants?
- What type of sampling will you be using?
- How will you get informed consent from your participants?
- How will you ensure individuals cannot be identified and will remain anonymous?
- How will you respect participants rights to privacy and confidentiality?
- Will there be any potential negative consequences to individuals who participate?
- If you are working with children, how will you introduce yourself?
- How will you establish a professional rapport with the children?

Link to companion website

https://bloomsbury.com/cw/successful-dissertations-second-edition/student-resources/chapter-3/

Recommended reading and further sources of information

Alderson, P. and Morrow, V. (2011, 2nd edition), *The Ethics of Research with Children and Young People*. London: SAGE.

British Psychological Society (BPS), http://www.bps.org.uk/

British Sociological Association (BSA), https://www.britsoc.co.uk/

Grieg, A., Taylor, J. and Mackay, T. (2013, 3rd edition), *Doing Research with Children: A Practical Guide*. London: Sage.

Harcourt, D., Perry, B. and Waller, T. (2011). *Researching Young Children's Perspectives: Debating the Ethics and Dilemmas of Educational Research with Children*. Abingdon: Routledge.

MacNaughton, G., Rolfe, S. A. and Siraj-Blatchford, I. (2010). *Doing Early Childhood Research: International Perspectives on Theory and Practice*. Maidenhead: Open University Press.

Moss, P. and Dahlberg, G. (2005). *Ethics and Politics in Early Childhood Education*. London: Routledge.

Oliver, P. (2010). *The Student's Guide to Research Ethics*. 2nd edn. Maidenhead: Open University Press.

Sargeant, J. and Harcourt, D. (2012). *Doing Ethical Research with Children*. Maidenhead: Open University Press.

Social Research Association (SRA), http://the-sra.org.uk/

Takacs, D. (2003), 'How does Your Positionality Bias Your Epistemology?' *The NEA Higher Education Journal*, Vol. 14, No. 2, 27–39.

4

Doing Your Literature Review

Janet Kay

Chapter Aims

By the end of this chapter you should know how to

- draw on relevant literature to formulate and refine your research question or hypothesis;
- plan and structure a literature review appropriate to your topic;
- select relevant references from appropriate sources;
- critique other studies in terms of their validity and reliability;
- use the literature review to contextualize your own study.

The literature review is a large section of any undergraduate dissertation. Experienced tutors know that writing a good literature review is not always straightforward and requires a range of skills and knowledge to achieve success. In this chapter, the purposes and process of producing a good literature review are discussed. Strategies for accessing references are covered as are ways of ensuring these are relevant to the topic and from appropriate academic sources.

Planning and structuring the review and relating the review to your own study and findings is also addressed.

What is a literature review?

The literature review is a discussion of selected items from the range of (mainly) published material available in a given subject area. It involves reading the literature available and ensuring that you have a very good knowledge of the main issues, arguments, controversies and gaps in knowledge within the topic area. From doing your literature review you should become knowledgeable in the topic area, not just in terms of facts but in terms of the methodological approaches commonly used in that particular field and the impact of previous studies on practice and policy.

A literature review is not simply a sequence of short commentaries on each piece of literature that you have read as this would constitute more of a book catalogue or annotated bibliography rather than a literature review. Instead what you are trying to create is a themed discussion of your topic which sets the context and elaborates on key issues by drawing on the literature available. It should summarize the views of others in the field certainly; literature reviews do involve giving information and pulling together what the different sources say, but they do more than just this. A good literature review will also organize this information into themes or subtopics so that the content of different materials can be compared or considered together. A good literature review should raise relevant questions and place your own study within the wider context. This involves synthesizing the literature to develop a coherent discussion about the subject and identifying key debates and critical issues within the area. A good literature review will also critique some of the sources that it draws on in terms of their significance or their validity.

In the majority of dissertations involving some firsthand data collection much of the literature review is completed before the data is gathered but in projects where a grounded-theory approach is used the literature review is carried out later on as part of the data (Punch, 2014). You may also be asked to produce a limited review of key literature as part of a research proposal to show that your research question has been informed by the literature and that you understand your topic.

The range of sources used will vary depending on what the topic is in terms of the types of materials, the quantity available, the sources and contexts but it should include examples of established scholarship in the field that you are planning to research. Sources should have been selected for their relevance and significance to your research question(s). It is worth noting that not all published material will be suitable for a literature review and certainly any items on which you are basing conclusions or claims need to be academically respectable. One of the key issues for any dissertation is to ensure that the literature review links closely to the rest of the project and the aims and outcomes of your data collection.

The purpose of a literature review

There are a number of interrelated reasons for reviewing the literature as part of your dissertation. These include

- to help you to decide on your final research question;
- to explore what has already been written in the field and to place your study in the context of other similar studies;
- to improve your critical awareness by identifying the disputed areas of your topic and to help you to make sense of your findings during data analysis.

Using the literature to help you decide on your final research question

Initial reading is crucial in determining your topic and the title for your dissertation, but more than that, the literature review creates the context for your own study by locating it within existing research on your chosen theme. A key question for you to consider is how your study will add to or complement existing knowledge in the area. The literature review will help you to locate your own study in the existing body of research in the field (Roberts-Holmes, 2014). It should also be viewed as the means by which you begin to narrow your focus so that you can develop research questions suitable and doable for your study (Mac Naughton et al., 2010). Your initial search of the literature will enable you to find out what others already know on the topic, to determine your own research question and to design your own study (Mac Naughton et al., 2010).

It is usual for students to start thinking about a general area of interest for a research dissertation and then to develop this initial idea until a title is agreed with the dissertation supervisor. This development process involves moving from a broad area of interest to a specific aspect which the student thinks is interesting and appropriate for a study and which is feasible in the time and context available (see Chapter 2). Reading the literature at this time is essential to inform yourself of the issues in the field and to help you to focus on an area you wish to do your study on. It will help you to spot areas that have been well-researched in the past and where an original dissertation may be more difficult to achieve. It will also help you to identify key issues and contested areas in the field and enable you to refine your thinking about which aspect you wish to consider in your own work (as the box below outlines). Reading around the subject at this time can feel a little unfocused and possibly wasteful of time as some of the reading may not inform your eventual literature review.

However, early reading provides a useful means of identifying where your topic area may be too narrow resulting in a limited number of available references. You may need to look at broader questions in the same topic area or even a different topic area if it is too difficult to find relevant reading (Roberts-Holmes, 2014). The aspects you choose to reject are as important as those you choose to include in your own study and taking time to consider the range of literature in the field will help you to identify a good theme or question.

Case Study – Using the Literature to Help Formulate a Research Question

Saima wanted to explore gender and play in Early Years settings but when she started to read the existing literature in the area, she found that there were already many studies that identified the age at which children started to play more exclusively with their own gender and which identified differences in the types of play and play materials often used by boys and girls.

Saima felt at this stage that she may have nothing more to add to this discussion. However, she continued to read around the area and eventually read an article about the influence of peers on gendered play. She became interested in the idea that gendered play was linked to children's need to conform and 'fit in' with peers. She began to think about whether gendered play in group settings was determined by this need to conform. She was curious to know whether this desire to 'fit in' was affected by the context in which the play was taking place. Saima's final dissertation explored whether children in a Year 1 class (age 5–6) in a local primary school played differently in school and out of school, in terms of playmates, materials and types of play.

Exploring what has already been written and placing your work in context

One of the worst things that can happen in a research study at this level is to completely miss a crucial piece of research or theory that is central in the field and that has a significant impact on knowledge and understanding of the issues and critical aspects of the topic. Initial reading around the area provides you with an opportunity to map progress in thinking in that area and to start to identify key theorists and major pieces of research that have contributed to that thinking. In other words, to start to get a feel for the main aspects of the field, the research and the theory which underpins current debates within it and which studies have been most influential in determining thinking in the area. This initial reading should also lead you to other references that are relevant to your eventual research question(s) and it should also help you to identify what types of sources are most likely to provide you with relevant literature for your completed literature review. The key issue is to be clear about the main features of the existing research in your chosen area.

As you start to focus more on a particular aspect of the field, your reading should become more specific and selective in order to ensure that what you read will contribute to both your understanding of the issues involved in your study and the discussion of your findings. The transition from the general to the specific usually takes place as you start to refine your ideas from a general topic area to the specific research question(s) discussed earlier. This more selective reading will help you to focus your discussion on what is relevant and enable you to locate and position your dissertation within the wider body of knowledge. You need to read studies that directly relate to your research topic. You will be looking out for what is interesting about the field you have chosen. However the challenge is to maintain your focus and not to become distracted by things that are interesting but are not directly relevant. International and cross-cultural comparisons offer a good example of this. International perspectives may be the central theme of some dissertations requiring an examination of material from a range of cultures to explore the similarities and differences between them. However, using studies from other national and cultural contexts to make or support a point in a dissertation that is not about international comparisons may not always be helpful. The differences between the contexts may invalidate the point being made. If such comparisons are made, the discussion must include some acknowledgement of the differences between the studies and the contexts as well as the significance of the findings.

Point to Remember – Don't Get Distracted by Things That Are Interesting but Not Relevant

Comparing school starting ages between European countries may be a useful way of showing that children in the UK start formal schooling at an earlier age compared to their peers in similar countries. However you would need to exercise great caution before deciding that such differences imply that one approach is 'better' than another. Such educational policy differences are the product of cultural and historical factors and simplistic policy borrowing in which it is argued that one country should copy the policies and practices of another in order to solve all its problems without any reference to its own history and traditions is naive.

Using the literature to improve your critical awareness and inform data analysis

In your earlier reading around you will have identified some of the disputed areas, the central arguments and the critical issues in your subject area. You now need to read and think about these in more depth in terms of their relevance to your own study and specific field of research. You may need to set out why you have focused on one aspect and not another. Your reading should determine what evidence there is to support different aspects of debates that are relevant to your project. This should help you to decide where you stand in any debate relevant to your chosen topic, what evidence you have for your position and help you to ensure that you are offering a balanced view of the competing views in the field. Below is an example of the sorts of competing viewpoints that your literature review may well throw up.

Case Study – Identifying Critical Debates Relevant to Your Study

Having read extensively Andy was interested in the development of government social policy which supported or exhorted mothers to join or rejoin the labour force. These policies were characterized by allowances, financial incentives and other initiatives to encourage unemployed women with children, particularly single parents to seek work and/or training. Andy wanted to explore the debate about these policy decisions. For some commentators these incentives and initiatives were regarded as a positive development for mothers and their children that would improve their economic well-being, standard of living and aspirations. For others the same developments constituted unwelcome and ill-judged pressure on mothers to return to work against their wishes or before they were ready and which risked condemning young children to long periods in childcare environments of variable and sometimes dubious quality.

In the later stages of your study you will be expected to discuss your findings to determine their meaning (see Chapter 8) and to consider what they suggest for future studies or possibly for practice in the field. The key task here is to compare your findings and conclusions to those from other studies. At this stage you will draw on those previous studies and theories that you first discussed in your literature review to draw parallels between your findings and others 'or to highlight differences between your findings and others'. It may be that your findings are in line with or at odds with those from previous studies. From this you can draw some conclusions both about the value of your own study such as how it has added to existing knowledge in the field but also about practice issues or further research questions.

Starting your literature review

Conducting a good literature review takes time and is highly likely to involve a few false starts, cul-de-sacs and U-turns on the way. It is important not to see these as failures but as part of the process of refining your approach to your study and developing your ideas about what you are going to research and why. This may even mean reading some literature early on in the process, making notes and then later discarding these as no longer relevant. This need not be time wasted, however, as the process of reading widely will have contributed to the development of the final research question. It is important that you agree the structure of your literature review with your supervisor and ensure that it is appropriate to your study and meets the guidelines you have been given. Remember, a good literature review will

- be concise and summarize the key debates and aspects of the topic;
- produce a coherent discussion that brings together or synthesizes the various themes within the topic;
- be analytical and critique the literature used and the ideas and debates within the topic area;
- be original by linking the review to the planned research study.

One way to start the process of reviewing the literature is to seek answers to certain questions which may help you to focus on the key aspects of the available research in this area. Thinking about these questions as you start your search for literature should help you to develop a general overview of what issues and debates are significant in the area you wish to study. For example:

- Who are the key theorists and researchers in this area?
- What sort of methodologies are used in the research you are reading?
- What seems to be well-known and established in the field and what is new?
- Where are the contested issues and controversial areas and what are the arguments about?

Another way to start the process off is to make yourself aware of what the final literature review will probably look like, albeit in very broad terms (see the box below). A good way of doing this is to look at examples of literature reviews in any previous dissertations held by your university library for reference purposes. This may give you an idea about what the 'finished product' will look like and may also help you to find material for your own review. An alternative technique is to look at articles and papers in the refereed journals that publish studies in your topic area as these usually have literature reviews. They will provide examples showing how a literature review is used to contextualize a study and how the discussion about the findings of the study is related to items in the literature review. However, you cannot assume that all published literature reviews are going to be of the highest standard so you should not be afraid to read them with a critical eye.

Points to Remember – Structuring Your Literature Review

The majority of literature reviews will follow a fairly standard pattern:

Introduction
Describing briefly what the review will cover and the scope of the literature included. This may also indicate how the review is organized or structured.

Main Body
This section is where the literature selected is discussed, analysed, compared and critiqued according to your chosen structure.

Conclusions
In this section the main themes emerging and their significance for your study are summarized and discussed leading the way into your own research.

If you are still not entirely sure about what is expected of a literature review on your course then you should look again at the relevant course or module handbook containing guidance on your research project to see what it has to say on the subject. Each university, faculty, school and department or even course will have developed a particular view on what your literature review should include and look like. This chapter cannot encompass all the possible variations so you will need to be sure that you have found out what is expected of you on your particular course. Not all guidelines are at course or module level so you may find university guidelines on your institution's websites or in the library or key skills materials. Check carefully, ask your tutor or supervisor and make sure you have copies of all the guidelines available and relevant to you and that you have read these. Although guidelines for dissertations do vary there are some common features of a good literature review. An effective literature review will

- compare and contrast different authors' views on an issue;
- group authors who draw similar conclusions;
- critique aspects of methodology;
- note areas over which authors are in disagreement;
- highlight significant or exemplary studies from the past;
- highlight any gaps in research;
- show how the study relates to previous studies;
- show how the study relates to the literature in general;
- conclude by summarizing what the literature says (University of Melbourne, 2007).

Identifying and obtaining the sources that you might use

At the start of your research project you may already have some ideas about what you would like to study; these may be quite specific or rather vague at this stage. However, regardless of the extent to which the focus of your study is clear or not at this time, the reading you do early on will help to refine it. You may find that there are texts that you have read previously which have informed your choice of topic and which you could revisit to help focus your interest. These may be readings that were part of your course reading list or which you used for an earlier piece of course work. It can be useful to start with these by rereading and taking notes from them. However, many students worry that when they start to look for relevant literature by themselves they will struggle to find the right type and quantity of sources or that they will struggle to select from a sufficiently wide range of possible sources. It is helpful to try and narrow your topic down as soon as you are able so that you can make your ongoing search increasingly well targeted and specific.

There are a number of approaches which can be used to find literature relevant to your topic. These are complementary, not mutually exclusive. The extent to which you use each approach will depend on your topic and the best sources of material for it. Almost certainly your main source of literature will be your university library so make sure you are familiar with the location of the materials that you need and the systems in place for carrying out searches. University libraries usually have an integrated resources search tool such as Library Search which allows you to access books, journal articles, theses, media and other materials, with direct links to online material. They are also likely to have subject area specific guides pointing to discipline relevant journal article databases for more in-depth searches.

The exact nature of the different sources of support for students trying to develop their literature search skills will vary according to the institution so you need to enquire about what is available for you but the librarians are a key source of expert help when it comes to literature searches. You might find that your library offers face-to-face or online tutorials with information skills advisers or subject specialists who will be able to point you towards key resources in your field. This is in addition to the advice and guidance on how to carry out literature searches that may be offered by your dissertation supervisor. It is also possible that your supervisor may direct you to other academic specialists in the faculty or department who could offer some insight and advice on the sources that you need to consider. To get the most out of any guidance session you would be well advised to prepare first by considering which keywords you might use beforehand; databases often provide a thesaurus of keywords and your guide can help you to use this more effectively. The following sections discuss some of the main activities when searching for suitable literature. However, the list is not definitive and you need to make sure you have discussed approaches to searching for relevant literature with your supervisor.

Making a list of keywords and/or phrases

Keywords and phrases should be selected from your dissertation title, your research question(s) or your chosen theme and should cover all aspects of the topic that you are researching. It is a good idea to include a range of variations and alternatives at first so that the initial searches are broad and comprehensive. As a starting point you could try to write a short statement which summarizes your research topic. The keywords you start with can be drawn from this statement and then used to start searching your library catalogue or the internet.

Case Study – Choosing Keywords

Jane's dissertation focused on how best to support ethnic minority pupils in Key Stage 2 (age 7–11) through the appropriate choice of learning and teaching approaches. For her initial review, she showed her supervisor two studies she had looked at. One explored communication difficulties that young children experienced in nurseries with particular reference to ethnic minority children. The other focused on an evaluation of the performance of the UK government's Sure Start scheme in relation to ethnic minority communities. Jane's supervisor pointed out that although either study might provide useful general background information neither matched Jane's specific focus, that is ethnic minority pupils, Key Stage 2 and learning and teaching approaches. Jane explained that she had found a mass of material through a keyword search and had been overwhelmed with choices. Her supervisor suggested she picked more specific keywords to narrow her search more and try again.

The keywords and phrases you have identified can be used to start your search and to get an overview of what is 'out there'. Initial steps can include

- searching the internet using your keywords;
- searching your library catalogue using your keywords;
- searching online academic databases in your chosen field to find journal articles and other papers and reports.

You are likely to want to refine your search by narrowing it or widening it using different keywords, or placing limitations on your search such as date restrictions or removing these if you are not finding enough items. It is usually clear fairly early on if you need to narrow or broaden your keywords and phrases in order to find enough sources to select from without having so many 'hits' that you cannot possibly select. The key test is whether the keywords you use are leading you to literature relevant for your topic which you can use in your literature review. If not, you need to refine your search until the right type of literature is appearing. In each case you will also need to make some preliminary assessments about the items that you have found and their suitability for inclusion in an academic literature review by asking yourself whether

- each item is directly relevant to your study;
- as far as you can tell, the author is knowledgeable – if he/she has published or written elsewhere on a similar or related topic, for example;
- the study seems methodologically robust and therefore academically respectable and trustworthy and
- the source of the information is reputable – well-known publishers, refereed journals and authoritative organizations could, for example, be considered reputable.

Points to Remember – Finding the Right Literature

It is important not to just give up trying and decide to change your topic if you are struggling to find the literature you need. You may need to do that eventually but if your supervisor has agreed your topic it is probable that the literature is available and you just have not found it. It is also important to ask for help if you are struggling to get the 'right' keywords. Sometimes at this stage you need to persevere by trying different keywords and combinations. It is also important not to use what you can find even if it is a poor fit with your topic. This will damage your dissertation from the start. Remember also that if you find any relevant articles or texts then use items from the reference lists from these to extend your reading.

What type of material can be included in a literature review?

Most of your sources will be available online although some may still be paper-based items which are relatively easily accessible in your own library. However, you may need to do additional work to get hold of some of the sources you have identified and they may take longer to access. On occasions items have to be ordered from another site if your institution is on more than one campus. Other items may not be held by your own institution at all and getting hold of these may require you to use an interlibrary loans system which means that things may take even longer before they are available to you. Getting the material you are going to use in your literature review therefore will take time and effort and may involve a 'trial and error' approach at first so allow plenty of time for the activity rather than leaving the search until the last minute. In the early stages of the process you can cast your net quite widely. Potential sources for your literature review could include sources as varied as:

- Books
- Previous dissertations and theses
- Academic journals

- Professional periodicals and magazines
- Press reports
- Internet material
- Conference papers
- Electronic information databases
- Government publications, for example Illinois Department of Children and Family Services (DCFS) research reports, green papers, white papers, Acts of Parliament
- International research reports on education-related topics, for example Organization for Economic Cooperation and Development (OECD), United Nations Children's Fund (UNICEF).

Make sure you search widely but be aware that not all the items you find will be appropriate for a literature review in a dissertation; you need to be selective and critical about what you include. In short you will need to make sure that your dissertation does not rely on low-level, poorly researched opinion pieces. It must instead make good use of appropriate academic research studies and a range of other reliable sources of information and evidence such as government reports or the findings of independent research, all of which have been subject to scrutiny and criticism. At this stage you need to go beyond your preliminary assessment to make a more thorough assessment. Not every source you find will be suitable when you need material that represents research completed to high academic standards (Cresswell, 2014). At the same time although academic respectability is an important criterion for determining whether to include an item in your literature review there are other criteria too. Some of the ways in which you can determine the standard and quality of the work and its suitability for your literature review are discussed below. You can select sources according to their academic quality, their credibility and/or their recency. If in doubt about the status and value of a document you could ask your supervisor or library adviser to give you their assessment.

Points to Think About – Assessing Your Sources

Ensure that you make a thorough assessment of your sources:

- What are the findings, claims or arguments contained in this source and how do they inform your study?
- Does this work inform the background to your study or does it relate directly to the research question(s) you are asking?
- What theoretical basis/methodological approach underpins this work (if any) and how does this relate to the theory/methodology that you are using (if any)?
- Where does this work fit into the literature map that you are developing? Does it fit a theme that you have already identified or does it indicate a new theme that you could consider?
- Is the context of the work relevant to the study that you are doing, for example a similar type of sample?

Selecting sources for their currency/recency

The age of an item may or may not be significant in determining whether you should use it or not. A reasonable rule of thumb is to use the most up-to-date studies unless there is a specific reason not to. During your initial search put filters on to exclude older studies so you can identify the latest sources. You can always go back and look at older studies later if there is a reason to think this may be helpful. All research builds on previous knowledge and findings so the most recent studies should be the most accurate and revealing. Older studies may confuse the issues as the debates and critical issues in the field may have moved on. Older studies may also reflect policy and legislation that has been superseded by more recent developments or they may reflect cultural norms from the past, which would no longer be acceptable. However, some dissertations that are specifically about exploring past issues may examine items that are from chosen time periods precisely because they come from that time. Alternatively it may be important to compare and contrast recent theory with theories that dominated past thinking; for example, a dissertation on attachment theory may well start with early theorists from the 1950s. History of education projects often focus on documentary evidence from the past but would also include more recent commentaries or discussions on the original materials.

Other dissertations may explore the development of theory or thinking in a particular field over time, starting at an identified point in the past and tracing developments through until the present time. In an education and social care dissertation charting the development of how children have been looked after by local authorities over the last 50 years, for example, it may be very interesting to explore the development of theories which have influenced changes from residential care, such as orphanages to family care. However, in critiquing the quality of care through time it would be important to recognize that some of these theories may not have existed in the past. For other research projects key theories may have been established in the past that still have significance now. In primary and Early Years education, the work of theorists such as Vygotsky, Bruner and Piaget still inform and shape educational approaches now and are therefore significant in a study on current educational policy and practice. However, it may be important to recognize how older theory is applied today in such a study to make clear the current relevance of older theory. The following sections expand on some of the different sources available to you and outline some of the pros and cons associated with their use.

Books

There will not be many undergraduate education dissertations that do not make use of a book at any point. Books may contain references to a wide range of studies which are worth following up, or they may discuss a single study in depth. It is sometimes good practice to try and find the original study, rather than quote it from a secondary source, although this may not always be possible especially if the original material is very old and is now out of print. You should however try to gauge the 'levelness' of the book to make sure it is appropriate for undergraduate study and bear in mind that some books may be too general in their discussion. Books that do not draw on recent studies may be less relevant as they may be at a lower level than you need. Books by their very nature can also be very detailed and give you a lot to read and sometimes you will find the same studies summarized in a journal article which is much shorter and may be more accessible. You do not always want or need everything contained in a book. Another pitfall to watch out for is to rely too heavily on a single text book at the expense of wider reading and reflection.

Refereed journals

Much of what you will be looking for when researching the literature is other studies that have been conducted within established academic research processes and many of these are published in refereed journals. Refereed simply means that the articles have been examined by a review board and have been critiqued in terms of the validity and rigour of their research design (Punch, 2014). It is useful to get to know the titles of and to browse the journals in your field of study so that you can identify the most useful and keep monitoring the latest issues for relevant items (Mac Naughton et al., 2010). Published studies in refereed journals are considered to add to the body of knowledge in the area because they are based on tried and tested academic research processes. One advantage of refereed journal articles is that they tend to be relatively short in comparison to books. They also usually have abstracts which are quick to read when you are trying to decide whether something is likely to be of use. The majority of journals are online with some online and paper-based. Online journals can be searched via journal sites, but perhaps more usefully via databases that cover the many titles in a subject area. It is worth considering setting up email alerts for new articles in a keyword search as most databases have this facility. Another approach to extending your range of sources is to consider looking at articles within the same subject areas in the reference list of an article you have already found and also to search for any articles that cite the article you have just read. One potential disadvantage of journal articles, however, is that some studies can be very small in scale and may therefore be hard to generalize from or be too specific to be of use. If you find a study that is useful but small then you can include it but ensure that you discuss its limitations as part of your critical analysis of the literature.

Online databases and other internet sources

In addition to online journals there is a myriad of other material available via the internet including e-books, research reports, government documents, briefing papers and press reports that are often very up-to-date and which you can access easily and quickly. Both general internet search engines and more specialized search tools such as Google Scholar can be used to identify key researchers and commentators in a particular field as well as any generally available sources of information. Just as with library searches you will need to give consideration to potential keywords and combinations of keywords to get the best results. There are also online academic communities which provide chat rooms and discussion boards for debating and information exchange on particular topics including publicly funded evaluations and research groups (Clough and Nutbrown, 2012).

You can also use online databases of research, such as the Education Resources Information Centre (ERIC), to carry out searches across a wide range of electronically available and academically respectable sources, of which there may be several to choose from. You may need to access a number of databases to get the information you need as some topics may draw on different disciplines. For example, if your dissertation focuses on youth and community work you might need to draw on psychology and education as well as social work databases. Such databases can help you to get quick access a wide range of sources including journal articles, conference papers and abstracts of articles, books or papers. Guidance from your supervisor and/or your library staff will help you to identify those databases that will lead you to the best material for your dissertation and can help you to master the varied operating characteristics and features of each.

The internet can be particularly useful for providing access to government papers and the documents of non-governmental organizations with an interest in education and related matters. However, remember to distinguish between independent research publications and documents produced by governments and other 'interested parties', such as think tanks with particular viewpoints and perspectives. Government reports, for example, tend to outline policy goals and may therefore take a particular 'line' on a topic that is not always shared elsewhere. That said, government websites often include national evaluations of government policy, with targeted studies on particular policy developments which may be very useful. It is sometimes possible to sign up for alerts such as local government information or Ofsted reports which have links to new key government documents. These automatic alerts can be useful in keeping you up-to-date with developments in your topic but they may also offer you a great deal of information you neither need nor want.

Case Study – Department of Education website

The Department of Education website has many materials on it relevant to children's services and schools, including evaluation reports and other publications, policy and legislation, announcements, consultations and statistics. If you were writing a literature review in this field you would, therefore, want to look at this site as a starting point to make sure you have the latest information. However, you would also want to consider the perspective much of this material comes from and how independent it may be. You would want to see how relevant policies and practice had been evaluated as well as searching independent sources such as refereed journals to see what others have said.

The sheer volume of material available on the internet can cause problems. An overwhelming number of items identified in a single search may make it difficult to determine which are the most appropriate sources to look at. Equally the quality of internet sources needs to be carefully considered before using any item in your work. While some articles may be from an academic journal that is refereed, others may appear as drafts or be from more mysterious or even dubious sources. Information acquired via the internet can be highly variable in its quality (Walliman, 2004). The extraordinarily democratic nature of the technology means that all manner of scribblings, ravings and unsubstantiated prejudices and polemics written by some 'eye-wateringly blinkered' and bigoted individuals are easily available and can appear alongside the work of internationally respected scholars and organizations. You must not make the mistake of thinking that any such proximity is evidence of equivalence. You need to satisfy yourself as to the accuracy, authority, detail, recency and potential bias when using internet sources (Walliman, 2004). You can avoid this by using respected databases via the library web or use Google Scholar which edits out most of the dross. Cross-checking with other sources can also help you here.

Although exercising your critical and evaluative skills is not unique to the use of the internet, it is particularly important when using online sources especially when the origin of those sources is in doubt or if it seems likely that they have not been through any editorial or peer review process (Creme and Lea, 2003). If you think the material is useful, try and check where it came from and if uncertain ask your supervisor or library staff for advice. The following questions from the University of Melbourne (2007) can be used as a set of prompts to help you to be more critical when using websites:

- Who are the authors of this piece? What do you know about them?
- What is the perspective of the writer(s)?
- Why does the site exist?
- How old is the material? When was the site last updated?
- Are the arguments logical?
- Is there reliable evidence to support the arguments and claims made?
- Is the material correctly and fully referenced or linked to other online sources?

Conference papers

These can often be found on conference sites on the internet (see above). Most are based on the presenters' own research, some of which may be published and some not. Although they are likely to be fairly up-to-date and may group a number of similar studies together within the conference theme, which is often helpful, the quality may be hard to judge and the studies may vary in size and generalizability. Conference papers may refer to large-scale, well-funded projects or to small single-person projects and every kind of project in between and so you will have to make a judgement about the quality and relevance of any conference papers reviewed. Unfortunately, sham or vanity-based conferences with little or no academic vigour are on the increase so be aware that not all conference papers are acceptable.

Previous dissertations and theses

Some university and college libraries retain copies of students' dissertations as reference copies in their collections. Not only can previous dissertations offer you useful pointers as to key authors and sources for your own literature review they may also offer useful models for your work as they may be of a similar size to your project and written according to similar or the same guidelines. However although they may be quite useful for background reading, reference lists and tips on layout and structure it is important to remember that you cannot always be sure of their quality and reliability. You are unlikely to know, for example, what mark or grade they were awarded.

Managing your reading

Reading efficiently

The thought of all the reading that is involved in a literature review can be quite daunting. To avoid the reading for a dissertation becoming an overwhelming burden it is helpful to set aside time to read regularly and to read little and often. It is not a good idea to try and read very large quantities of material in a single sitting as you will become tired and miss things. It is important when you are searching for items to develop strategies which help you to determine quickly whether something is likely to be of use to your literature review or not. Where you are using journal articles or previous theses and dissertations try reading the abstract first for a brief summary of the study. It is what the abstract is there for and it could save you a lot of time. If an abstract is not available then an alternative way of checking quickly whether a particular source might be worth reading in more detail is to skim read the beginnings of chapters or specific sections to get the gist of the content. For example, sometimes you may turn first to the conclusions section of an article or chapter and what you read there will help you to decide whether you need to read the rest of the document. Where you have very large research reports and government publications you often find that they will provide an executive summary of the contents (usually found at the beginning of the report). These too can provide you with a quick way of deciding whether you need to read the whole report or not.

Make sure you keep a list of full references of all the items you have looked at or are thinking of reading as part of your literature review right from the start. If you have had referencing problems in the past or if feedback on other pieces of work suggested that you were not referencing correctly then you need to address this issue urgently as incorrect referencing will affect your mark for the dissertation.

Check the referencing guidelines that you have been given and ask for help from someone such as your supervisor, study support and academic guidance advisers or library staff.

When you find a likely source you will need to make sure you either have a copy or can locate the source again easily so you can read it and make notes. Most online material can be saved as a PDF file or you can print it thought this may be costly. If you do not have time to do any of these things, make a note of its location so that you can return to it quickly later on. Check with your library referencing guide what information you need to record for a reference. Your reference list can also note the location of the item (e.g. web address, library catalogue number, name of online database) if you have not yet saved it. A surprisingly large number of students (and other writers) do not do this and then have to waste precious time later on tracking down the sources of their notes or finding full references. You may end up with items on your list that you do not use in the finished dissertation and which, therefore, have to be removed from your final list of references. However this is preferable to a desperate last minute hunt for the source of a quote that you jotted down in a hurry months ago. If you do not discipline yourself to record every reference in full as you go along you will almost certainly struggle to return to specific sources again at a later date.

Reading critically

Once you have identified sources that you need to read in more detail this work too needs to be managed efficiently. Reading without a clear plan of what you are trying to find out may be acceptable and even quite useful when you are first reading around the wider topic but once you are clearer about what you want to focus on then you need to read with more purpose. Reading critically can be seen as concerned with content, analysis and appreciation. Clough and Nutbrown (2007; 2012) discuss the concept of 'radical reading' which encompasses a critical approach to the material you engage with. They suggest that the following questions should be considered when reading:

- What is the main point/central argument?
- Who is the audience?
- Why has this account of the research been written?
- What is the author trying to achieve?
- What evidence is offered to support claims?
- Is this evidence acceptable?
- What is your view and what evidence do you have for it?
- Does this account fit with your experience and knowledge and therefore should it be part of your study? (Clough and Nutbrown, 2007, p. 102).

Ideas to Use – 'Radical' or Critical Reading

Summary and context	
Research questions addressed	
Key terms and concepts	
Methods of data collection and analysis	
Claims made	
Assessment of claims	
Critical appreciation	

Another strategy you can employ if you find yourself referring to similar sources as some of your fellow students is to try to act as critical friends for one another (see the guidelines below). Remember, though, that if you do this you will need to be very careful not to overstep the boundaries between collaboration and collusion (see Chapter 9).

Ideas to Use – Reading Critically: Being a Critical Friend

The purpose of the exercise is for you to help one another to

- get to know the content (what the source *actually* says);
- comprehend the methodology/method(s) of the author(s);
- evaluate how trustworthy any claims are;
- consider how worthwhile the source is.

Individually

1. **Getting the 'gist'**
   Read/scan the paper fairly quickly.
   Working in pairs/small groups discuss:

2. **What's the paper about?**
   How would you summarize the paper?
   What is the research question(s)?
   Note down/discuss any key terms and concepts.

3. **Data and analysis**
   How did the author gather any data and analyse it?
   Why did he/she do it this way?
   What were the advantages/disadvantages?
   What claims does he/she make?

4. **Your assessment/evaluation/appreciation**
   What do you think of any claims made?
   How far is the source successful in its own terms, that is in relation to the author's own research question(s)?
   What implications, if any, does the paper have in general and for your dissertation in particular?
   What issues or questions remain unresolved or unasked?
   What effect, if any, has the paper had on your own thinking about the issues or anything else?

Note-taking and summarizing

As you read you will need to make notes and to summarize the material effectively. Summarizing is part of the process of getting your items organized and grouped by theme as a start to analysing their content and methodology and turning your items of literature into a well-written review (Punch, 2014). A summary should include

- any research questions the study set out to answer;
- brief contextual information if appropriate;
- a short statement about the methodology and sample where appropriate;
- the main findings and claims and how they were interpreted;
- key quotes, phrases and terms (explained and defined where necessary);
- comments on the quality of the source and whether any conclusions drawn are reasonable or useful.

Examples – Good Note-taking and Summarizing

Sought to evaluate the strategies used to support language development with 3–5-year-olds in nursery classes.

Research carried out in nine nursery classes in a socially and economically deprived area in north of England.

Data gathered through interviews with staff in each nursery and observations of nursery sessions in each setting.

Main findings = there needed to be more focus on planning and delivering specific language development activities in the classes and more support for child-initiated play in the sessions.

Sample is very small and the nurseries were all drawn from the same social context therefore difficult to generalize from the study.

Note-taking is a crucial skill and it does take practice, it can be surprisingly difficult to take notes that make sense later on when you return to them. You are aiming to précis, summarize and comment on the contents and not to copy them out in their entirety. Taking notes needs to be a focused activity that leaves you with information you can use in your literature review, not page after page of redundant information. Use keywords and phrases as prompts and make sure you put the page and possibly line number next to them so that you can locate them again quickly if you need to check back at a later date. You should not be afraid to put things in your own words albeit interspersed with keywords, phrases and concepts taken verbatim from the source. Remember that any such material should be clearly distinguished from your own words, for example, by using quotation marks and page numbers. However good notes do not just record or rewrite existing text they also include a reflective dimension in which the content of the source is questioned, explained, interpreted, commented on or linked to other sources. This could include a critique of the methodology, size and choice of sample and any factors that might affect validity of the findings. It may also critique the extent to which the findings support any conclusions or recommendations arising from the work.

Ideas to Use – Alternative Approaches to Note-taking

Jot things down sequentially as you go through the document from start to finish. Make some evaluative comments at the end.

Take notes sequentially but use two columns. In the first column note down factual information about the source. In the second column make some commentary/ remarks on the content as you go along.

Try breaking a document down by summarizing each page in three sentences and then summarizing all your sentences in one paragraph.

Read the document noting down only a few headings that represent the key themes and issues raised. Then return to the text and make more detailed notes under each of your headings.

Try a question and answer with a critical friend following the sample summary outline verbally, then write it down.

Once you have begun to find, select and summarize some sources, the next step is to organize your notes. To begin with it is a good idea to keep your notes together so that they are easily available when you need them. Summarize each source you are planning to use (or think you may use) as soon as possible. It is a personal decision as to whether you make notes by hand or on a computer file but whatever you do you need to file the notes as soon as they are completed. As the file fills up you can start to group the notes according to common themes for your review.

Organizing and structuring your literature review

A key skill for writing a good literature review is to be able to structure and organize the material effectively. One of the ways that you can manage and develop the structure of your literature review is to use a 'literature map' which is a visual or diagrammatic representation of the themes within the relevant existing research.

Case Study – Using a 'Literature Map'

Rowena was studying the gender differences in play both at school and at home in a group of 6–7-year-olds. She included in her literature map the following themes:

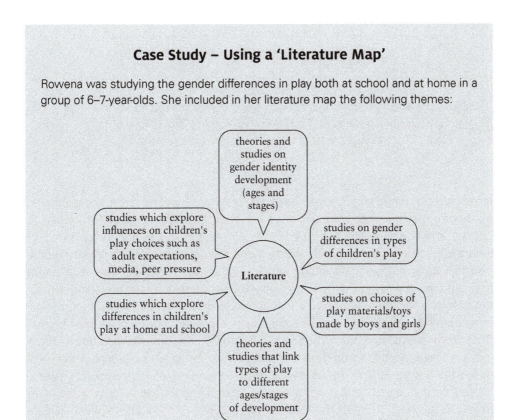

Often these maps feature interlocking circles, spider diagrams, flowcharts or hierarchical charts. The aim is to order your literature review using categories to group the studies found (Cresswell, 2014). The map may develop over time as new categories and sources are identified. It allows you to see what issues you need to address, what sources you are going to discuss under each category and where the gaps are. Subtopics are likely to emerge within the main topic and these may include groups of studies that support a particular viewpoint and/or build on each other's findings. There may be several groups of these which may represent different or opposing views on a topic. The map should be developed as you read and be added to as the shape and content of your literature review becomes clearer. It is not something you include in your finished review but provides you instead with some scaffolding to help you to develop the final structure of that review.

Ideas to Use – Developing a Literature Map

Using the model provided above:

(a) write a list of themes that have emerged from your reading so far;
(b) draw a literature map for your review to include these themes;
(c) start to group your readings under the themes on the map.

Irrespective of whether you make use of a 'literature map' or not it is essential to make sure that the final structure of your literature review is logical and relevant. Literature reviews should not look like a commentary on a random selection of readings listed in no particular order. The items discussed need to be linked in some way that suits the particular study and makes sense. There are several different forms of literature review, depending on the focus of the study you are doing. One of the simpler ways of organizing your literature is to place the sources in chronological order starting with the earliest. This approach may seem logical, but it may be that this merely produces a 'book catalogue' of commentary on unrelated items. There may well be a place for a brief historical account of progress or events in the field, to set the scene, outline the context or provide some useful background material for your own study, but this is not the same as ordering the whole of your literature review in this way. Three of the most common types of literature review include a thematic approach, a theoretical approach and a methodological approach; although many undergraduate dissertations will have literature reviews that have elements of more than one form.

A thematic approach to a literature review

Probably one of the most common methods of organizing a literature review is through themes which connect or group items in the review (Punch, 2014). This approach is characterized by organizing your readings according to the issues that you feel are the most significant themes in your topic area (Mac Naughton et al., 2010). This type of literature review seeks to discuss and integrate material about the topic to provide context, background and a summary of key research and areas of debate within the topic area. If you adopt a thematic approach then the various themes within the topic are discussed in a logical sequence and linked together to provide a systematic review of the studies, issues and arguments in the field. The focus is on the content of the area you are discussing and the themes obviously need to relate to your overall topic and specific research questions. The themes used should emerge from the reading and relate to more than one source.

Case Study – Using a Thematic Approach

Kai was studying the extent to which parents were encouraged to get involved in their children's learning by staff in a Year 3 class in a primary school. His literature review focused on discussing key themes arising from this area which were drawn from a range of sources. The themes included

> research into parental involvement and 'models' of partnership;
> the development of UK government policy on parent partnership;
> strategies used by schools and parents to support children's learning at home;
> communication issues between teachers and parents;
> potential barriers to parental involvement in school.

Each of the themes was discussed using material from a range of sources including research papers in refereed journals, government policy documents; press reports; books; professional magazines and websites of schools and parents groups.

A theoretical approach to a literature review

This type of literature review focuses on the main theories within the subject area and discusses these in relation to each other and the key debates in the field. The purpose is to identify, compare and possibly challenge the theories that determine thinking in the topic area and to develop an argument that may support certain theories as a basis for a study which focuses on theory testing or theoretical development. Clearly there is a crossover with some aspects of a thematic review which may also discuss theory. However, this type of literature review is more likely to be found in a study where the focus is examining, testing or expanding upon the theoretical basis of the field.

Case Study – Theory Testing

Sara is studying the extent to which babies in a private day nursery are showing attachment behaviours to their carers in the nursery. Sara wants to test the theory that securely attached children are better able to make attachments to other carers beyond their primary attachment to a parent or main carer. She wants to explore what stages babies go through on separation from their main carer and how they make attachments to other carers as part of this separation process. Sara is exploring a range of theories about children's attachment behaviour starting from John Bowlby's original work on attachment and the development of his theories from the 1950s onwards.

A methodological approach to a literature review

Some literature reviews are organized around the methodology or methods used in the sources discussed and the value of different methodologies for exploring particular issues or topics. These types of review focus not so much on the themes within the topic as the approaches used in key studies to gather data about those themes and the appropriateness and effectiveness of these in terms of achieving the aims and objectives of the study in question. Methodological literature reviews examine and critique studies from the starting point of how they were planned, designed and carried out. The key questions will be whether the methodology used was robust, reliable and valid for achieving the planned outcomes of the study or whether alternative approaches may have produced better results. For example, a study on the methods used to gather data from young children would have a review which focused on the methodological, ethical and data-gathering approaches. Key aspects of a study like this would include the ways in which researchers engaged with the children, how 'informed' consent was obtained and the steps that were taken to ensure that the data-collection methods used were appropriate for the age of the participants.

Case Study – Focusing on Methodology and Methods

Geraint's dissertation focused on adoption and in particular the incidence of adoption breakdown. He wanted to look at the approaches to seeking this information and the criteria used in different studies for determining whether an adoption had broken down or not. He was aware that in the UK some studies were based on government figures for children returned into the care system which might not have included all the children whose adoption had failed. He was also aware that some studies depended on parental reporting which involved varied criteria for what was defined as a 'breakdown'. For example, where a 16-year-old was living away from home, albeit with adoptive parental support and involvement, that might be regarded in some quarters as a failed adoption. Geraint intended to critique the available studies in terms of their methodological approaches and the extent to which these produced reliable and valid results.

Once you have gathered and read a significant number of relevant sources and mapped them by theme, theory or methodological approach you will in be a position to start editing and pulling the different sections together into a coherent whole (see Chapter 9). You may not, at this stage, have all the items you are eventually going to include in your literature review, so assume you will at some stage be doing supplementary searches to fill the gaps identified as you write. A literature map should have made some of the gaps obvious; so, make sure you continue to search as you write. However, this should be a clearly focused search at this stage, based on a definite idea of what additional sources you need to include. Your writing plan should cover the order in which you will discuss the themes, theories or issues you have identified and the links you are going to make within sections and between sections. If possible, get your supervisor or another appropriate person to look at your writing plan before you start.

Summary of key points

- Start reading early on and keep your reference list up-to-date right from the start.
- Check to see if you already have relevant material from elsewhere on your course or from other sources. Use the reference lists or bibliographies from these materials to find other items.
- Make sure you discuss your plans with your supervisor(s) and seek other expert support as required, for example library advisers.
- Choose your keywords carefully to ensure you find the main studies in your chosen area. Be prepared to revise your search terms if you are not successful first time round in your searches.
- Start a literature map as soon as themes begin to emerge and extend it as you continue to search and read.
- Group your chosen items under the themes in your map as you find them and extend your themes as new ones emerge. Note any gaps in your map and fine-tune your literature searches to fill them.
- Ensure all items used are relevant, academically respectable or in some other way appropriate for your study.
- Be prepared to abandon irrelevant and/or out-of-date material.
- Make sure your review makes links and connections between themes, theories and issues.
- Make sure your review contains critical discussion of the sources chosen and the themes, theories and issues identified.

Reflective task

Choose a study on a previous piece of research that is relevant to your research topic and read it:

1 What was the methodological approach and how well did it work to gather the required data? Could it have been done differently and if so how?

2 What was the sample size? How could this affect the influence of the study on your own work?

3 How old is the study? Why is this important and how do you need to reflect this in your literature review? Was anything different about the context when this study was done?

4 How was the data analysed? Does the analytical approach work well to produce answers to the research questions? Could it have been done differently?

5 Do the conclusions and/or recommendations accurately reflect the findings? Can you see how the author(s) reached their conclusions? How do they contribute to knowledge in the field?

6 How does this study fit with other studies in the field? Are there similarities? Are their differences in findings and if so what may be the reasons?

7 What was the methodological approach and how well did it work to gather the required data? Could it have been done differently and if so how?

8 What was the sample size? How could this affect the influence of the study on your own work?

9 How old is the study? Why is this important and how do you need to reflect this in your literature review? Was anything different about the context when this study was done?

10 How was the data analysed? Does the analytical approach work well to produce answers to the research questions? Could it have been done differently?

11 Do the conclusions and/or recommendations accurately reflect the findings? Can you see how the author(s) reached her/his conclusions? How do they contribute to knowledge in the field?

12 How does this study fit with other studies in the field? Are there similarities? Are there differences in findings and if so what may be the reasons?

Link to companion website

https://bloomsbury.com/cw/successful-dissertations-second-edition/student-resources/chapter-4/

Recommended reading and further sources of information

Your university should have online advice about writing a literature review and there may be course-level advice as well.

Ridley, D. (2012), *The Literature Review: A Step-By-Step Guide For Students* (Sage Study Skills Series) London: Sage.

Wevers, J. and McMillan, K. (2011, 2nd edition), *How to Write Dissertations and Project Reports* (Smarter Study Skills). Essex, England: Pearson Education Ltd.

5

Research Methodologies

Jonathan Wainwright

Chapter Outline

Chapter Aims

By the end of this chapter you will

- know what terms such as methodology, ontology and epistemology mean;
- understand the distinction between quantitative and qualitative methodologies;
- be familiar with a number of different methodological approaches to research, including
  - an experimental approach;
  - an ethnographic approach;
  - a phenomenological approach;
  - a grounded-theory approach;
  - an action research approach;
  - a narrative approach;
  - a case study approach;
- be able to make methodological choices suitable for literature-based dissertations.

As soon as the word 'methodology' is heard, confusion and concern seem to follow and words like phenomenology, interpretivism and positivism can appear very intimidating at first. This chapter aims to provide you with an understanding of methodology and some of the terms used. It deals with two of the key issues in methodology: how we think the world is and how we explain it. It will also help you to make a clear distinction between methodology and methods and allow you to outline your own position on the research you plan to undertake for your dissertation. Understanding these concepts will enable you to make convincing arguments for your chosen research methods.

Methodology or methods?

In defining methodology perhaps the first distinction to make is that between *methodology* and *methods*. The term *methods* describes the techniques or procedures used to gather data related to your research question or hypothesis. Chapters 6 and 7 offer more detailed information about a range of data-collection methods that you may wish to consider. *Methodology* however is the framework and rationale around which your project is structured. Among other things your methodology will determine the relationship between your literature, the data you have collected and your subsequent analysis. The methodology informs your decisions on how you set about the task of choosing methods and analysing data. The methodology should underpin every aspect of your dissertation and your choice of methodological approach will be determined by your values and beliefs which will in turn influence your views first on how you think the world is (the nature of reality and being) and second how you explain the world (what counts as knowledge).

Points to Think About – Four Levels of Understanding

Porter describes research as being founded on four levels of understanding:

Level 1: Ontology – What is the nature of reality?
Level 2: Epistemology – What counts as knowledge of the real world?
Level 3: Methodology – How can we gain an understanding of reality?
Level 4: Methods – How can we collect evidence about reality?

Source: Porter, 1996, pp. 113–22.

Ontology

Ontology is the study of 'being'. It is concerned with the question 'What is the nature of existence and reality?' and our ontology is our view of how we think the world is. Ontology has strong links to epistemology (the study of knowledge – or how we explain the world) and the boundaries can become blurred on occasion. In the interests of clarity of understanding, however, this text will treat the two things as distinct from one another. Stainton-Rogers offers a brief overview of ontology; she refers to the nature of what things are and their being in the world as 'what it consists of, what entities operate within it and how they relate to each other' (Stainton-Rogers in Porter, 2006, p. 79) or, more straightforwardly, as whether the social world is regarded as external to social actors or as something that people are in the process of constructing (Bryman, 2016).

Put in its simplest terms there are three broad traditions within ontology. On the one hand there are those who argue in favour of an objective approach to the search for the truth, sometimes referred to as 'realists' or 'objectivists'. Those taking an alternative position, sometimes referred to as 'constructivists', argue instead that ideas, thoughts and social interactions are also real and have meaning. There is a third ontological position which is purely subjective and suggests that knowledge is generated from the mind with no external reference. However, it would be difficult to take a completely subjectivist approach in your research as this position implies that any claim you might make can be neither true nor false, or that what is said is really just reflecting your state of mind at the time.

For the objectivist the world is a place that is governed by the laws of nature which, through reasoned analysis and experimentation, we can discover. Things just 'are' and are completely independent of human meaning. When objectivists research the world they can be, as the title suggests, completely objective about it. A tree makes a noise when it falls, it does not matter if anyone is there to hear it or not.

When students talk about 'findings' in dissertations they are often using language that reflects this objectivist stance, that is there is something that has always been there, it has just not been discovered before. Objectivist ontology says that the things we see in the world are measurable and can be explained in a scientific way. In other words, the only way that claims of knowledge about what things there are in the world can be justified is through observation and testing. Such claims have to be

- reliable, in that the same procedures, experiments or actions carried out in another place and at another time would produce the same result(s);
- valid, in that the research is really measuring or observing what it claims to be;
- and generalizable, in that the work and its outcomes are applicable and/or useful to people in similar situations elsewhere (Swetnam, 2004, p. 23).

Example – An Objective Reality

You may remember from your school science lessons that when you set fire to magnesium ribbon, it flares up; it always flares up, not just now and then. What is more, there is a rigorous and well-tested chemical explanation for this phenomenon ($2Mg + O_2 = 2MgO$) which is readable all over the world. It is all to do with energy and oxidation and scientists can do the calculations to prove it.

From a social science perspective the objectivist or realist ontological position implies that *social phenomena confront us as external facts that are beyond our reach or influence* (Bryman, 2016, p. 29). All social phenomena and categories are viewed as existing beyond the control of the people involved in them and their actions and are separate from any meaning we might put on them; in other words the truth is out there regardless. For example, if you were interested in the characteristics of good educational leaders, such as head teachers or children's centre managers, an objectivist ontology would suggest that such characteristics are clearly identifiable, that they are clearly measurable, that your view of these characteristics would be the same as everyone else's and that these characteristics would always prove effective no matter what the situation. However, you need only compare the distinctly different characteristics of say, Margaret Thatcher and Mother Teresa, both of whom might be described as having been effective leaders, to see that there are some issues arising with this approach. An alternative way of viewing the nature of being, therefore, is the 'constructivist' position.

The constructivist view holds that there is no objective reality, only models of it. Knowledge is constructed rather than being discovered. Unlike the objectivist approach where the researcher seeks things which have not yet been discovered, the constructivist approach would argue that just finding things out is not enough to explain what there is in the world. It does not deny the world, a world of 'death and furniture', but it does challenge the idea that all we have to do is to *strip off the veils of human ignorance in order to reveal facts about the-world-as-it-really-is* (Stainton-Rogers, 2003, p. 28). From this ontological perspective meanings are socially constructed by people as they engage with the world (Crotty, 2003, p. 43).

According to Bryman, constructivism asserts that *'social phenomena and their meanings are continually being accomplished by their social actors ... [and] are in a constant state of revision'* (Bryman, 2016, p. 29).

As an example, the way in which childhood is seen by society varies both over time and with culture. Historically, children were 'not treated any differently or recognised as being of particular concern because of their young age' (Clark, 2013, p. 17) as a result they dressed in the same way as adults and were expected to work. Our perspective on childhood is now constructed very differently.

A constructivist ontology means then, that meaning cannot be described as objective in the way that an objectivist would. Meaning is built or made from what is already there around us and this ontology represents the way in which we interact with the world, not seeing ourselves as separate from it.

For the purposes of your dissertation therefore it is possible to consider the world either as a place where you can find out things which have always been there and measure them through observation or experimentation and/or as a place where you influence the construction of reality and need to interpret what has been constructed. This is where you make your first choices since once you have established your view of what the world is like, you can start to think about how you can explain that this is the case.

Epistemology

As we have already seen it can be difficult to separate 'being' from 'knowing' and epistemology refers to how we can know things and what counts as knowledge (Crotty, 2003). In other words, what can we know and how can we know what we know? As with the debates over ontology there is more than one epistemological standpoint. One of the ways in which you could try to determine which epistemological tradition you might be coming from is to consider whether you think the social world, that of people, can be studied in exactly the same way that we study the natural sciences (Bryman, 2016). If you think the answer is yes you could be said to be taking a positivist position. This is not unlike the objectivist way of looking at the world that was outlined in the previous section and confirms how difficult it can be to separate ontology from epistemology. Positivism is rooted in a number of key principles:

- Knowledge has to be gained through, and confirmed by, our senses.
- Research must generate hypotheses that can be tested.
- Knowledge is arrived at through gathering facts which enable laws to be established and predictions to be made.
- Research must be conducted in a way that is value free (Bryman, 2016, p. 24).

This approach results in a position where researchers are trying to explain human behaviour by looking for the forces that act on people and identifying the causes of their actions. This approach to knowledge implies that every researcher who looks at something will see that thing in the same way. It is easy to see why a positivist approach can seem like the sensible approach to all research as it appears to offer clear, trustworthy and 'scientific' explanations. However, if things were that simple and there were universal laws governing social situations, then people would not need to argue about the significance of events. Yet clearly we do argue and disagree about all manner of social situations, everything from international summits between world leaders to who will win the 'X Factor'. The positivist approach can even run into difficulties in relation to the natural sciences. For example, take the burning magnesium example mentioned earlier; observers might argue about how brightly it burned, or how noisy it was despite being able to produce objective measures for these characteristics. You might also remember the black and blue dress, which many saw as white and gold (or the other way around, of course). [1]What one person sees may well be very different from what another sees and can be influenced by their own ideas, motivations and view of the world.

Positivism forms one end of an epistemological continuum where it is argued that there can be a certainty of knowledge which we gain through our senses, knowledge which is 'value free', detached from the researcher and which offers explanation and predictable rules.

At the other end of this continuum lies interpretivism. Where natural science looks for laws, interpretivism looks for human explanations and as everyone is very different we see the world in very different ways. The interpretivist researcher's interest in this world then is likely to centre on individuals and groups of individuals and their unique perspectives. This perspective suggests a real difference between social science and natural science. This difference comes from the idea that social reality matters to people and they behave in a way that is influenced by others and reflects what matters to them.

As Schwandt (2001) suggests, human action is inherently meaningful and in order to *understand a particular social action, for example, friendship, voting or teaching, the inquirer must grasp the meanings that constitute that action* (Schwandt, 2001, p. 191). What it is important to realize is that social actions have different meanings in different societies and contexts, and they can be carried out with different intentions. For instance, tears may indicate sorrow or joy or, in the case of crocodile tears, deception, just as raising one's arm could be variously interpreted as voting, hailing a taxi or asking for permission to speak (Schwandt, 2001). As researchers, it is our job to 'gain access to people's "common sense thinking" and to interpret their actions and social worlds from their point of view' (Bryman, 2012, p. 30).

Interpretivism, then, describes approaches to knowledge which require us to understand what particular social actions mean. Inevitably, though, as a researcher, we have to put our own meanings on to social actions in order to write about them; indeed, this is where the term interpretivism comes from.

Methodology

Methodology has been described as a 'plan of action' (Crotty, 2003, p. 7) and your view of the world and the nature of knowledge, therefore, will influence your decisions

---

[1]See Wikipedia 'The Dress'. This was a viral internet picture from 26 February 2015 where there was disagreement over whether a dress was black and blue – or white and gold.

about how to go about answering your research question. This standpoint will help to determine which methodological approach you adopt (Crotty, 2003; Cresswell, 2013). Your question too will have implications for the decisions you make about which is the most appropriate methodological approach to adopt depending on whether you are seeking to describe something, to explain something, to quantify something and/or to change something. The methodology sections of your dissertation will be rooted in your epistemological and ontological standpoint and will set out why you chose the research methods that you did, how you used them and how you set out to analyse the data that they produced.

None of the methodological traditions covered in this chapter is immune from criticism; all have their strengths and weaknesses and you will need to assess which approach offers the 'best fit' for your research question (Denscombe, 2007). Broadly speaking, your methodological approach is likely to fall into one of three or four categories or 'paradigms'. Your research methodology could be located in objectivist, positivist traditions, often characterized by the collection of quantitative data, such as statistical tests and correlations. Alternatively, your methodology may be constructivist and interpretivist in nature, often characterized by the collection of qualitative data such as narrative or visual data. Table 5.1 discusses the differences between qualitative and quantitative approaches.

A third tradition is variously described as critical, transformative or emancipatory. This includes such things as feminist theory, queer theory, cultural theory and critical

Table 5.1 Differences between qualitative and quantitative approaches to methodology

Qualitative	Quantitative
The aim is a complete, detailed description.	The aim is to classify features, count them and construct statistical models in an attempt to explain what is observed.
You may only know roughly in advance what you are looking for.	You know clearly in advance what you are looking for.
The design emerges as the study unfolds.	All aspects of the study are carefully designed before data is collected.
You are the data gathering instrument.	You use tools, such as questionnaires or equipment to collect numerical data.
Data is in the form of words, pictures or objects. This approach is more 'rich', time-consuming and generally not intended to be generalized.	Data is in the form of numbers and statistics. This approach is more efficient and able to test hypotheses. You are trying to find things that are generalizable.

Source: Miles and Huberman, 1994, p. 40.

race theory. This tradition originates in Marxism and makes use of both positivist and interpretivist approaches arguing that both are incomplete as a result of their failure to engage with issues of power and domination in society. Researchers from a critical tradition aims to shed light on the operation of power in society and to contribute to increasing social justice (Kincheloe and Steinberg, 1998). Horkheimer (1937) suggests that critical theory must explain social problems, offer practical solutions to them, and then make the change. Researchers from the critical tradition therefore often adopt methodological approaches and styles such as action research aimed at effecting change and bringing about perceived improvements in people's situations.

Emancipatory Research: Feminist Perspectives

Feminism is difficult to define but is basically both a concept and a movement, which focuses on acknowledging and working to identify and change gender inequalities. The concept of gender inequalities is central to feminist approaches to research. These are based on the belief that ways of knowing the world are gender-biased and feminists challenge the *knowledge that is validated* in a gender-unequal world (Brayton, 1997, p. 2). Feminist epistemology challenges the qualitative versus quantitative classification of research methodologies and argues that both approaches are based on patriarchal assumptions (Anderson, 2009). There is no simply defined feminist methodology (Punch, 1998). Feminist research is a broad field with many diverse groups (e.g. liberal, Marxist, radical, etc.) and there is some difficulty in knowing what identifies particular research as feminist. It is a complex and changing field; earlier concepts of women as a homogenous group have given way to recognition of the interconnections between gender and other factors such as ethnicity and class in determining women's experiences and perspectives (Olesen, 2005). In general though, feminist research starts with women's experiences and viewpoints and then actively seeks to challenge and change gender inequalities; as such, it is characterized by

- conscious efforts to reduce the power imbalance between participants and researchers;
- attempts to ensure research reflects the participants views, experiences and standpoints faithfully;
- a recognition of the role of the researcher in determining the structure and outcomes of the research;
- a focus on research as a means of bringing about active social change for women (Brayton, 1997).

In the past there has been a tendency in research to see these different methodological paradigms as fundamentally and irreconcilably opposed to each other. Quantitative approaches tended to be associated with natural science, objectivism and positivism; qualitative approaches were seen to be related to constructivism and interpretative ways of thinking, while emancipatory approaches included action research. The language used on occasions, for example 'hard' and 'soft' often hinted at the underlying worth attached to different approaches by different authors. This is probably less the case now and there is greater recognition that each type of research has its place. Miles and Huberman (1994) argue, for example, that the quantitative and qualitative traditions need each other, though of course there will always be those who put their trust in large-scale quantitative research over what they might see as a more subjective qualitative approach and vice versa. Perhaps therefore a fourth approach might be termed *mixed* or *pragmatic* in nature. You do not have to be a 'purist' to produce a high quality dissertation and this approach draws on any and all of the various traditions in response to the research question or theme (Crotty, 2003, p. 215).

Common methodological approaches

The remainder of the chapter will provide an overview of some of the more common methodologies adopted by undergraduate education students when doing their dissertations. Some of the key questions and issues that need to be thought through in relation to particular methodological approaches will be outlined and suggestions offered about further reading. It is worth noting that the boundaries between some of the different methodologies open to you can become blurred on occasion and your methodology may have characteristics associated with more than one approach; for example your research could be a case study and ethnographic at the same time. It is also worth pointing out that the descriptions here cannot hope to deal with all the possible different variations under a particular heading. For example, there are different types of experimental designs and there are alternative approaches in phenomenology. For this reason having outlined some of the broad features of these different methodological approaches the chapter makes some suggestions about further sources of information to consult once you have decided what your methodology will be. The approaches covered include experimental design, ethnography, phenomenological research, grounded theory, action research, narrative research and case studies. Table 5.2 shows the various common methods in this regard.

Table 5.2 Common methodological approaches

	Focus	Common methods
Experimental research	Finding out how things happen	Scientific experiments
Ethnography	Describing a culture	Observations and interviews, other artefacts
Phenomenological research	Understanding the essence of experience	Interviews
Grounded theory	Developing a theory grounded in data from the field	Interviews with a significant sample size
Action research	Developing your own practice	Interview, documents, observation, self-reflection
Narrative research	Exploring the life of an individual	Interviews and documents
Case study	Developing an in-depth description	Interviews, observations, documents

Experimental research

Experimental research is positivistic in nature; it draws on research traditions in the natural sciences and aims to produce results that are predictable and repeatable. Researchers who adopt an experimental methodology must seek to control all the factors or variables that might influence the results of their experiment. By doing this they intend to test a theory or hypothesis and to make judgements about the different variables. In an experiment of this kind the researcher tries to design an approach where there is only one factor or variable which can impact on the results. Experimental researchers must attempt to control all the independent variables so that any effects observed during the experiment can only be as a result of the dependent variable (see Chapter 6 for more on variables). This sort of research design is likely to involve a control group which is not involved in the research activity. For instance, in testing a new drug among a number of people, all of the participants may be given a tablet but only some of them will be given a tablet which contains the active ingredients. Everyone else receives a placebo which has no effect on the human body. The researchers can then look for differences between those receiving the drug and the control group who have been taking the harmless fake tablets.

An experimental methodology presents researchers with a number of issues to be resolved when the experiments involve living participants. One of the first challenges, particularly for those working in educational contexts, centres on the ethics of control groups. Imagine for one moment that you believe that a new reading scheme will improve young children's ability to read. To test the impact of this new reading scheme you could introduce the new approach to half of the children in a class while continuing with the old approach with the rest of the class who would act as the control group. However if your hypothesis, that the new scheme was better, proved to be true you would have advantaged one half of the class over the other half and condemned that control group to poorer performance as a result.

One response to the difficulties of establishing control groups is to make the observations and then use the data from those observations to create the groups. This is sometimes referred to as 'quasi-experimental research'. For example, if you wished to measure the link between illness and the number of cigarettes smoked daily then in a true experiment you might ask one group of participants to smoke 20 cigarettes a day, another group 40 cigarettes a day and a third group 60 cigarettes per day and so on. However, this would clearly be unethical as you would be harming your participants; an alternative, therefore, is to ask people who already smoke how many cigarettes they smoke each day and then create your groups that way. This approach may have an added advantage of being a quicker and less expensive way of identifying your samples too, although it would depend on your participants' accuracy and honesty when discussing their smoking habits.

Other potential difficulties facing those adopting an experimental methodology centre on threats to the validity or trustworthiness of the research. In some instances, events in between your observations that are beyond your control such as illness among your participants or even bad weather may affect your results. This problem is sometimes referred to as 'history'. Another issue facing education students is the problem of maturation. Taking the reading scheme example from above it may be that any improved reading scores might be the result of the children's natural growth and development rather than the impact of the new reading scheme. Yet another issue to be thought through concerns pre-testing and the effect that your early observations may have on your later observations. Your participants may become sensitized and more aware of your purpose and may alter their responses and behaviour as a result. Another challenge is sometimes referred to as 'experimental mortality' and refers to the loss of research participants. For example, if your experiment centres on the experiences of children with EAL and a number of your participants leave to visit Pakistan for an extended period during your research you may not be comparing like with like.

If you decide that experimental research is the approach that best fits your research question you will need to clearly articulate your hypothesis, design an experiment in which all the variables apart from the dependent variable can be held, conduct a pilot, revise your design if necessary, carry out your experiment, measure your results, analyse your data and draw your conclusions.

Ethnography

Ethnography is rooted in interpretivist epistemologies and has its origins in cultural anthropology. An ethnographic methodology seeks to understand humans in context, that is where they live, how they live, why they live. The approach sets out to offer an account of the *social life and culture in a particular social system based on detailed observations of what people actually do* (Johnson, 2000, p. 111). Ethnography developed originally from researchers living with groups of people in pre-industrial societies and conducting participant observations on them – examples of this type of research include the works of Margaret Meade in Samoa and Bronislaw Malinowski in the Trobriand Islands in the 1920s. However, ethnographic approaches have also been used to research human society and culture much closer to home, such as Evans' (2006) study of Educational Failure and Working Class White Children in Britain. Evans spent nearly two years researching a failing primary school and working-class families and neighbourhoods in Bermondsey and showed that while families and schools blame each other for educational underperformance among many working-class children, the real problems are that many children are unprepared at home for school-based learning and the issue of 'problem families' is overstated; street culture is, especially for boys, likely to be as, if not more, significant a cause of educational failure than problems in the family home (Evans, 2006).

Using an ethnographic methodology a researcher will focus on a particular group or community, for example a nursery, a school, a children's centre or a youth club and will seek to immerse herself/himself in the culture of that situation. While there she/he will get involved either overtly or covertly in that community over an extended period of time by watching and listening to what is said and done, by asking questions and by collecting *whatever data are available to throw light on the issues that are the focus of the research* (Hammersley and Atkinson, 1995, p. 1).

> If you want to understand what motivates a guy to take up skateboarding, you could bring him into a sterile laboratory and interrogate him … or you could spend a week in a skate park observing him interacting with his friends, practising new skills and having fun. (Yu in AIGA, 2009, p. 4)

In an ethnographic study data is collected through participant and non-participant observations, interviews and, in situations where documentary evidence is involved, content analysis. Interviewing becomes an iterative approach where interviewees are spoken to many times often using information obtained from other interviews. This enables the researcher to probe deeply into the issue being studied and helps to develop a collective understanding. An ethnographic methodology may seek to understand the situation from the perspective of an 'insider' (emic approach) or it may take the opposite tack and aim to offer the perspective of an unbiased observer who is an 'outsider' (etic approach).

As with all of the methodologies outlined in this section this one has challenges associated with it. It is common for ethnographic researchers to spend a significant amount of time, months and even years, immersed in the culture under study. This poses a considerable problem for an undergraduate researcher who will probably only have nine or ten months to complete her/his dissertation and so will have a very limited amount of time in which to conduct any field work. This might make becoming an 'insider' impossible in many situations. One criticism that is sometimes made of ethnography concerns the trustworthiness of the research. Cresswell (2013) suggests that ethnography is a challenging approach not just because of the time involved, but also because of the possibility of 'going native' and thus being unable to complete the study.

Those opting for an 'insider' approach may find that being a participant presents challenges in collecting data, for example being a 'player' in children's role play may require you to stay in role and prevent you from noting down observations. Being a participant in young people's lives may also present other dilemmas, for example being invited to take part in antisocial or illegal activity. Alternatively, adopting the role of dispassionate 'outside' observer may make participants less inclined to trust and open up to you or more likely to exclude you from things. In some contexts trying to maintain the non-participant outside observer role can be difficult. In some instances you may feel compelled to intervene (e.g. if you think a child is at risk). In other situations your status as non-participant observer might not be recognized or acknowledged by some of those being observed. For example, trying to engage in non-participant observations in a nursery setting can be very difficult in the face of young children's enquiries about who you are, what you are doing there and/or whether you can help with something.

A further criticism levelled at ethnographic approaches is that their focus on specific groups and communities makes it impossible to make generalizations based on the results. However, it could be argued that this criticism is not entirely fair as many ethnographic studies do not set out to demonstrate repeatable results in the same way that positivist methodologies might attempt to do. Provided the data are robust and valid then the research can be regarded as trustworthy. Chapter 5 offers further advice and guidance in relation to positionality and reflexivity and you will need responses to questions such as those listed below if and when you decide to adopt an ethnographic methodology.

Points to Think About – Key Questions for Would-be Ethnographic Researchers

- Can a research methodology or approach ever be free of values?
- Can the methods or tools used in carrying out your research be separated from your values, feelings and emotions?
- What should be declared and in how much detail? How does a researcher's 'positionality' impact upon her/his research and how, and to what extent, should it be made explicit?
- Where and how should 'reflexivity' (see Chapter 5) work within your research design, data collection, data analysis, writing and reporting?

Source: BERA, 2004.

Phenomenological research

Phenomenology sets out to study and describe the meaning of experience, and to understand social and psychological phenomena through the perspectives of the individuals involved (Groenewald, 2004). The approach may be particularly useful if your research question seeks to understand the motivations behind people's actions and behaviours. This object of human experience could be almost anything, children's experiences of a reading scheme, the experiences of single parents or the experience of starting university. The approach requires that data are collected from people who have first-hand experience of the particular phenomenon under investigation and the researcher's job is to describe and interpret the common features arising from these individual perspectives to get at the essence of that experience (Cresswell, 2013, p. 76). This description and interpretation will consist of 'what' those involved experienced and 'how' they experienced it. A key feature of a phenomenological methodological approach is the need to try and 'bracket' your previous experience and knowledge. In other words the researcher has to put aside all preconceptions, prejudices and expectations from his/her mind in order to describe the phenomenon as accurately as possible, as though seeing it for the first time.

Phenomenological approaches may involve single cases or they may extend to include a much wider, larger range of participants. They often draw on data-collection methods similar to those listed above under ethnography, that is interviews, observations and content analysis. The approach tends to emphasize depth rather than structure. Although rapport, empathy and trust are all essential if you hope to get participants to share their experiences and opinions openly and honestly especially when the topic under observation or being discussed is hugely important to those participants, at the same time researchers using this methodology must take care not to influence the outcomes. For example, if your research focuses on teachers' practices and attitudes and you are seeking the teachers' perspectives on these then you must be aware of how sensitive a topic this is likely to be for your participants.

Challenges to phenomenology have been made in a number of quarters. One criticism levelled at the approach concerns the concept of bracketing. Many researchers have questioned the ability of anyone to completely clear their minds of existing knowledge, preconceptions and biases. Should you opt for a phenomenological methodology, therefore, you may wish to respond to this criticism by making your own positionality clear as part of your discussion (see Chapter 5). Another difficulty for undergraduate students can result from phenomenology's emphasis on depth. Phenomenological approaches often produce large quantities of rich, thick data that can be messy and hard to categorize – for example, interview transcripts, post-it notes and audio-visual recordings. As with ethnography, phenomenological research projects are unlikely to result in findings that are generalizable from a statistical perspective and given that the approach requires the researcher to interpret as well as report, it leaves itself open to charges of subjectivity and bias.

Grounded theory

Grounded theory is a research methodology located in interpretivist traditions which, at first glance, appears to turn the norms of research practice on their head. Grounded theory begins with data collection. The approach was developed by Glaser and Strauss in the late 1960s as a challenge to the idea that qualitative research was not as scientific as it might have been. The thinking behind grounded theory was that knowledge could be increased by developing new theories as opposed to analysing data using existing theory. The theory which is developed as a result therefore is 'grounded' in the data that comes from participants who have experienced the process being studied.

In grounded theory the stages of research differ, starting with the identification of the question, followed by data collection, then data coding and categorization so that connections and causal relationships can be made coupled with the generation of a hypothesis. Software packages such as NVivo and SPSS (Statistical Software Package for the Social Sciences) are sometimes used to support this process. The final stage is the validation of that hypothesis (Strauss and Corbin, 1990). Key features of grounded-theory include coding, 'memoing' and a review of the literature that emerges as the research progresses. By examining the data repeatedly, grounded theory researchers are trying to 'spot' ideas, categories and patterns. This coding activity happens at a number of levels. Open coding is essentially a descriptive process in which you identify 'what' you have got. Axial coding involves looking for connections and relationships. Thirdly comes selective coding as you attempt to identify what is the core category involved in your research around which everything else revolves. 'Memoing' describes the process of noting down your thoughts and ideas throughout the research process as you gather, code and analyse your data, and as you make links between your data and the literature.

Case Study – Coding and 'Memoing'

Data:

'Pain relief is a major problem when you have arthritis. Sometimes, the pain is worse than other times, but when it gets really bad, whew! It hurts so bad, you don't want to get out of bed. You don't feel like doing anything. Any relief you get from drugs that you take is only temporary or partial.'

'Memoing':

'One thing that is being discussed here is PAIN. One of the properties of pain is INTENSITY: it varies from a little to a lot. (When is it a lot and when is it little?) When it hurts a lot, there are consequences: don't want to get out of bed, don't feel like doing things (what are other things you don't do when in pain?). In order to solve this problem, you need PAIN RELIEF. One AGENT OF PAIN RELIEF is drugs (what are other members of this category?). Pain relief has a certain DURATION (could be temporary), and EFFECTIVENESS (could be partial).'

Source: Strauss and Corbin, 1990, p. 78.

The relationship between grounded theory and literature is interesting. At first glance it might appear that a grounded-theory dissertation would mean that you could forego the need to do any reading and move straight to data collection. The reality is likely to be more complicated; reading too much, too soon might risk closing your mind down to certain possibilities when coding and 'memoing'. On the other hand, however, the literature is just as likely to point the way to new ideas and is an indispensable part of every dissertation, particularly for undergraduate students who may be engaging with themes and topics for the first time. The likelihood is, therefore, that if you adopt a grounded-theory methodology your reading and the data collection, coding and 'memoing' are likely to run in parallel rather than sequentially, with you not always knowing ahead of time which sources you will need to go to until the relevance of those texts emerges from your data.

Grounded theory may be useful in situations where there is no existing theory to explain the thing you are researching or where the theories were developed among participants very different from those you might be interested in. However, in order to generate new theory, it is likely that research would have to involve a lot of participants in order to fully develop (or 'saturate') the model. Cresswell (2013) suggests this may involve between 20 and 60 interviews, which would probably be beyond the capacity of most undergraduate students in a nine- to ten-month period. Grounded theory therefore is not an easy option for those who have a relatively limited amount of time in which to complete a dissertation and who may benefit from adopting methodologies that put reading ahead of data collection in the sequence of events. A grounded-theory approach will also need the support and understanding of your supervisor.

Action research

Action research is a methodological approach focused on changing practice. It is widely acknowledged to have developed from the work in the 1940s of Kurt Lewin, who suggested a seven-step approach to the process:

1 Identify the research question;

2 Find out what you can about it;

3 Plan what you intend to do (i.e. the action you are going to take);

4 Do it (take the first action step);

5 Evaluate what happened as a result of your action;

6 Revisit the plan for action – or plan the next step;

7 Do it (take the second action step) (Lewin, 1946).

Individuals identify an aspect of their practice that they feel could be improved on and then set out to find a solution and to understand their practice better. Self-reflection is a central part of action research and the 'action' term implies that you will continue to learn and develop. McNiff and Whitehead (2006) suggest that action research does not have a hypothesis at the start but then neither does it have a particular end point, which they argue distinguishes it from other forms of research. In addition, because the researcher herself/himself is part of the focus of the research, anyone opting for an action research methodology needs to be clear about why they want to do what it is that they want to do. These reasons will reflect their values, aspirations and beliefs and so their positionality (see Chapter 2) and will need to be made explicit in a dissertation based on action research. As Carr and Kemiss put it:

> Action research is simply a form of self-reflective enquiry undertaken by participants in social situations in order to improve the rationality and justice of their own practices, their understanding of these practices, and the situations in which the practices are carried out. (Carr and Kemiss, 1986, p. 162)

In principle, therefore, action research becomes an iterative process, that is you keep doing it over and over again. It is a process that will look very familiar to teacher training students who will have engaged in lesson-planning processes and are therefore familiar with cyclical models such as plan-do-review or plan-act-monitor-evaluate. Although action research tends to involve individuals, those individuals often work as part of a larger team and therefore changing and improving their own practice must take those relationships into account. Action research may well lead to *new understandings and actions from people working together in new ways, and their influence on one another, that is, how they learn with and from one another* (McNiff and Whitehead, 2006, p. 18). Distinctive features of action research are the notions of interdependence, dialogue and 'critical friends'. For an action researcher things cannot be understood in isolation, and understanding can be facilitated through discussion with someone else who, while supportive, will pose questions, challenge assumptions and widen the scope of the debate.

There are risks associated with action research, not least the danger of taking on too big a task. For educational practitioners creating the time and space alongside their daily tasks and duties can be a challenge; however, it is worth noting that as a student working in a placement setting your circumstances are different. If the practitioners are not actively involved in your research project it is questionable whether it could be called true action research. What you may find is that you have a methodological approach that borrows some aspects of action research, such as the intention to change practice, but which is not action research in the traditional sense because it is not your practice that is being changed, it is someone else's. A further challenge to action research and action research-like projects centres on their validity and the dangers of bias during data collection and analysis. Furthermore action research is inherently very specific in nature and is therefore incapable of producing any statistically generalizable results, although as with methodologies like ethnography such criticisms may miss the point that action research does not set out to make such claims.

Narrative research

The term narrative research might be used to describe any text or conversation but with a specific focus on storytelling (Cresswell, 2013). These stories might be provided through interviews or literature or through written observations or through letters (Lieblich et al., 1998). Web-Mitchell suggests that everything is held together with stories which are a way in which people make sense of themselves and the world around them. Narrative is crucial in understanding human life *for all that we are, and all that we do and all that we think and feel is based upon stories, both our personal stories and those of our communities* (Web-Mitchell, 1995, p. 215). If you think about your own day-to-day conversations with others you will realize that you often communicate through stories. For example, you might tell your friends about a difficult journey to university and the things that happened to you, all told in the form of a chronological account with a beginning, a middle and an end, albeit one 'to be continued'. Everyone tells stories, whether it is young children in the role-play corner or teenagers awkwardly trying out roles to figure out their place in the world; for adults too, *the true and imaginary stories we wish to tell and believe suggest what we value most in this world. In a real sense, stories make people* (Shannon, 1995, p. 11).

As a research methodology narrative research can involve biographical studies written about the experiences of another person, autobiography, personal essays or oral history and life history. A narrative methodology seeks to try and put them into a story line where causal links can be identified and themes and knowledge emerge. Mishler (1991) suggests that there are three such themes involved in narrative research. The first is to identify the relationship between the order in which events happened and the order in which they are referred to in the telling of the story. The second is to look at the language used in putting the story together while the third is to consider and examine the place of the particular story in the society in which it is told. Unlike some of the other methodological approaches outlined previously, the focus of narrative research is very often on an individual, although this does not have to be the case.

Example – The Title of a Dissertation Using Narrative Methodology

'Becoming a head teacher: the story of Sam's journey'

Adopting a narrative research methodology will affect the structure of your dissertation as you will have to provide your readers with some biographical information about your speaker or speakers as well as outlining the circumstances in which the narration took place. You would also have to think about how much time you would need to spend with your narrator(s) to carry out this type of research. Interviewing can be tiring for everyone involved and the process will produce a considerable amount of data to be transcribed, which will generate a large amount of very time-consuming work. A further issue arises from a consideration of the ethics of the process. As narrative research may involve eliciting deeply felt and personal experiences from people there are sensitive considerations to be faced in relation to ownership of the story, anonymity and confidentiality. Trust and a willingness to reveal things to you are essential if your dissertation is to be a success using a narrative research methodology and yet your conclusions could be critical of or unpalatable to your narrator(s). This could present you with an interesting dilemma especially if in the interests of ethics you have previously agreed that your narrator has the power to veto what you can and cannot use in your thesis.

Case study

Case studies are an approach to research design whereby an individual, a group, an institution or a wider community is investigated to answer specific research questions in order to inform judgements or decisions. The basic idea is that 'one case ... will be studied in detail, using whatever methods are appropriate' (Punch 1998, p. 150). Research projects using a case study methodology try to offer plausible and accessible explanations of examples of human activity located in the real world, which can only be understood and studied in context. Case studies can penetrate situations in ways that are not always susceptible to purely numerical analysis, illuminating subtleties and complexities in the process (Cohen et al., 2007).

A case study seeks to explore significant features of the case in question, to build up an argument supported by the literature, to communicate that argument clearly to an audience and to provide an evidence trail (featuring numerous sources) by which the argument can be checked or challenged. Case studies tend to draw on multiple sources of data such as interviews, documents and observations and these multiple sources of data allow the development of a very 'rich' picture. Case studies are likely to try and answer 'how' and 'why' questions and are used to generate theories in response. Flyvbjerg (2004) suggests that the detail generated by case studies and the descriptions of real life that they generate are important for two reasons; first, because they develop a realistic view of how people are and how they behave; and second, because they help researchers develop their skills. Our interest in education might offer us the opportunity to study the 'case' of a single child or a group of children, a teacher or a practitioner or classroom or a school.

Yin (2014) suggests that each case has boundaries that must be identified at an early stage of the research , each case will be something that you are interested in – so that interest must be defined early on, and the research question must be identified to match the specific features of the case that interests you.

One criticism of the case study approach is that by focusing upon a single 'case' it is not possible to generalize. However, although all qualitative methodologies have been criticized for a lack of statistical analysis and emergent design, these features do not automatically equate with an absence of rigour (Denscombe, 2002). Equally, criticism of case study and other qualitative methodologies for being unable to provide generalizations could be seen as flawed because the term generalization is being defined scientifically or statistically in the first place. In educational settings such claims will always be suspected no matter how big the sample. For Bassey, case studies offer the possibility of reaching 'fuzzy' generalizations about an instance and hence from an instance to a set of instances due to the fact that case studies often present research and evaluation data in a more publicly accessible form (Bassey, 1998; Cohen et al., 2007). It is true that there is no certainty of the relatability of findings from one situation to another, but because the single cases concern 'particular' rather than 'unique' experiences, the value of the comparison is that it may stimulate worthwhile thinking. Case studies therefore offer the potential at least for research outcomes that are credible and authentic for people. They can generate 'naturalistic', 'inside-the-head, propositional' or qualitative generalizations that hold up to the reader a picture of events (Bassey, 1998, p. 6). It is for the reader then to consider the extent to which this picture has relevance for her/his setting:

> Sometimes we simply have to keep our eyes open and look carefully at individual cases, not in the hope of proving anything, but rather in the hope of learning something. (Eysenck, 1976 in Flyvbjerg, 2004)

Most undergraduate dissertations in education that involve some form of primary data collection could be viewed as case studies in one form or another. This is simply because most education students undertaking an undergraduate dissertation will not have either the time or the resources to conduct research beyond more than one or two settings or contexts.

Methodology and literature-based research projects

In some cases students decide or need to conduct a literature-based dissertation. Some topics could be potentially very 'high risk' in relation to primary data collection and therefore in the interests of the safety of students and the emotional well-being of potential research participants it may be decided that the best approach is to opt for a literature-based study. A good example of this would be any dissertation where the focus was on child abuse, 'stranger danger' or a similarly highly emotive and charged topic. In other cases the decision to opt for a literature-based study may be rather more pragmatic, for example a minor injury might prevent field work or alternatively a placement might be withdrawn at the last moment due to an unexpected Ofsted inspection.

Rather than requiring primary data collection literature-based research projects draw solely on data that has already been collected and analysed. Such an activity may feel a little like an oversized essay; however, there is still a need to consider and set out your methodological approach. If you are completing a literature-based dissertation it is a good idea to search government reports and refereed journals in education and other social science disciplines for literature reviews as these will contain examples of methodologies on which you can base your own approach.

In such a dissertation you will need to ensure that you address a number of headings when setting out your methodological approach. To begin with you will need to make a clear statement about the aims and purpose of your project and to clarify what has and has not been included. For example, you may decide that you are only going to draw on sources from a particular period in time or from a particular standpoint and these decisions need to be made explicit and explained. Secondly you will need to set out the more detailed objectives of your research. If an aim is what you hope to have achieved at the end of the process then the objectives are the building blocks of that achievement. Do not have too many objectives as you run the risk of not being able to do justice to all of them. It is impossible to give a figure for how many objectives you should have as this will be determined by the focus of your research but if you find you have more than half a dozen you might need to sharpen your focus a little more.

Example – Aims and Objectives in Literature-based Dissertations

Aim
To review government policy and guidelines in relation to parent partnerships in primary schools

Objectives
To identify and review key sources on the concept of 'partnership' in education
To review the development of government policy on parent partnerships from 1997 to the present day
To examine any relevant international comparisons

Having established your aims and objectives you will then need to set out how you propose to go about the task beginning with the identification of keywords and themes probably involving a preliminary literature search. This preliminary work may focus on a key text of some kind – such as an Act of Parliament, a Government White Paper or an influential and/or controversial research report. This will help to set the scene and provide you with the necessary background understanding with which to identify key themes and ideas. Having agreed these keywords and themes with your supervisor you will then need to engage in analysing and appraising the literature fully. At this point you may decide to use a proforma or template of some kind to help you record and manage this process more effectively (also see Chapter 3).

Checklist – Recording and Managing Your Reading

Reference	
Relevant chapter(s)/page numbers	
Main points/claims	
Author position/perspective	
Links to other sources	
Key quotes	
Comments/thoughts	

When setting out your methodology in a literature-based dissertation you will also need to set out any particular theoretical standpoint or perspective that you plan to use to help you assess and analyse the data gathered from all the different sources. The example below sets out the theoretical underpinning in Ben's dissertation for an analysis of the development of City Academies under the Labour Government after 2000 drawing on the work of Levin and others. In the third stage of the process you will need to pull together and synthesize your findings and to map these against your original aims and objectives (see Chapters 8 and 9). By this time you may be in a position to point to unresolved issues and/or gaps in the literature that could lead to possible future research opportunities.

Case Study – Ben Sets Out His Theoretical Standpoint: 'Distinguishing those facts that will shape the future is much easier said than done.'

Levin refers to this phenomenon (using Dror's phrase) as fuzzy gambling (Levin, 2001). At the same time Broadfoot challenges the assertion that education practice can be proved to impact directly upon subsequent economic performance (Broadfoot, 2000). Hargreaves meanwhile challenges the focus of some policy initiatives aimed at promoting the knowledge economy and/or knowledge society (Hargreaves, 2003). In his view these are often misguided in their attempts to educate children in the knowledge and skills for a particular kind of economy. Instead he argues that such initiatives should be aimed at developing a population's capacity for learning in order to be able to adapt and respond quickly and flexibly to economic change.

Levin's model is characterized by 4 phases in the process of policymaking and reform. The first is described as origins and centres on the ideas and beliefs that lie behind changes in policy. The second stage of adoption focuses upon the evolution and development of a policy between its original conception and its final incarnation, examining the events and factors that led to these changes and developments. The third stage, implementation, concentrates on the difficulties of translating policy changes into practice and seeks to identify what Levin refers to as the policy levers involved. Finally the model considers outcomes. Any policy may result in a range of outcomes both intended and unintended. Levin cautions the reader against assuming that the origin of government policy is entirely rational and objective due to the limits of human capacity to understand and solve problems (Levin, 2001).

Like all stage theories, Levin's model implies a logical progression from A to B, or in this case from origins to outcomes, which can belie the complexities involved. Levin himself acknowledges this fact, stating that the use of such models should not blind the researcher to the fact that in reality the stages overlap and interact with one another in subtle and complex ways rather than constituting distinct and discrete phases. In spite of this complication, such a model can be helpful in illuminating the messiness of policy to practice. This dissertation will apply Levin's four stage model of educational policy making to the development of the Labour Government's City Academies.'

A possible structure for a literature-based dissertation may well echo that of an empirical work, but the detail will be different. The example below has been adapted from the NIH:

Title: The title should accurately reflect the topic under review. Typically, the words 'a systematic review' are a part of the title to make the nature of the study clear.

Abstract: A systematic review usually has a structured Abstract as would any other dissertation.

Introduction: The Introduction summarizes the topic and explains the reasons why the systematic review was conducted. Possible reasons for this are given above.

Methods: The Methods section is the most crucial part of a literature-based dissertation. The methodology followed should be explained clearly and by logically discussing the following areas.

- Which types of literature you used and why you chose those sources
- Which search terms you used and why
- Which limits you applied to the data – for example, nationality, age, methodological standpoint
- Which databases you used and why
- A commentary on the quality of the data
- Your approach to data analysis

Results: The Results section should also be explained logically. You can begin by describing the search results, and then move on to the study range and characteristics, study quality and finally discuss the effect of the intervention on the outcome.

Discussion: The Discussion should summarize the main findings from the review and then move on to discuss the limitations of the study and the reliability of the results. Finally, the strengths and weaknesses of the review should be discussed, and implications for current practice suggested.

References: The References section of a systematic review article usually contains an extensive number of references. You have to be very careful and ensure that you do not miss out on a single one. You can consider using reference management software to help you tackle the references effectively.

Summary of key points

- It is important to be clear about the distinction between methodology and methods. Your methodology is the framework around which your project is structured and is informed by your views on reality and knowledge. Your methods are the techniques and procedures used to gather data.

- Broadly speaking methodologies can be positivist, interpretivist, transformatory or pragmatic in nature.
- Any methodology has its strengths and shortcomings and you will need to demonstrate that you understand these in your dissertation and can justify your eventual choice.
- Methodology is not just an issue for students involved in primary data collection. Literature-based and other secondary-data projects also present you with methodological considerations.

Reflective task

Consider some questions about how you see the world:

1 Do you think we can study people in the same way that we can study things?
  In what ways might this be possible, in what ways not?

2 Has everything always been there, just not yet discovered – or does the presence of people give new meanings?

Look at previous research which uses specific methodological approaches;

1 Why do you think this approach was taken?

2 Would other approaches have been possible?

3 Would another approach have led to different outcomes?

Link to companion website

https://bloomsbury.com/cw/successful-dissertations-second-edition/student-resources/chapter-5/

Recommended reading and further sources of information

Bryman, A. (2016, 5th edition), *Social Research Methods*. Oxford: Oxford University Press.
Cohen, L., Manion, L. and Morrison, K. (2011, 7th edition), *Research Methods in Education*. Abingdon: Routledge.

Cresswell, J. (2013, 3rd edition), *Qualitative Inquiry and Research Design: Choosing among Five Approaches* (Paperback). Thousand Oaks, CA: Sage.

Crotty, M. (1998), *The Foundations of Social Research: Meaning and Perspective in the Research Process.* London: Sage.

Denzin, N. K. and Lincoln, Y. S. (2014, 4th edition), *The Sage Handbook of Qualitative Research.* Thousand Oaks, CA: Sage.

Robson, C. and McKarten, K. (2011, 4th edition), *Real World Research.* Chicester: John Wiley.

Silverman, D. (2013), *Qualitative Research.* Thousand Oaks, CA: Sage.

6

Data Collection Using Qualitative Methods

Janet Kay and Jonathan Wainwright

Chapter Outline

Chapter Aims

By the end of this chapter you will

- know about the use of individual interviews in qualitative research projects;
- be aware of the advantages and disadvantages of using focus groups as a means of gathering qualitative data;
- know about a range of observational techniques in qualitative data collection including structured, unstructured, participant and non-participant observations;
- know how to use questionnaires to obtain qualitative data;
- know about the range of creative methods of data gathering available and how these can be used to enhance your study.

In this chapter some of the more common methods of gathering data in qualitative research, including individual interviewing, focus group discussions, observations, questionnaires and creative methods, are discussed. Each of the five types of methods discussed is described and some of the advantages and disadvantages associated with the approach are explored. This chapter also makes suggestions about the methods appropriate for different types of study as well as commenting on some of the practical considerations associated with their use. Clearly, there are many methods of gathering qualitative data, but we have chosen to focus on those most likely to be used in undergraduate qualitative dissertations.

The choice of a qualitative method should be made as part of your research design and choice of methodology. It is not random, and there is a process of decision-making from your interest in a topic, to your choice of research question, to the methodology and methods, underpinned by your 'philosophical stance' (Edwards and Holland, 2013). The method you choose to gather data should fit in with your design and, most importantly, must enable you to gather the data that you need to answer your research question. The choice of data-gathering method or methods should also be made in conjunction with your choices about how you are going to analyse the data. Data analysis of qualitative data is not usually an endpoint activity as it is normally something you start to do as soon as first data is gathered. This chapter should, therefore, be read in conjunction with the discussion on qualitative analysis in Chapter 8.

It is also important to remember that some studies lend themselves to more than one data-gathering method – for example, starting with a focus group to explore a topic and get a good understanding of the issues and then conducting semi-structured interviews to get more detailed data. In a case like this, the findings from the focus group would inform the interview schedule at the next stage of data gathering, having been analysed before the interviews start (see Chapter 8 for discussion on qualitative data analysis). However, if your research requires gathering data from more than one group of participants you may need to use different methods to suit the needs of each group – for example, interviews with professional adults and observations with children. In some cases, data gathering using more than one method is a strategy for confirming the credibility of the data – for example, using creative methods to gather visual data such as photos or drawings and then interviewing the participants about the meanings of their materials.

Finally, with all these methods, materials to be used to gather data, such as interview, observation and questionnaire schedules, need to be piloted beforehand. This means trying them out on a couple of individuals who meet the criteria for your sample but are not in it. The data gathered needs to be scrutinized to make sure it answers all of your research questions that it is expected to, and that the data-gathering materials produce the right data without bias or omissions. You then need to make changes and possibly even pilot again if the original materials were very ineffective. This is important because gathering a lot of data that does not answer your questions is a mistake made by some students and the outcome is not a happy one!

Interviews

Interviews are the most commonly used method in qualitative data gathering and are generally seen as a cornerstone of qualitative research (Edwards and Holland, 2013). It is common to think of interviewing as primarily a face-to-face experience but in fact there are many ways of interviewing. These include telephone interviews, group interviews, email interviews and completing questionnaires with the participants. This section is primarily concerned with one-to-one interviews of various types. If your methodological approach involves grounded theory, phenomenology, ethnography, discourse analysis or a case study, you may well find yourself interviewing as part of your data collection. Gathering data using *direct verbal interaction between individuals* (Cohen et al., 2011) gives you the opportunity to explore participants' views, experiences and perspectives on specific phenomena in their lives (Denscombe, 2014; Kvale and Brinkman, 2015). Interviews give you the chance to gather data on participants' own subjective views and feelings on aspects of their own lives. There are different ways of interviewing and different types of interviews reflecting the diversity common to qualitative research designs. That said, although there are different types of interviews it is the interaction between the interviewer and the participant that is the common and key element of this method. This interaction between interviewer and interviewee is significant because it makes it possible to *obtain a rich, in-depth experiential account of an event or episode in the life of the respondent* (Fontana and Frey, 2005, p. 698). The approach allows you, therefore, to hear directly about participants' experiences, the meanings they place on those experiences and to ensure that their views and opinions and feelings and responses are accurately reflected in your findings (Punch, 2009).

Points to Think About – Using Interviews in Qualitative Research

- The interviews are recorded and presented descriptively not numerically;
- The interviews are focused on particular events;
- The interviews explore participants' views and experiences of those events.

Source: Kvale and Brinkman, 2015.

Some advantages and disadvantages of interviews

Interviews are certainly time-consuming in terms of preparing the interview schedule, finding and recruiting the participants, seeking consent, making practical arrangements for doing the interviews and carrying out the interviews. Transcribing interviews can also be very time-consuming, as can the data analysis and interpretation processes

(Robson and McCartan, 2016). However, other costs and resources are relatively cheap and may offset the investment in time needed (Denscombe, 2014).

Points to Think About – Planning Interviews

Interviews require careful planning to ensure they are successful and that the data gathered is what is required. Some of the questions that you need to consider include

- How will you gain access to the participants and are there going to be any ethical issues which may impede access?
- What are the ethical issues around consent and confidentiality and how will you handle these?
- Where will the interviews take place and will this be the best venue for ensuring that your participants are comfortable and relaxed?
- What sort of interview are you going to conduct and is this approach right for your study and the participants involved?
- How long will each interview be?
- How will you record each interview and could this influence the outcomes?
- How will you present yourself as the interviewer?

However, perhaps the main advantages and disadvantages of interviewing both lie in the same characteristic of the method; it involves face-to-face interaction between the researcher and the participants (Robson and McCartan, 2016; Cohen et al., 2011). This interaction allows the interviewer to draw directly on the participants' views, feelings and understandings. There are a number of skills that you should consider developing in order to make the most of interviewing. When using unstructured or semi-structured interviewing, listening and asking questions with an 'enquiring mind' are key skills to develop (Robson and McCartan, 2016; Cohen et al., 2011). If you want to get the most out of your interviewees, then you will need to be quick-thinking and logical, to have a good memory and be genuinely interested in what the other person has to say (Legard et al., 2003). Establishing a good rapport and helping the participants to feel at ease with the process is important as is your ability to follow up issues raised sensitively and knowledgeably (Legard et al., 2003). In some types of study, the data is seen as a product of the interaction between the interviewer and the participant. The checklist below outlines a few techniques that can be very effective at encouraging your interviewees to talk to you.

Points to Think About – Getting the Most Out of Your Interviewees

- Use prompts, probes and follow-up questions to elicit further information or to seek clarification.
- Use affirmative noises such as 'mmmm', silence or non-verbal signals such as nods, glances and 'quizzical looks' to encourage people to say more or keep going.
- Paraphrase what someone has just said to you as a means of checking with them that you have understood something correctly.

Source: Denscombe, 2014.

One of the criticisms made of interviewing is that it is less reliable than some other methods such as questionnaires because the interviewer's influence on the outcomes may produce inconsistencies (Denscombe, 2014). As a consequence, data from interviews could reflect the biases, preconceptions and beliefs of the interviewer (Fontana and Frey, 2005; Kvale and Brinkman, 2015). The issue of bias can be viewed either as something to try and eliminate in an interview or, instead, as something to be acknowledged as an integral part of interviewing as a method. For example, in more structured interviews the interviewer can try to control or remove possible sources of bias (see Chapter 6). Alternatively, when using unstructured or semi-structured interview approaches, researchers acknowledge the risk of bias in the interviewing process, take steps to minimize that risk and then acknowledge the risk when writing up the findings of the research (Cohen et al., 2011). For example, in any type of interview the researcher's choice of topic, their research design and overall control of the interview process can create power differences between interviewer and participant (Kvale and Brinkman, 2015). In such circumstances, there is the possibility that the participant may be inhibited from giving full and frank responses by the researcher or by the context. The interviewees might even feel that the interview is an invasion of privacy if it is poorly handled (Denscombe, 2014). Yet these risks can be reduced in impact if the interviewer is skilled and the preparation is thorough and includes a consideration of any ethical issues.

Types of interviews

Interviews are differentiated according to the extent of their structure. There are thus three types of interviews – structured interviews, semi-structured interviews and unstructured interviews (Fontana and Frey, 2005). Although, it is worth noting that it might be best to view these three types as points on a continuum rather than as three completely separate and distinctive types (Edwards and Holland, 2013). The choice of interview type depends on what the research question is and what data you need to gather. For example, if you want to gather data that can be quantified by eliciting standard answers that fit into preset categories, then more structured interviews are the way forwards. These are often used in market research. On the other hand, if you want to explore a topic with an open mind, no preconceptions and no boundaries, then a more unstructured approach is indicated. Most interviews fall between these and are to varying degrees, semi-structured. In this section, the three types of interviews will be discussed further with some additional emphasis on semi-structured interviews as it is one of the most commonly used approaches in qualitative undergraduate dissertations.

Structured interviews

Structured interviews are based on a predetermined interview schedule, which is fixed and unchanging for each interview in the set. The interviewer *asks all respondents the same series of pre-established questions with a limited set of response categories* (Fontana and Frey, 2005, p. 701). The questions are answered in the same order in each interview and there is little or no flexibility. The answers are recorded in a preset coding system. The aim is to standardize the interview process and to minimize variations (Punch, 2009). This sort of interview is used in studies where a high level of structure is needed and the answers need to fall into clearly defined categories. They tend to be more common in quantitative studies (see Chapter 6); however, it is possible that you might wish to use more structured approaches as part of a qualitative project.

The interviewer's role in a more structured interview is to minimize variations and to follow the interview schedule in a standardized fashion, trying to keep any variations between interviews to a minimum (Fontana and Frey, 2005). To do this you need to behave as neutrally as possible, using a standardized explanation to introduce the interview and not deviating from this or from the set question schedule by using the same wording each time. You need to try to conduct each interview in the same manner keeping your involvement with the participants to the minimum (Edwards and Holland, 2013).

The main perceived advantage of structured interviews is the reduction of bias as you seek to minimize the impact of your presence and involvement on the interviewing process. However, this also means that the interview is less interactive. You will not be able to seek clarification or follow up on interesting but unplanned issues or to ask for more information. This may reduce the depth and richness of the data gained. In addition, by determining the categories for responses prior to the interviews you may limit the voice of the participant in the outcomes. Although validity, reliability and trustworthiness are apparently increased by the lack of variation in the questions and the minimal interaction, many qualitative researchers would argue that validity and reliability in interpretative studies comes from truly representing the participants' voices. In addition, the neutral stance of the interviewer may not be entirely successful, participants may still be influenced by their need to please or give the 'right' answer, and there is always a risk that the interviewer may not follow the script (Fontana and

Frey, 2005). In view of these factors the structured interview may not be as useful in many qualitative studies as less structured approaches.

Unstructured interviews

There is no schedule as such in unstructured interviews, just some opening enquiries and prompts around the topic chosen. The unstructured interview is often used in ethnographic studies or oral histories and is in depth. There are no predetermined categories and much of the data is gathered through informal conversation. As the interviewer, your aim is to encourage participants to discuss the issues relating to the topic with very few prompts or formal questions. The approach is very informal and although you may have some idea about what sort of topics might be discussed, this is open-ended and not predetermined. When using unstructured interviews, it is quite likely that you will be interviewing participants in their own environment and you will need to blend into this environment to a certain extent. As Fontana and Frey (2005) state, 'One might have to buy a huge motorbike and frequent seedy bars in certain locations if ... attempting to befriend and study the Hells Angels' (Fontana and Frey, 2005, p. 707). Hopefully, as an education student you can avoid the temptations associated with seedy bars and conduct your interviews in less risky settings, such as classrooms, staff rooms or youth clubs.

One of the main problems with unstructured interviews in undergraduate ethnographic studies is gaining access to the environment and participants within it. Unstructured interviews work best when you have had an opportunity to establish a rapport and trust through prolonged contact with your participants. Without this relationship, it may not be possible to gather any useful data in this way. In many such studies building a relationship with an 'informer' or 'insider' in the community studied, someone who can act as your guide to the cultural and other issues involved, is useful. This process may also involve the interviewer in changing their own behaviour and lifestyle to become involved. However, on an undergraduate degree course your ability to build up such relationships over an extended period of time may be very limited; time is short and there may be some types of behaviour that you cannot emulate in your efforts to become accepted by the group – for example, criminal activity. Recording your data may also be difficult, as in naturalistic settings electronic recording may be inappropriate or impossible. Note-taking may not capture all the relevant details and it may not be easy to do without introducing an unwelcome formal note to the process. Unstructured interviews can also produce a mass of data which can be very difficult to analyse and organize. Making comparisons across the data or between interview data and other forms of data may also be difficult if there are wide variations in the content of the interviews.

The main issue in unstructured interviewing is the extent to which the interviewer's involvement may bias the data. It may be difficult to discuss your findings because of the extent to which your participation and perceptions have shaped the data. If you opt for unstructured interviews as your data-collection method, then you must examine your influence. In order to look at data, your *biases and taken-for-granted notions* have to be made explicit in your thesis or, as Fontana and Frey say, *exposed* (Fontana and

Frey, 2005, p. 714). To do this your data analysis section will need to address not only 'what' was found in the study but also 'how' it was found, as the content of the data collected will depend on the interaction between you and the participant. Reflexive accounts are often included in this type of study to explore the interviewer's role and involvement (see Chapter 2). These accounts enhance the work by showing how the interviewer influenced and was in turn influenced by the participants.

Semi-structured interviews

Semi-structured interviewing falls between the structured interview, which seeks to minimize variation or exploration beyond the clear boundaries of the question schedule, and the unstructured interview, which has almost no limits (Kvale and Brinkman, 2015). A semi-structured interview schedule is structured but not rigidly. It has initial categories and themes, drawn from the literature and possibly from earlier data gathering using other methods, with room for the introduction of new themes within the parameters of the research questions overall. Data gathered can include information about behaviour (what the participants do) and beliefs (what they think and feel) (Robson and McCartan, 2016). Your role is to explore the participants' actions, views, beliefs and meanings through flexible use of the interview schedule, asking additional and probing questions to gather more in-depth data. While keeping the interview within the boundaries of the research questions overall, you can follow up interesting themes and ideas and ask additional questions. Perhaps most importantly there is a sense of dynamic between the interviewed and interviewer in terms of the development of new meanings and understandings on both sides. Kvale and Brinkman refer to this method as 'inter views ... where knowledge is constructed in the interaction between the interviewer and the interviewee' (Kvale and Brinkman, 2009, p. 2). The outcome of the interview is therefore influenced by the choices and actions of the researcher and the results are an 'active co-creation of the researcher and participant' (Fontana and Frey, 2005, p. 696).

Case Study – Semi-structured Interviewing

Naila is interviewing teaching assistants in an SEN team in a large secondary school. She is trying to find out what strategies they think are most successful when working one-to-one with dyslexic children. Naila has a list of topics she wants to cover but her focus is on getting the teaching assistants to talk about their work with dyslexic children and their own views on what works for them. Naila asks some questions but she mainly listens, giving some prompts to move the conversation forward and asking for clarification when she needs it. The interviews are quite informal and relaxed. The teaching assistants comment afterwards that the interview process has helped them to clarify and understand their own approaches to this work and to make sense of some of the issues related to supporting dyslexic children.

Using semi-structured interviewing gives you an opportunity to explain and expand on questions to ensure that participants have understood what has been asked of them. This can encourage more considered responses than might be possible using other approaches (Cohen et al., 2011). The semi-structured interview is also very flexible, as the aspect under discussion can be adjusted during the interview itself and relevant subtopics followed up. The depth and richness of the data gathered is a significant advantage of a semi-structured interview, as is the opportunity to explore meanings as they arise (Denscombe, 2014). You can check your data during a semi-structured interview to ensure that you have understood what the participant means. Being able to check and confirm data in this way may enhance its validity or trustworthiness. This communicative validity is based on an honest discussion with participants about meanings and shared understandings (Denscombe, 2014; Kvale and Brinkman, 2015).

However, although semi-structured interviews provide some consistency between participants, they are also criticized for allowing variable responses (Cohen et al., 2011). Participants need to have a clear understanding of what is being asked in order to maintain validity. Another concern is that an interviewer might overwhelm the data with their own viewpoint, rather than trying to ensure that her/his part in the co-construction is to illuminate the participants' views. In semi-structured interviewing, you must ensure that you do not shape the data according to your own biases or preconceptions, nor must you seek to influence the responses you get during the interview. The impact of non-verbal messages is a point for consideration as these may encourage particular responses from the participant if you are indicating approval or disapproval for particular answers non-verbally. The aim is to ensure that the interview process produces findings which reflect the phenomenon studied and genuinely represent the voices of the participants. In order to achieve this there must be careful consideration of the quality of the interview planning and processes (Edwards and Holland, 2013).

Reliability too is complex in semi-structured interviewing as the actions considered by some to be most likely to increase reliability (i.e. closed questions, high level of structure) are not compatible with the in-depth approach of this type of interview (Cohen et al., 2011). To enhance reliability the sampling, questioning, recording and coding of the data must show consistency throughout the study (Lewis and Ritchie, 2003). As such, there must be a clear 'audit trail' from first data gathering until analysis is complete to show how the researcher has been faithful to their participants' voices throughout. The key elements in achieving good standards of reliability without compromising validity in this type of interview are the skills and integrity of the interviewer and attention to consistency rather than rigidity in the processes (Kvale and Brinkman, 2015).

Case Study – Improving Your Interviews through Planning and Preparation

Graham has decided to interview young people who attend a youth centre located on their estate to get feedback on the activities offered and to try and find out what sort of sessions and approaches would benefit the teenagers most from their own point of view. Graham has decided to attend some of the sessions offered to ask the teenagers face-to-face if they will be interviewed as he does not think a letter will get much response with this group. Graham has a consent form and further information that he goes through with any of the young people who respond positively to his request. They are also asked to get parental consent by taking the form home and getting a parent to sign. Graham realizes that he will have to ask a lot more of the young people than he actually wants to interview as some will say no before or after discussion and some will not get parental consent either because they forget to ask or their parents refuse.

Graham has also asked for and been granted permission to do the study by staff in the centre. Youth workers in the centre have given their consent and Graham has arranged with the manager to have a small room available at various times which he can use for the interviews. He has devised a semi-structured interview schedule which he piloted with two young people and then subsequently revised. This semi-structured approach gives some flexibility for the young people's views and opinions to emerge but also some structure to base the analysis on. Graham records the sessions with a digital recorder so he can listen and not have to take notes. Graham dresses neatly but casually and tells the teenagers about himself in terms of being a student and interested in youth work. He wants them to feel relaxed with him but he does not try to present himself as one of them. During the interviews he asks questions and prompts but tries in the main to listen and not talk too much. He uses attentive listening skills to convey interest and is relaxed, friendly and open in his manner.

Table 7.1 lists the strengths and limitations of the various interviewing techniques.

Table 7.1 Strengths and limitations of interviewing techniques

	Strengths	Limitations
Structured interviews	May reduce the risk of bias and enhance the levels of reliability as the interviewer attempts to be more 'neutral'.	May not be possible to seek clarification or to follow up on interesting but unanticipated responses. May limit interviewees' responses.
Unstructured interviews	Gives interviewees huge scope to talk about what is important to them in contexts where they feel comfortable and confident. Often produces very rich and detailed data.	Building trust and gaining access to locations and participants may take a long time. Can be hard to record and may produce large amounts of data that are difficult to organize and analyse.
Semi-structured interviews	Enables interviewers to respond to interviewees, questions and to seek clarification of responses. May encourage more considered responses than might be possible using other approaches. Very flexible as the aspect under discussion can be adjusted during the interview itself and relevant subtopics followed up. The depth and richness of the data gathered is a significant advantage.	May suffer from a lack of consistency and variable responses. Interviewers may influence interviewees' responses through verbal or non-verbal cues.

Focus groups

Another potential method for gathering qualitative research data is the focus group. In some ways a focus group is a type of group interview; however, unlike a group interview which tends to have a question-and-answer format, a focus group seeks to engage participants in high levels of discussion as much among themselves as with the researcher. The difference is highlighted in that though you could still be described as an interviewer, the terms moderator or facilitator are more common since you are aiming to facilitate a discussion and it is the discussion, with its interaction, that will provide you with a richness and thickness of data.

A focus group usually consists of between 6 and 12 participants brought together to discuss and comment on your research topic. It is likely that the group members will have something in common – maybe they are all children in a particular class or children carrying out the same activity, or perhaps they are staff members in a setting where you are exploring attitudes towards inclusion. The use of focus groups in social science research is relatively recent, although they have been used in market research for many years (Smithson, in Alasuutari et al., 2008). Television companies, for instance, commonly use them to learn about people's opinions on their programmes. They are also used by political parties to test people's reactions to policy proposals.

The advantages and disadvantages of focus groups

Using focus groups could offer you a number of advantages. The first of these advantages is the amount of time needed in comparison to conducting one-to-one interviews with an equivalent number of people. Somewhere between 30 minutes and an hour would probably be a sensible length to aim for, depending on your experience and the numbers of participants involved. Facilitating a focus group well does require practice and listening intently is always a very tiring process. This does mean, however, that you have the potential to collect a large amount of data over quite a short time period. Secondly, focus groups can be a useful first step in a research project as a means of gaining an overview of participants' thinking about the issues; information which you could then use in designing follow-up interviews where you might probe in more depth. Thirdly, they act as an opportunity for research participants to build on and develop each others' ideas, *collectively, bringing forward their own priorities and perspectives* (Smithson, in Alasuutari et al., 2008, p. 359). Group situations make it possible, in theory at least, to move beyond the thoughts and actions of individual interviewees in isolation, to the thoughts and actions of individuals in relation to others (Field, 2000). They have the potential to involve participants in an iterative learning process in which people's views evolve, change, are shared, debated and challenged (Litosseliti, 2003). Discussing topics with others in this way offers both the researcher and the participants the chance to refine their thinking through the act of putting thoughts into words and in the light of the views of others. In this sense, therefore, focus groups constitute a learning process for the participants as well as a finding-out process for the researcher. This can be very helpful if you are taking a grounded-theory approach and are keen to hear the language and specific stories that belong to the participants you are working with.

You might also consider using a focus group to provide additional supporting data to increase the reliability of your study.

Case Study – Using a Focus Group

Farah is interested in finding out about the impact of introducing an outdoor play area in a children's centre. She gathers together a group of participants for about 40 minutes. The group she has invited consists of a teacher, a health worker, a family support worker, an Early Years practitioner and the setting manager. Her questions focus on what the participants have noticed about how children use the area and if they have noticed any differences. She needs to listen carefully to what is said (though she is recording the discussion) and to ensure that only one person is speaking at a time. She asks for clarification if she does not understand something or if people are using expressions that she thinks others might not understand. She tries to summarize what has been said every now and then to ensure that everyone understands; this also helps to add to the reliability of her study. The participants state that they find the process a useful way to hear the views of others which they might not have heard before.

As with any data-collection method focus groups also have drawbacks. To begin with they involve people's personal stories which may or may not be reliable. You also need to be aware of the dangers of 'groupthink' where a group can *strive for unanimity while ignoring information inconsistent with these views* (Chioncel et al., 2003, p. 503). Focus groups can have the opposite effect though and lead to conflict and there is the danger that the loudest person will be heard more than the quieter participants and result in the over-reporting of individual articulate group members rather than the collective opinions of the group. This could be the case particularly when you are working with children – inevitably some will be shyer than others. Roberts-Holmes (2014) suggests that when conducting focus groups with children, you might ask one child to select the other participants. Because of the homogenous nature of the participants, you might find that the outcomes of group discussions can be misleading because opinions are shared. To counter this, you may want to hold more than one group. (Field, 2000). Power relationships can also be a factor and some participants may be nervous about speaking out in front certain people, they may be concerned about what others think of them or they may worry about the quality of their opinions. Facilitating a group of people all of whom have something to say but some of whom may be worried about saying it is a potentially difficult task requiring sensitivity, resilience and perseverance. The issue of power relationships – and hence ethics – also extends to the relationship between you and the group. The group nature of the method may mean that you dominate the group discussion or lead respondents in a particular direction, whether this is conscious or accidental. One way of responding to this is to develop a group contract before starting. There is no guarantee that 'what goes on tour, will stay on tour', however you will at least have made your ethical stance explicit.

A further difficulty can arise as the group setting can encourage idle chatter unrelated to the purpose of the meeting, particularly when you may be struggling to control the discussion anyway. Not only will this not inform your research but it will add to the already considerable task of transcribing. You also need to consider the ethics of the focus group approach. Confidentiality and anonymity of the participants' information will be out of your control and it may be very had to predict how participants might respond to each others' comments. You are unlikely, for example, to want to use focus groups where sensitive issues form the basis of your research or where you are looking at more in-depth personal narratives (Smithson, in Alasuutari et al., 2008). For example, if you were researching young people's experiences of bereavement a focus group may be far too public a forum for handling such an emotional and sensitive topic.

If you decide that you want to use a focus group a number of practical things have to be taken into consideration. In trying to use focus groups, it is easy to come unstuck because of some fairly down-to-earth but nonetheless serious problems associated with the hectic nature of many people's lives. As with any other form of research, you will need to choose a sample group. Getting groups together can prove very difficult. Your participants may simply be too busy at different times making it impossible to find a time when everyone is available. Even when people do agree to come together it is impossible to predict who will actually turn up on the day. Things happen and people's best intentions can be derailed by 'events'. Although smaller groups provide more space for people to talk and enable you to delve into more detail, they also make you more vulnerable to these 'events'. If you end up with fewer than four participants you are likely to lose the conversation, interaction and debate which distinguish a focus group from a simple group interview (Smithson, in Alasuutari et al., 2008). With focus groups it could be argued that validity comes from the competence of your participants to answer the questions and reliability comes from their ability to provide a range of responses (2Chioncel et al., 2003). Clearly therefore a poor turnout could threaten this.

Points to Think About – Running Focus Groups

- You will need to find a suitable room, ideally one where there are no distractions, where it is quiet and where there is enough space for people to be able to interact.
- You will need to find a time when people are available to talk, one which will cause your participants as little inconvenience as possible. This could prove quite difficult if, for instance, you are researching in a busy environment, such as a school.

Points to Think About – Cont'd

- You will need to keep your principal research question in mind. This will be the *focus* of the group, and will help you to produce a list of topics which will form the basis of the discussion.
- It is unlikely that you will be able to be highly structured in your approach because you never quite know where the conversation will lead. Like any other conversation, there will be pauses and times when people will speak over each other.
- You will need to think about your role as the facilitator (sometimes referred to as the moderator) in the group, it is a crucial role requiring a number of well-developed interpersonal skills, such as listening and behaving in a non-judgemental way. It will also require a degree of confidence and it might be a good idea to pilot this approach with a group of friends first so that you can practice:

  - letting people know why you are there and the purpose of the session;
  - managing a group and asking questions in ways which will keep the conversation flowing;
  - probing for meanings;
  - ensuring that everyone who wants to gets a chance to speak.
  - listening not just for the content of the conversation but also the feelings, contradictions and tensions (Grudens-Schuck et al., 2004).

- You will need to think about how best to record the proceedings. You could take notes, you could audio record or you could video record the discussion(s). With smaller groups it is easier to recognize individuals' voices; with larger groups this can become quite confusing. Video recording might be the best option but not everyone likes the idea of being videoed which could reduce the number of volunteers that you get.

Observations

In this section, types of observations most often found in qualitative studies are discussed. Other types of observations used in quantitative studies have already been covered in Chapter 6. Observation is the process of looking at and listening to participants' activity, behaviour, interactions and other social phenomena in chosen environments with a particular purpose in mind. Observations in research are a more considered process than observations in everyday life. If you opt to use observations as a means of data collection you will have to look and listen critically and actively and will be expected to challenge assumptions about what you have observed (Roberts-Holmes, 2014). Observations can be one of the least obtrusive methods of data collection (Edwards, 2001) and along with interviews, are a very common method of data collection in qualitative studies. Observation is a key data-gathering method in ethnography (both participant and non-participant) and it is also used in case studies, action research and phenomenology. Observation can be used to explore a situation or context and to develop research questions which can be followed up through further, more focused observations, or through other data-gathering methods, such as interviews. The method is often combined with other methods to provide the opportunity to contrast and compare data (10Roberts-Holmes, 2014). Observation can be a very useful data-gathering method with young children, especially where conversation, behaviour and social interaction are being studied.

The advantages and disadvantages of observations

Observations offer you the chance to see for yourself what is going in a specific situation or context. This can be very useful in a study where other data has been gathered through methods that focus on the experiences and views of the participants, such as interviews. Observation can be used effectively to support an initial exploration of a situation or behaviour with the purpose of drawing research questions from these preliminary findings. Unstructured observations can provide rich data to draw on and develop further through more focused observation or other data-gathering methods. Observations are valuable when the study is focused on the behaviour of participants rather than their views and opinions as the researcher can see for themselves what participants actually do rather than what they say they do. This makes observation especially useful when studying children who may be too young to interviewed.

However, observation only allows you to note behaviour and verbal contributions. It does not necessarily give you any insight into what the meanings, purposes, intentions and rationales behind the behaviour are. One of the key skills of an observer is to try and record her/his observations from a neutral standpoint, avoiding comment, opinion or use of terminology which is subjective or judgemental (Mac Naughton et al., 2010). Access may be a further source of difficulty as consent is required from all possible participants and from gatekeepers (Punch, 2009). When observing children, for example, consent may be given by the parents but the child may not assent or be involved in the observation. Another possible disadvantage of observation is the impact that your presence as an observer may have on the participants' behaviour and conversation. At first they may act and talk differently because they know they are being observed. This effect can be reduced if you can make a number of observations over a longer period of time while maintaining a relatively unobtrusive presence until your participants get used to you being there. Recording may also be a challenge. Using written notes can leave you trying to write quickly and extensively in longhand while simultaneously continuing to observe. Becoming good at making notes and observing at the same time takes a lot of practice; it can be exhausting and may limit the extent to which all the action is recorded sufficiently. Audio or video recording may be a possibility but in some contexts it can be highly distracting to the participants and may also be more expensive as an option. Becoming a good observer depends on being alert and there is likely to be a limit on how well and for how long you can maintain this level of concentration.

Case Study – Observing in a Nursery

Harry wanted to do some observations on practitioner behaviour in a nursery setting. His focus was on observing the extent to which the adults involved themselves in play with children. Initially Harry thought he would only have to get consent from the practitioners, but after discussion with his supervisors he realized he would have to secure consent from all the parents too as the children were part of the observations. When he did a pilot observation, Harry used a video camera to record the observation. However, the children were completely distracted by the camera and spent a lot of time asking Harry how to use it and if they could use it or look at the recording. Harry tried again using notes only, making himself unobtrusive and ensuring that he was a familiar presence in the setting before trying to observe.

Observation needs to be carefully planned in order to ensure that the data gathered is relevant to the research questions and is manageable. As was clear from the previous paragraph, key issues to consider when planning include gaining access, determining the focus of the observations and deciding how best to record (Punch, 2009). Clearly your planning will vary according to the extent to which your observations are structured. Some observations involve carefully planned and piloted observation schedules while other more exploratory studies will need much less structure. As with any qualitative data-gathering method, observations also carry a risk that their trustworthiness might be undermined by observer subjectivity or bias. These risks too can be lessened and validity and reliability improved as a result, if you think carefully beforehand about the planning and implementation of your data gathering.

Skills for observing include being able to note down behaviour and utterances accurately, without interpreting them or distorting what actually happened or was said. Being unobtrusive is important in some observations. Observers also need to have a very clear idea of what behaviours and utterances are important to their study and to be able to focus on these alone and not be distracted by other events. As such, a very good understanding of the types of data you are gathering is needed.

Points to Think About – Planning Observations

- What will you observe and why?
- How many observations will you do? Will you be observing on a number of occasions over time or will they be one-off snapshots?
- Who will the participants be?
- Have you got consent from any gatekeeper(s) and all possible participants?
- How will you record the observations in ways that are effective and detailed but not intrusive?
- Will you use a predetermined observation schedule or adopt a more open narrative recording style?
- Will you be a participant or non-participant observer? How will you minimize your impact on the observed situation?
- How quickly can you write up/transcribe your observations?
- How will you analyse your observation data?
- How will you tackle the threat of bias or preconceived assumptions? Will your observational data be compared to other data gathered through different methods? Could you ask participants if they think that the observation influenced their actions?

Types of observations

Like interviews, observations can take a number of forms and there are various ways of categorizing the different approaches. Some are highly structured, others much less so, some feature the observer as active participant, others depend on the observer remaining a neutral non-participant; some are based on a continuous narrative while others rely on a series of snapshots taken at key points in time. The remaining sections outline some of the alternative approaches in a little more detail.

Structured and unstructured observations

Highly structured non-participant observations used in quantitative research studies are discussed in Chapter 6. However, this categorization can be misleading in that some qualitative studies will include observations which have structured observation schedules, but which do not collect numerical data, for example learning stories. Learning stories are narratives of a child's learning to support understanding and development (Carr, 2001). Observations are a key element of learning stories and are partly written as narratives of the child's actions. However, they are also structured to focus on how to support learning development and are often linked to curriculum outcomes.

Case Study – Learning Story Observation Schedules

Learning Story: Max Smith, 3 years and 2 months	
What was seen and heard?	Max approached the home corner and stood for about 2 minutes watching two girls playing with the cooker. The girls were role-playing making tea with one being mum and the other the child. The 'mum' noticed Max and said, 'Do you want to be the baby?' Max shook his head but didn't move. He stayed watching the girls for a few more minutes and then walked forward and stood at the table until one of the girls handed him a bowl and said, 'Eat up.' Max watched the other girl and copied her 'eating' out of the bowl.
What learning was noticed?	So far Max has not joined in play with other children since starting nursery 2 weeks ago. However, today he started to learn about social role-play through observing other children and copying them.
How can this learning be progressed?	Find out more about Max's interests and ensure role-play materials are available to meet these.

Child's name: JG
Date:
Teacher:

Strands	Goals	Learning story	
Belonging	**Taking an interest** • Finding an interest • Recognizing the familiar and enjoying the unfamiliar • Coping with change	JG built a tower with the bricks	JG played with the Lego bricks with D. He searched for and found some wheels and a base and said, 'I'm making a car.' JG added some bricks onto the base and said, 'This is where the people sit.' JG struggled to disconnect two Lego bricks but he didn't give up and used his teeth to pry them apart before separating them fully with his hands. JG carried on a conversation with D about his car using vocabulary such as 'wheels', 'bonnet', 'tyres' and 'exhaust'. After 10 minutes JG pronounced his car finished and began to roll it around on the carpet.
Well-being	**Being involved** • Paying attention • Feeling safe • Trusting others • Being playful with others and materials	JG paid attention for a sustained period	
Exploration	**Persisting when difficulties arise** • Setting and choosing difficult tasks • Using a range of strategies to solve problems when 'stuck'	JG separated the bricks	
Communication	**Expressing and idea or feeling** • Communicate in a range of ways – for example, using oral language, gesture, music, art, numbers and patterns, telling stories, etc.	JG used lots of language to convey his ideas	
Contribution	**Taking responsibility** • Responding to others, activities and events • Ensuring that things are fair • Self-evaluating • Helping others • Contributing to the programme	JG evaluated his work – 'It goes fast!'	

Case Study – Cont'd

Evaluation/What's next	Parents'/Child's comments
JG was really involved in his building. He demonstrated a lot of knowledge about the different parts of cars. Staff to introduce JG to some of the non-fiction books about cars, vehicles and transport in general.	JG's really interested in his dad's car at home. He's always asking questions about it and likes to sit in the driver's seat and pretends to drive.

The less or unstructured observations associated with qualitative studies are usually made in participants' normal, everyday settings and events are recorded as they occur naturally rather than in any predetermined way (Punch, 2009). This method may be adopted in situations where the data to be observed are part of wider social activities and patterns of behaviour in a particular environment and there is a need to focus down on particular aspects of that activity. In some studies, unstructured observations are the starting point of the data gathering and therefore may be less specific at first becoming more focused as the research questions emerge and are refined (Roberts-Holmes, 2014).

Case Study – Observing a Play Situation

Jenna wants to observe how children who are playing in groups with the construction materials respond when another child tries to join the established play. She observes children in a nursery setting at times agreed with the manager and during these times she records incidents where this event takes place. Jenna makes a note of the children involved, the sequence of events, what is said and the time the events last. She also records how successful different children are at negotiating entry to the group play and how long this takes. As part of this she notes down the strategies children use to join in and the responses of the other children. Jenna starts to build up a picture of how children respond in this situation and what strategies work for children wanting to join the construction play.

Participant and non-participant observation

At first glance participant and non-participant observations might appear to be polar opposites. In non-participant observation, the researcher is not involved in the action but observes events from the 'outside' in a detached fashion. As a non-participant observer, you have to try not to influence the behaviour and actions of your participants' but instead must remain neutral and unobtrusive, standing back from the events and allowing the participants to act as naturally as possible. In contrast during participant observations the researcher is involved and embedded in the environments and activities being observed. As a participant observer, you must have sufficient local knowledge and information to become part of that situation. This approach is more typical of ethnographic studies where the researcher is essentially taking part in or joining social activities in order to research them from the inside.

However, it may be an oversimplification to view these types of observation as opposites. It seems more likely that they sit somewhere on a continuum of levels of involvement depending on the extent to which *the researcher intrudes into the situation during data collection* (Punch, 1998, p. 188). Complete participant and complete non-participant roles are problematical when it comes to observation. In the case of the complete participant, the observer may 'go native' and become fully part of the observed group rather than continuing in the researcher role. In the case of the complete observer meanwhile, he/she has no interaction with the observed and so may have difficulties drawing from the data and interpreting it (Cohen et al.,2011).

Points to Think About – Gold's Continuum of Participant/ Non-participant Observation

- complete participant
- participant-as-observer
- observer-as-participant
- complete observer

Source: Gold, 1958.

Qualitative observations conducted as part of undergraduate education dissertations are more likely to be closer to the non-participant end of the continuum. This is because true participant observation can involve a very long process of gaining access and becoming involved in the social setting as the observer seeks to minimize the effect of her/his presence on the interactions in the situation. In many cases therefore the timescales are too long to fit easily into the final year of a degree.

Narrative observations

These are descriptive observations which document and record a particular sequence of events that take place over a set period of time. Narrative observations can be used to explore behaviour, consequences and the context in which these take place, in terms of the particular issue under study. If you opted for this kind of observational data-collection method you would record events as a continuous narrative flow rather than using a schedule with themes and headings under which to organize your data.

This approach is sometimes called a running record and if you use it you will have to jot down either in note form or in longhand everything you see as it occurs (Mac Naughton et al., 2010). The advantages of this approach are the richness of the data gathered and the authenticity of the directly observed record. However, it can be difficult to record everything that happens and the running record may only reflect part of what went on as you can miss things while noting other things down. A further risk is that consciously or unconsciously you might start to filter what is noted down or seen as significant; although this problem can be reduced once you have clear research questions that distinguish what aspects of behaviour are to be focused on and recorded (Mac Naughton et al., 2010).

Narrative observations can be used to explore an issue or phenomenon early on in a study to find out more about what is going on and to develop research questions from the outcomes. Narrative observations can also be compared with interview or other data to confirm or challenge existing information about a particular issue. These types of observations also supply good material as cases or vignettes to illustrate the discussion in the data analysis section of your dissertation (see Chapter 8). Cohen et al. (2011) suggest that if you choose to use narrative observations to collect your data then you need to make sure that your record captures:

- events and actions;
- non-verbal communication;
- time and timing of events;
- information about the context;
- comments on what is taking place (Cohen et al., 2011).

Case Study – Using Narrative Observation to Gather Data

Maria wanted to observe the behaviour of children in a particular part of the playground where there were two benches to sit on. She wanted to know which children used the benches and for what purpose. Maria went out at breaks and lunchtimes and positioned herself near the benches and wrote down what happened there, who was involved and what they did. She focused on how long children stayed at the benches, what they did and the groupings they were in and how these changed and evolved.

Maria discovered that there was a core of older girls who 'occupied' the benches for the majority of breaks. Other girls came and went, sometimes 'hovering' nearby until invited explicitly or implicitly to join the core group. Only a few boys came near the benches or were invited to stay, although one group of boys frequently 'bated' the core group from a slight distance. Some specific individuals and pairs of girls were vociferously 'driven off' if they approached the benches by members of the core group who shouted at them and told them to go away.

Time-sequenced observations

Time-sequenced observations are made and recorded at predetermined intervals to gather data about the behaviour and/or conversation of an individual or small group. The aim is to get a picture of what they are doing over a period of time by looking at the different snapshots as a whole. Edwards (2001) suggests the target-child approach as an example of this type of observation. In this approach, a child is observed and his/her behaviour recorded using a predetermined code at timed intervals to get an overview of what he/she is doing over a period of time (Sylva et al., 1980). A number of such observations would take place to monitor aspects of the child's behaviour and to note any issues or concerns.

Case Study – Time-sequenced Observations

Target child

Child: JG Age: 2 years 8 months		Date: 21/7/10	Time: 10.00	
Minute	**Activity**	**Language**	**Task**	**Social**
1	*Construction play (Duplo). TC selecting bricks. SOL play within SG situation.*	*TC → A 'I building tower'*	*Construction play (Duplo)*	(SG)
2	*Moves round table to access new bricks*	*F → TC 'Hey! No!' A F 'We can share. Here you are F' (A passes new bricks to F)*	*Construction play (Duplo)*	(SG)
3	*Stands next to tower and watches other children*	*TC → A 'Can I have bricks?' A passes bricks to TC TC → G 'I making big tower'*	*Construction play (Duplo)*	"
4	*Returns to building*	*TC → All 'Look! Look at my tower!'*	*Construction play (Duplo)*	"
5	*Protects tower and pushes F away*	*F → approaches tower TC → F 'No! F. My tower!'*	*Construction play (Duplo)*	"

Social codes

TC	Target child	SOL	Solitary
A	Any adult	PAIR	Two children together
→	Speaks to	SG	Small group of 3 to 5
(SOL)	A circle drawn around grouping indicates adult involvement	LG	Large group

Event sampling is another time-sequenced approach to observation. In event sampling the observation is focused on a particular phenomenon or behaviour. Using this system you would observe but would only note things down whenever the event or behaviour that you are interested in takes place, at which point you record something about it such as, *what happens, who does what, how long the event lasts* (Mac Naughton et al., 2001, p. 228). The purpose is to focus on one aspect rather than on a more general observation. This type of observation can be time efficient and is useful when you can be very clear and specific about exactly what it is that you wish to observe. Event sampling can also be used as a quantitative approach where a tally system is used to note the frequency of particular behaviours (see Chapter 8).

Table 7.2 lists the advantages and disadvantages of the various types of observations.

Table 7.2 Strengths and limitations of different types of observations

	Strengths	Limitations
Structured/Non-participant observations	Your 'detached' status may reduce the risk of your actions or statements influencing or altering the behaviour of those being observed.	It may be difficult to remain a non-participant in many contexts. Your non-participant status may itself affect the behaviour of those being observed if they are aware that they are being observed.
Semi-structured/ Participant observations	Your involvement and participation may encourage those being observed to be more accepting of you and to be more open and honest in their statements and behaviours.	It can be very difficult to observe, record and participate simultaneously. Important events may be missed.
Narrative observations	Can produce very rich and insightful data about particular individuals and/ or events.	Can be very hard to capture everything as it happens. You need to be careful to record everything faithfully and not to 'edit' as you go.
Time-sequenced observations	Can be a useful approach in isolating and focusing on particular behaviours.	May be too narrow in focus and may miss events and behaviours that happen at times other than those when recording is taking place.

Questionnaires

Chapter 6 contains considerable advice and guidance on using questionnaires in quantitative research projects. Much of this advice holds true for qualitative questionnaires too, for example some of the advantages and disadvantages of questionnaires in general as a means of data collection. In a qualitative project, however, the type of question asked is different. In purely qualitative research questionnaires you need to have open questions, questions which do not close down the debate by limiting respondents to a predetermined set of responses or that produce purely numerical information. In a qualitative questionnaire you need to offer participants the opportunity to include whatever information they feel is relevant in their attempts to explain their answer to the question. For instance, if you were to ask, 'How do you feel about being asked to fill in questionnaires?' you would be inviting a full response and would not be restricting participants' answers in any way. Analysis of the responses to this type of qualitative questionnaire should reveal information about participants' feelings towards and their understanding of the area being researched.

Advantages and disadvantages of qualitative questionnaires

As with quantitative projects, questionnaires in qualitative research projects offer a means of gaining access to data from a larger number of people, in a shorter period of time and less expensively than could be interviewed on a face-to-face basis. They can be carried out either over the phone or sent out by post, email or administered online as self-completion/self-administered questionnaires (Bryman, 2016). Qualitative questionnaires are subject to the same limitations in relation to response rates (see p. 225), identity of respondent and question design (see p. 226) that affect quantitative questionnaires. They also offer similar advantages (see Chapter 6). Sometimes it is easier to write than to talk and the absence of an interviewer may lead some respondents to be more confident in answering questions honestly that are quite personal or where an interviewer might appear judgemental. For instance, Tourangeau and Smith (1996, in Bryamn 2008) found that people admitted to a greater use of drugs, alcohol and the number of sexual partners in questionnaires than they did in interviews.

Case Study – Using a Qualitative Questionnaire

Richard is interested in the experiences of being a male worker in Early Years settings. In theory, he could send his questionnaire to every man in the country who works in Early Years. Given the scope of his dissertation, he does not have the time, resources or desire to do this, so he must select a sample from this population. He decides to select a group of men who work in settings in Sheffield. This is because he knows most of them and he believes that they will be supportive of his efforts. He tries to

Case Study – Cont'd

get in touch with as many of them as possible because he takes into consideration the number of responses he is likely to get, and how much time he has to spend in analysing the results. He realizes that analysing data always takes more time than he thinks it will. When he sends out the questionnaire out, he lets people know how long it will take them to complete and thanks them for taking part. He feels that personalizing the form will make people feel more engaged with his work.

Perhaps one of the biggest issues to consider in relation to qualitative questionnaires is the type and volume of data that open-text questions can produce. Certainly, it is possible that some respondents may give you one word answers to open-text questions that are very difficult to interpret. However, the reverse can also cause you some difficulties as when people write at the length the data produced is so rich and deep that it can be quite a challenge to analyse. When you get the responses back, you will need to think about how the data will be analysed and how long it is likely to take. You should expect to be presented with a lot of text much of which may be hand-written and not always easy to read. Like any form of textual data, it will need to be coded in order for you to make sense of it and to try to identify what the research is telling you against the themes that you have been asking about (see Chapter 8). Pure qualitative questionnaires, therefore, can produce a considerable volume of data to be processed and you need to bear this in mind when thinking about the number of questions you wish to ask and how large your sample can be before it ceases to be realistic and manageable.

Ideas to Use – Qualitative, Open-text Questions

What sorts of games do you play with your child?

_____
_____
_____

Are there any other comments you would like to make? (Please continue on a separate sheet if necessary)

_____
_____
_____

What do you think are the three most important things that education should do for pupils and why?

_____
_____
_____

Framing your questions in a qualitative questionnaire is every bit as important as in a quantitative questionnaire. You need to give careful consideration to the purpose of your research and the nature of the information that you need to get from your participants in order to answer your research question(s). The questions you design need to provide you with the information necessary to answer your research question. Where the questions asked do not provide the data being sought this is sometimes referred to as 'specification error' (de Leeuw, in Alasuutari et al., 2008, p. 315). This may seem obvious but it is very easy to get side tracked into thinking that you have a great question only to find afterwards that it has not given you any useful data.

Points to Think About – Think About What You Want to explore

Your questions must enable you to gain data for what you set out to explore. There is no point asking about 'physiotherapy in a specialist school' if you are interested in 'the role of the school nurse', in spite of the occasional overlap between the two.

Keep things simple

The Plain English Campaign suggests that an expression such as '*High-quality learning environments are a necessary precondition for facilitation and enhancement of the ongoing learning process*' might be replaced by '*Children need good schools if they are to learn properly.*' (www.plainenglish.co.uk)

Don't muddle up the issues with multiple questions

The question 'How can we improve students' attendance and writing skills?' is in fact two questions.

In designing your questions it is also important that you avoid ambiguity and use straightforward words and expressions. Multiple questions, where two or more questions are conflated into one, are not helpful either. For instance, 'How do you feel about the reading and writing involved in your research topic?' Such a question in a questionnaire is unclear because you might enjoy the reading far more than the writing and would, therefore, be left uncertain about how best to answer the question.

A clear design and layout are equally essential in the absence of an interviewer. You need to make sure that your instructions are explicit and that participants will know exactly what is required from them. Even the smallest of oversights can catch you out; for example, not putting an instruction to turn over on a two-sided questionnaire could mean that a few of your respondents only provide you with answers to the questions on the first side – it has happened.

When you think about the phrasing, design and administration of your questionnaire, you need to keep in mind those who you hope will be responding. Once you have a first draft you must pilot your questionnaire. Many students ask flatmates, work colleagues, friends and relatives to try it out. Ideally though the questions and layout should be tested with a small sample of people who are as similar as possible to the actual participants who will take part in your research. You might even use a focus group to do this. The aim of a pilot is to check whether your questions generate the kind of responses that you need, whether your instructions are clear and whether or not people feel comfortable in responding to them. The following guidance sets out some useful questions for you to consider when designing and piloting a qualitative questionnaire.

Points to Think About – Writing and Testing Your Questions

Comprehension and interpretation of the question being asked – Will your participants understand the words of the question and be able to work out what information you are looking for?

Retrieval of relevant information from memory – Are you asking for simple factual information and/or deeply held views which participants can usually remember and articulate quite easily?

Integrating information into a summarized judgement – Are you asking about more complex matters (e.g. feelings, attitudes, events that happened some time ago)? This may take more thought on the part of your respondents and the responses may be less precise.

Reporting judgements using the means offered – Will your participants be able to write down their answers in their own words (e.g. using open-text boxes or spaces)?

Source: de Leeuw, in Alasuutari et al., 2008, p. 316.

Creative methods

The research methods discussed in this chapter so far rely on either numbers or words, whether spoken or in the form of text. While it is difficult to separate ourselves from language, the reliance on more 'traditional' forms of data means that we limit our choice of methods. Creative approaches tend to rely on art – this could include creative writing, music, photography, sculpture in fact, almost any art form and this section briefly explores these approaches.

Visual research methods (VRMs) have become increasingly widely used throughout the social sciences and are now firmly entrenched in major fields of inquiry, including sociology, health and nursing studies and in particular for us, in educational research. They can be used in both qualitative and quantitative research.

Many of you will have come across 'the Mosaic approach' described by Clarke and Moss (2001) where getting children to take photographs provides part of the data collecting process.

VRMs use visible artefacts to explore research questions. There are very many examples of these methods, such as photographs, diagrams, graphic novels and cartoons. Some methods use materials provided by the researcher, others by using images created by the research participants.

Gillian Rose (2016) suggests a number of reasons for using VRMs. She suggests that having visual images which are discussed in an interview increases the amount of evidence presented, for instance she cites a project which found that it was the photographs and drawings that it asked children to take, rather than conversations with those children, that revealed the importance of pets to children's lives and especially to the physical activities they undertook.

Examples:

Chloe wants to explore how children spend their play times. She asks them to take photographs of their favourite places. This then provides her with a focus for her later interviews with them and gives her rich insights into what children enjoy doing and why.

Rose (2016) suggests that in research using participant-generated images, the participant is situated as the 'expert' in the interview as they explain their images to the researcher and she cites Sweetman (2009) in suggesting that visual materials can *'reveal what is hidden in the inner mechanisms of the ordinary and the taken for granted'*.

Using images as data can be powerful, but it can also generate ethical concerns – for instance think about some of the issues around on what is published on line. However, the incorporation of visual methods into your research approach can lead to a richer source of data and can be a great way of really engaging people with your research.

As an example of another creative approach, David Gauntlett (2015) for instance, advocates the use of Lego as a tool for developing creative thinking. Such tangible objects, as Lego or Play Doh, can be used by research participants to construct representations of the focus of their research.

A recent doctoral study asked participants to build Lego models to represent how Early Years teachers experienced placement. *Sometimes, it is difficult for participants to put things into words – creative approaches can help them to 'create something where previously there was nothing' (Gauntlett, 2015).*

These approaches can seem to be out of the ordinary and quite challenging to do – however, as Kara (2016) points out, 'any non-research skills you have may be useful in the service of research and if you want to expand your methodological repertoire, you can do so one step at a time'.

Summary of key points

- Every data-collection method has its advantages and disadvantages and you must make a decision about which approach is the *best fit* for your dissertation in terms of gathering the data you need to answer your research question.
- Qualitative data-collection methods tend to produce very rich and complex data which while fascinating can be very hard to process and to analyse.
- The chosen data-gathering methods need to fit with the overall approach of the study and if more than one method is used these need to complement each other.
- Semi-structured interviews and focus groups are important data-gathering methods in qualitative studies.
- Observations and qualitative questionnaires are also useful tools but may need to be supplementary to other methods such as interviews to get sufficient data. Creative methods can be challenging, but offer the opportunity to get very rich data.
- Careful planning is the key to ensuring high levels of validity, reliability and trustworthiness using qualitative methods.

Reflective task

Ginny is thinking of researching language development in a nursery in a socio-economically deprived inner city primary school. She wants to know what teacher and teaching assistant strategies are used to promote children's talk and whether these are effective.

What sort of data-gathering method or methods would be of most use to her in answering her research question?

What might be the difficulties of conducting data gathering using this method or methods?

If you suggest more than one method, what order should the data be gathered in, and why?

Link to companion website

https://bloomsbury.com/cw/successful-dissertations-second-edition/student-resources/chapter-6/

Recommended reading and further sources of information

Bell, A. (2007), 'Designing and testing questionnaires for children'. *Journal of Research in Nursing*, vol. 12, no. 5, pp. 460–9.

Chioncel, N. E., Van der Veen, R. G. W., Wildemeersch, D. and Jarvis, P. (2003), 'The validity and reliability of focus groups as a research method in adult education'. *International Journal of Lifelong Education*, vol. 22, no. 5, pp. 495–517.

Edwards, R. and Holland, J. (2013), *What is Qualitative Interviewing?* London: Bloomsbury.

Folque, M. A. (2010, 2nd edition), 'Interviewing young children', in Mac Naughton, G., Rolfe, S. and Siraj-Blatchford, I. (eds), *Doing Early Childhood Research: International Perspectives on Theory and Practice*. Buckingham: Open University Press.

Gauntlett, David (2015), 'The LEGO system as a tool for thinking, creativity, and changing the world', in *Making Media Studies: The Creativity Turn in Media and Communications Studies*, New York: Peter Lang.

Grudens-Schuck, N., Lundy Allen, B. and Larsen, K. (2004), *Focus Group Essentials*. Iowa: Iowa State University. http://www.extension.iastate.edu/publications/pm1969b.pdf.

Jupp, V. (2006, 2nd edition), 'Documents and critical research', in Sapsford, R. and Jupp, V. (eds), *Data Collection and Analysis*. London: Sage.

Mukherji, P. and Albom, D. (2010), *Research Methods in Early Childhood*. London: Sage.

Oppenheim, A. N. (2001), *Questionnaire Design, Interviewing and Attitude Measurement*. London: Continuum.

Roberts-Holmes, G. (2014), *Doing Your Early Years Research Project: A Step by Step Guide*. London: Sage.

Rose, G. (2016, 4th edition), *Visual Methodologies: An Introduction to Researching with Visual Materials*. Maidenhead: Oxford University Press. www.ncrm.ac.uk.

7

Data Collection Using Quantitative Methods

Pam Dewis

Chapter Outline

Chapter Aims

By the end of this chapter you will

- be able to recognize when quantitative methods are appropriate;
- know how to make a variable or variables measurable;
- appreciate the need for care and attention to detail when constructing quantitative data-collection tools;
- know about some of the pre-existing quantitative data-collection tools that are available to you and how to access these;
- know what reliability and validity mean when using quantitative data-collection tools.

The aim of all research methods is to collect data which provide as true a reflection of a situation as is possible so that credible conclusions about that situation can be made. This chapter deals with some of the key ideas and themes associated with quantitative research methods. The main focus is on the fundamental logic behind their use as opposed to more technical issues, such as the detailed 'how to' of each of the methods outlined. This is done in depth elsewhere (see recommended texts at the end of the chapter). The overall aim of this chapter is to convey the essence of what is involved when using quantitative methods. The chapter begins by exploring the suitability of quantitative methods to an area of study. Variables, the mainstay of quantitative research, are discussed at length, in terms of how they are defined, categorized and measured. Quantitative data can be obtained in a number of ways, such as by asking questions (using questionnaires or interview schedules), observing and recording behaviour, and through reviewing existing documents. This chapter therefore outlines some of the key features of the more common methods used by undergraduate students, with reference to some of their strengths and limitations.

The what, why and when of quantitative methods

What are quantitative methods?

Quantitative methods are used to gather factual or attitudinal information in numerical form. Therefore, they are used to ascertain how much, how many, how frequently and/or, to what extent something occurs or exists, be this a fact or an attitude. It is worth noting that quantitative data do not necessarily start off in numerical form; they can often take the form of words which researchers later translate, by means of applying numerical codes, into numbers. Quantitative research conceptualizes reality in terms of variables and the relationships between them and relies on numbers, counts and measurements in order that these relationships can be portrayed using tables, charts and graphs. Data is generated through asking questions and getting responses (self-report methods) or by observing and recording past (secondary) or present behaviour.

Why and when is it appropriate to use quantitative methods?

Students are often unsure as to whether quantitative, qualitative or a combination of both methods are called for, hence the inclusion here of some information that will hopefully aid this crucial decision. Choosing correctly between the use of quantitative or qualitative methods, or indeed a combination of both (using a mixed-methods approach), is imperative to the success of a research project. It is likely that quantitative methods will be appropriate if some of the following apply:

- You accept the notion that reality can be understood (see Chapter 5) through discovering the distribution of and relationship between variables (read the section 'Variables' below before continuing through this list).
- Other researchers have dealt with the same or similar research topics/ questions as yours using quantitative methods.
- You want to describe the distribution of a certain variable, or variables, in a given population. The importance of such descriptive knowledge is often underestimated, compared to that of explanatory knowledge, yet this descriptive knowledge is often a prerequisite to explanation: *you can't explain something properly until you know what the something is* (Miles and Huberman, 1994, p. 9).
- You want to make standardized and systematic comparisons to demonstrate correlational or causal relationships between variables (these concepts are examined later in the chapter). You want to describe and/or explain a phenomenon in terms of what happened. You are not concerned with individuals' views on, attitudes towards or perceptions of the phenomenon, you simply want to describe and/or explain it.
- You want to generalize your results or findings to a reference population (a population from which a research sample has been drawn). Note, however, that such generalization requires a representative sample of the population under study, as well as the use of specific statistical techniques; for most undergraduate dissertations this is unlikely and any claims you make are likely to be restricted to the sample population itself.

If, having read the points listed above, you are still uncertain as to whether quantitative methods offer the best way to proceed, make sure you consult with your supervisor; do not take pot luck and hope for the best. Wrong methods are likely to produce the wrong data which in turn will be of little or no use to answering your research question(s).

Variables

A variable is anything that can differ across individuals or situations. As such, a variable can be absolutely anything you can think of that varies from individual to individual and therefore it would be possible to conjure up millions of examples. Quantitative researchers are interested in relationships between variables. These can be simply correlational, or otherwise causal (i.e. cause and effect), in nature. A correlational relationship exists where the action of two variables is in some way related. For example, Mrug and Windle (2010) found a relationship between exposure to violence at home and the manifestation of anxiety and aggression in adolescents. A causal relationship on the other hand exists when one variable causes the change in the other. This is more commonly known as a cause and effect relationship. Staying with the example above; a causal relationship would exist if it were the exposure to violence that actually caused the development of anxiety and aggression in the adolescents in question. While it is reasonable to assume a causal relationship in this event, in the absence of the use of a control group for example, it is not possible to establish causation because the effect (anxiety and aggression) could well have been caused by something else, unbeknown to the researcher.

If you plan to make use of quantitative data-collection methods, as well as understanding levels at which variables can be related (correlational or causal) you will also need to understand other fundamental factors about them. First, you will need to be able to define your variables both conceptually and operationally. Second, you will need to be clear about the types of variables you may have to deal with. Third, you will need to familiarize yourself with the different levels of sophistication with which variables can be measured.

Defining your variables conceptually and operationally

A conceptual definition of a variable tells you what that variable is; it defines it. An operational definition meanwhile provides a means of measuring variables by translating them into something that can be counted in some way (this is called operationalization). The variable aggression, for example, could be conceptually defined as, behaviour, either physical or verbal, which is intended to cause harm to others. However, in order to measure aggression you would have to decide what constitutes such behaviour, instances of which you could then look for; examples might include hitting, shouting at or insulting others. The importance of carefully selecting indicators that accurately reflect the variables of interest cannot be overemphasized. No matter how rigorous a piece of research, if the variables under investigation are not operationalized properly, the results of the study may be seriously flawed.

Types of variable

There exist two distinct types of variable; discrete and continuous. Discrete (also known as categorical) variables vary in kind only in that they have no possible values in between them, they are *only meaningful as whole numbers* (Calder and Sapsford, 2006, p. 208). The number of children per family is a classic example of a discrete or categorical variable; it is possible to have one or two children for example, but never one and half (obviously).

Other examples of discrete variables include the number of people in a group, the number of pupils in a school, the number of brothers or sisters that an individual has, marital status and so on. Continuous variables on the other hand vary in degree. Unlike discrete variables, they have possible values in between them. This allows for ranking or measurement to take place. Weight is a good example; an individual can weigh 60 kg or 61 kg, or any of an infinite number of weights in between. Attitudes towards certain phenomena are also examples of continuous variables. Children who enjoy learning mathematics, for example, will vary in terms of how much they enjoy it.

Variables can be measured at four different levels: nominal, ordinal, interval and ratio (Stevens, 1951). This order is hierarchical in terms of the level of sophistication, from the crudest nominal-level variables to the most sophisticated ratio-level variables. Understanding these levels of measurement is important due to the crucial part they play in determining what type of statistical tests can be applied (for more information about this see Chapter 6).

Points to Think About – Types of Variables and Levels of Measurement

Discrete/Categorical

- Nominal-level variables (e.g. gender, marital status) have no evaluative distinction in that they cannot be measured in terms of one being greater or lesser than the other. Their difference is therefore in kind as opposed to being quantitative.
- Ordinal-level variables do have evaluative distinction. Although, like nominal variables, they can fall into distinct categories and so are discrete in nature, unlike nominal variables, they can be ordered or ranked in some order of importance within that category. For example, individuals can perceive their state of health as excellent, good or poor. Similarly, classifications of socio-economic status are good examples of ordinal-level variables.

Continuous

- Interval-level variables are similar in nature to ordinal-level variables; the difference being that the distance between each value is equal. Temperature is a good example; the difference between 12 and 13 degrees centigrade is the same as the difference between 22 and 23 degrees centigrade, thus they are continuous.
- Ratio-level variables have the same properties as interval variables but differ in that they have an absolute zero point. Weight is a good example; there is no weight below zero kilograms in that zero kilograms denotes the absence of weight. Age is another example; there is no age below zero.

Talk of conceptual and operational definitions, discrete and continuous variables and nominal-, ordinal-, interval-and ratio-level measurement can seem bewildering at first but, if you are keen to make use of quantitative data-collection methods, then it is important to persevere. It can happen that a student finds herself/himself disappointed at the data analysis stage of their dissertation (when little or nothing can be done to remedy the situation) to discover that the data she/he has gathered do not adequately inform the research question. This can be due to inadequate operationalization of the variable(s) of interest, and/or through collecting data in a form that does not lend itself to the type of quantitative analysis required to answer the research question(s). It is important, therefore, to be clear about whether your research question requires that you examine the distribution of a variable or variables (a descriptive study), or whether you will be seeking to explain how or why something is happening (explanatory research).

Points to Think About – Do You Want to Describe or Explain?

The nature of your undertaking	Sample question
Describing the distribution of a variable	What are the breakfast eating habits of a group of 5-year-old children?
Describing a relationship between two variables	Is there a relationship between eating breakfast and school performance in a group of 5-year-old children?
Demonstrating a causal relationship between variables (explanatory research)	Do 5-year-old children who eat breakfast every day perform better at school?

Sampling in quantitative research

If variables are one of the key features of quantitative methods then sample selection is another, and decisions about how to approach sampling in quantitative research are largely dependent upon whether or not researchers wish to generalize their findings to the research population from which the sample was drawn. In other words, whether they want to claim that what was discovered from their research, based on a sample of the reference population, is true of the reference population as a whole.

If you have no intention of generalizing your findings, there is very little restriction on how you select your sample, other than the need for ethical considerations and to select a sample of participants who can provide relevant data in respect of your research questions. If you were to conduct a survey, for example, you might decide to include all the children in Key Stage 1 because you are doing a placement in a Key Stage 1 classroom and your research question relates to young children attending school. This type of approach to sampling is generally known as non-probability or convenience sampling, where the sample is selected at the researcher's convenience as it were. However, if you did want to generalize your findings, you would need a representative sample. Drawing on Key Stage 1 children from one setting alone would not suffice in this case, the obvious reason being that only the views of that particular age group attending that particular setting would be represented. In other words, the sample would be biased. In view of resource and access implications, it would be unlikely that an undergraduate researcher would be able to generate a representative sample from a much wider reference population.

Indeed, most commentators agree that in reality it is virtually impossible for anyone to produce a sample that is completely and truly unbiased and thereby one hundred per cent representative of a reference population. However, probability sampling techniques can be employed to keep this bias to an absolute minimum. Probability sampling methods are so called because they are used for the purpose of increasing the probability that the sample will be representative of the reference population. This is achieved by employing some sort of random selection, including

- Simple random sampling – as its name suggests, this is random sampling at its simplest level, just like drawing names from a hat. Basically, each member of the research population has an equal chance of being selected. Another example of simple random sampling is the national lottery draw where each number or combination of numbers has an equal chance of being selected.
- Stratified random sampling – differs from simple random sampling in that the sampling frame (e.g. all children attending junior schools in a particular city) is stratified in some way, into gender or age groups for example, and a simple random sample is then selected from each stratum. Stratification ensures a more representative selection of the research population.
- Systematic random sampling – if a group of researchers wanted to use systematic sampling to generate a sample of 360 primary school age children with asthma out of all primary school age children with asthma in a given population (the sampling frame) – let us pretend this is 3,600 – they would need to select every 10th name (3,600 divided by 360) from a register of children fitting the relevant age group and diagnosed with asthma. Systematic sampling also ensures better representation of the research population than simple random sampling.

Sample size is also linked to how representative of the reference population the sample is. The smaller the sample, the less representative it will be, even in the event of a systematic random sampling technique having been used. In basic terms, in order to generalize research findings, the bigger the sample the better. Denscombe (2014) recommends a sample size of anything between 30 and 250 cases as being adequate in social science research, as long as you acknowledge the limitations to your study of having a small sample. He also notes that any attempt at statistical analysis with a sample as low as 30 is foolhardy and could be misleading (Denscombe, 2014).

As an undergraduate student researcher, it is unlikely that you will be expected to undertake your project in such a way as to guarantee the generalizability of your findings, in which case you may not need to concern yourself too much with the science of probability sampling. However, if generalizations are what you plan to make then Dhivyadeepa (2015) provides excellent guidance on probability sampling. What is more likely is that you will be expected to explain in your dissertation why your findings cannot be generalized. This requires that you understand the difference between probability and non-probability/convenience sampling and can justify why you opted for the latter. Your reason will most likely be the avoidance of difficulties brought about by probability sampling, particularly the time it takes and potential financial costs. The fact that the use of a non-probability sample does not allow you to generalize your findings does not remove from the fact that your findings can inform further research as well as add to an existing body of knowledge (Bryman, 2016).

Asking questions in quantitative research

In this chapter the focus is on data collection rather than overall research questions of the kind covered in Chapters 1 and 2. Research questions guide the project. They indicate what data are needed to inform the dissertation and also provide a basis for choosing or formulating data-collection tools, and identifying any variables that need to be counted or measured. The data-collection questions which are dealt with here, however, are more specific; their aim is to operationalize those variables arising out of the original research question(s).

Quantitative research relies on structure at every stage of the research process, and self-report methods such as questionnaires and structured interviews are often used to achieve this. In quantitative research projects, these self-report methods generally use closed questions with a fixed response (sometimes called 'forced choice') format, which means that possible answers to a question are presented to respondents rather than allowing respondents to give their own answers as is the case in qualitative research. Although, there can also be an 'other' category to allow respondents to provide data that had not been anticipated. The fixed response format is used so that the same type of information can be gathered in the same way from all respondents, thus allowing for statistical analysis to take place. Most fixed response formats are precoded, that is each response category has been assigned a number prior to respondents making their choice (see Chapter 8). Various fixed response formats can be used depending on the type of information being sought and the level of measurement that needs to be achieved. Some of the more common formats include

- Choice of categories: respondents are asked to identify, out of a list of categories, the one which best describes them. More often than not, the list of categories includes an 'other' category. Information about marital status and ethnicity, for example, is frequently obtained in this way.

- Checklists: respondents choose, from a number of possibilities, all the items on a list that they like, dislike, are interested in and so on, depending on the question. For example, circling all the vegetables they like out of a list of ten.
- Ranking ('response scaling'): respondents are asked to place items in sequence, such as first choice, second choice, third choice and so on, depending on the number of items presented. An example would be to ask respondents to rank newspapers that they buy or would consider buying in order of preference. One downside of ranking is that the data cannot be averaged.
- Rating scales: these are procedures for the assignment of numbers to a series of objects. They differ from ranking/response scaling, in that the procedures to give items a numerical value take place independently of the respondent. Rating scales allow us to see differences in the degree to which a phenomenon exists and thereby provide more information. These scales can take a number of different forms. Using the Thurstone Scale respondents are presented with a set of statements that describe specific attitudes that people may have towards a variable under investigation. Each statement has a numerical value reflecting the degree of favourability towards it. Respondents have the option of agreeing or disagreeing with the statements. The Guttman Scale meanwhile uses statements that are ranked from least to most extreme attitude towards a variable. This scale is based on the premise that, if a person agrees with an extreme statement then he/she will also agree with the less extreme ones that preceded it. Probably one of the most commonly used scales in social research and one that you will very likely have already encountered somewhere is the Likert Scale. Likert Scales measure attitudes in terms of degree of agreement with a set of statements about the variable in question. Level of agreement is generally measured on a five or seven-point scale; ranging from 'strongly disagree' to 'strongly agree' through a central neutral option such as 'undecided' or 'not sure'.

Example – Likert Scales

Supportiveness of the University Environment

Thinking about your experiences during the current academic year, how far do you agree with the following statements:

I would contact my tutors/lecturers for help with academic work if I needed it.
Strongly disagree 1-2-3-4-5 Strongly agree

Tutors and lecturers are helpful and sympathetic.
Strongly disagree 1-2-3-4-5 Strongly agree

Example – Cont'd

There are spaces on campus where I feel comfortable working collaboratively with others outside of taught sessions.
Strongly disagree 1-2-3-4-5 Strongly agree

Support staff are helpful and sympathetic (e.g. course administrators, advisers in the Learning Centres and Student Academic Services Centres, security personnel).
Strongly disagree 1-2-3-4-5 Strongly agree

I feel I can ask for help with coping with responsibilities outside academic life (work, family, finances, etc.).
Strongly disagree 1-2-3-4-5 Strongly agree

Other students are friendly and supportive.
Strongly disagree 1-2-3-4-5 Strongly agree

Source: SHU, 2009c.

Such self-reporting methods can be used to ask questions about social properties – including factual variables such as gender, social class and ethnicity, affective variables such as feelings, opinions, views and beliefs – and behavioural variables such as exercise (Rosenberg, 1968). Questions can also be used to gauge respondents' knowledge of a particular issue, or to test their cognitive ability. Often respondents are asked to indicate their level of agreement with a statement or to indicate a category which best describes them as opposed to being asked a direct question.

If you decide to opt for a self-report method of questioning then you will need to consider how you will avoid or at least minimize the impact of some of the problems inherent in the approach. Problems associated with self-report methods include respondents misinterpreting questions and respondents struggling to remember past behaviours and events accurately. A further issue can be caused as a result of response style when rating scales are used and strongly opinionated people tend to opt for extreme responses, while more cautious individuals consistently opt for the more moderate responses. Fortunately, the overall effect of response style on the findings of a study is small.

Two of the most common challenges to self-report methods of questioning centre on the response set (Webb et al., 1966). Response set difficulties can happen in two ways; first, the acquiescence effect and second, the social desirability effect. Acquiescence effect occurs when respondents consistently respond to items in the same way regardless of the appropriateness of that response. For example, opting for one or other of the extreme response ends of a rating scale in a consistent way throughout a battery of such scales; opting for the 'strongly agree' option across a battery of Likert Scales for instance. The second type of response set problem is the social desirability effect, which, as its name suggests, refers to a tendency on the part of some respondents to respond according to the option that they perceive as being the most socially desirable. For example, when asked about how much reading a child does at home, parents may wish to impress the researcher by opting for the highest option when in actual fact this is not the case.

Eliminating response set effects entirely is not easy. As a researcher, you will never be able to say with complete certainty that these effects have been eradicated. However, there are steps that you can take to help you to spot it when it happens so that the data can be withdrawn. One way of doing this is to reverse the wording of the questions occasionally so that least and most favourable responses towards a variable vary in terms of which end of the scale they appear on. In this way, anyone who is ticking a particular box every time without regard for any of the questions is likely to be exposed by the contradictory responses. Guarantees of anonymity and confidentiality may help to minimize social desirability effects, so too may pleas for honesty on your part in which you stress how anything other than honesty will undermine the chances of success of your project/dissertation. Should you decide to opt for the latter of these two suggestions you are advised to craft the wording of your request with care and your supervisor should be able to advise you here. You do not want potential respondents being inadvertently made to feel dishonest.

It is all too easy to underestimate how challenging a task it can be to formulate and frame really effective data-collection questions. Common mistakes made by students when drawing up their data-collection questions include not providing sufficient instruction on how a question should be answered, using yes/no questions excessively and/or formulating closed questions that are not mutually exclusive (Bryman, 2016). The list below outlines some of things to watch out for when drafting your data-collection questions.

Points to Think About – Formulating Questions to Use in Quantitative Research

- You need to pitch your questions at the right level. This involves making sure that potential respondents have the necessary knowledge to answer them and that they fit their frame of reference.
- There is almost always the potential for ambiguity in any data-collection technique involving the written or spoken word, however you must keep this to a minimum by drafting and redrafting your questions to get them as clear and unambiguous as you can (Fontana and Frey, 1998). This means avoiding any unnecessarily complex phrases or potentially unfamiliar vocabulary. It is particularly important to make the meaning of your questions clear where clarification of potentially ambiguous questions is not possible, that is if your respondents are going to complete the questionnaire in your absence. Even if you are present it is possible that respondents might feel too embarrassed to admit to not understanding a question and might therefore just take a guess.

Points to Think About – Cont'd

- Keep your questions as succinct, concise and free of waffle as you can. Shorter questions have been associated with better response rates (Sallant and Dillman, 1994).
- Avoid double-barreled and, worse still, multiple-barrelled questions; for example, 'Please rate the staff in terms of friendliness and efficiency.' This is asking for two separate pieces of information; the staff in question could be very friendly but incompetent, alternatively they might be extremely efficient but not in the least bit welcoming. This question should therefore be divided into two separate questions: first, 'Please rate the staff in terms of friendliness,' and second, 'Please rate the staff in terms of efficiency.'
- Clear instructions for your respondents are essential especially so when you are using questionnaires and the instructions have to be in writing; for example: '*Please turn over page*,' '*Please tick all the answers that apply*,' or alternatively '*Please tick the answer that best describes your view*.' Rating scales in particular must be accompanied by clear instructions as to what is required of the respondent.
- When using a quantitative data-collection method, you will need to include enough questions to ensure the reliability (see p. 149) of that measuring instrument whether it is a questionnaire or an interview schedule. Reliability tends to increase with the number of questions. However, so does the time taken to answer them and so you need to balance the need for reliability with the need to get people to take part.
- Generally, less than 20 questions decreases the reliability of quantitative data-collection instruments and more than 30 tends to deter potential respondents.
- You must pilot your questions. Testing a questionnaire or an interview schedule can reap huge rewards. Piloting in this way will give you insights into any misunderstandings and problems with the first draft in time for you to take action. This includes identifying potential ambiguity in the wording of questions, removing questions that are unnecessary or potentially offensive and spotting any gaps where you need some additional questions. You can engage the help of your friends and family for this, but if possible it is far better to conduct your pilot with people who are representative of or similar to those in your eventual sample.

Reliability and validity

Reliability refers to the consistency of a data-collection method no matter how often it is used or by how many different researchers. Validity, meanwhile, is concerned with the truthfulness of the conclusions generated by a piece of research. In other words, has the research been conducted in such a way that we can believe its findings to be true? All data-collection methods have the potential for error. Thus, if you are constructing your own data-collection tools, you must make every effort to minimize such error as far as possible so as to enhance the trustworthiness of your findings.

Reliability

All data-collection tools used in quantitative research should, as far as is practicable, be reliable; *not like an elastic tape measure, measuring differently depending on how hard you pull it* (Malim and Birch, 1997, p. 46). Gauging the reliability of a quantitative data-collection instrument means considering whether it measures consistently within itself (internal reliability), when readministered (external reliability) or when administered by a different researcher (inter-tester reliability).

Internal reliability refers to the consistency of a measure in terms of its content. In other words, how well does each of the items (indicators) believed to reflect the variable under investigation, yield similar results. If some items produce markedly different results than others, the data-collection tool is flawed. Inter-tester reliability meanwhile is only an issue when there is more than one researcher, in that it estimates the level of agreement between two or more researchers rating the same phenomenon.

External reliability, often referred to as the stability of a data-collection instrument, refers to its ability to yield similar results over time and in similar situations. In other words, every time it is applied with similar participants it should produce similar results. External reliability can be estimated using a test-retest technique, which requires that the measurement instrument is administered twice to the same participants at different times.

Validity

A number of factors contribute to the validity of a study in quantitative research, of which measurement validity is one. Others include issues such as using the most appropriate design and controlling for possible confounding variables. Measurement validity refers to the degree to which a data-collection method measures what it purports to be measuring and is logically preceded by reliability (Davidson et al., 2000). In other words, validity presupposes reliability, in that an unreliable data-collection tool will not measure what it claims to be measuring. Reliability, however, does not equate to validity. For example, you might well have a state-of-the-art thermometer, proven time and again to yield accurate measurements of body temperature, but you could not use it to measure a person's blood pressure. The same is true in research, no matter how accurate and reliable a data-collection tool, it has to be fit for the purpose to yield trustworthy findings.

Common methods of quantitative data collection

Four of the more common data-collection tools used in quantitative research include questionnaires, structured interviews, structured observations and content analysis.

These are examined now with reference to some of their key features and some of the advantages and disadvantages associated with their use. The section concludes with a discussion of reliability and validity in relation to quantitative data-collection methods.

Questionnaires

Self-administered (or self-completion) questionnaires, so named because respondents fill them in by themselves usually without the researcher being present, are one of the most frequently used data-collection methods in education and social sciences research. Their most common usage is in survey research where large amounts of information are gathered about the distribution and relationships between variables (Punch and Oancea, 2014). The intention is to describe and/or explain statistically the variability of certain features of the population such as the distribution of characteristics, attitudes or beliefs (Marshall and Rossman, 2006).

Points to Think About – Questionnaire/Survey Types

- Factual, for example census, essentially descriptive;
- Attitudinal, for example opinion polls;
- Explanatory, for example to test theories and hypotheses;
- A combination of two or more of the above types.

Questionnaires can be administered in a variety of ways. You could opt for a postal questionnaire which would help to ensure the anonymity of your respondents, but this often results in fairly low response rates and carries a risk of bias as the respondents may have characteristics in common that non-respondents do not. For example, in a satisfaction survey it is possible that those who are most dissatisfied would be more likely to respond while those who are satisfied or reasonably satisfied might be much less likely to complete the questionnaire. An alternative to the postal method is to hand out questionnaires to a group of respondents to be collected once they have been filled in. The 'captive audience' tends to produce very high response rates and ensures that you get all shades of opinion; however, there is a danger of researcher bias as your presence may cause respondents to adjust their answers. A further option is to administer your questionnaire over the telephone; however, this can be a very labour-intensive activity and if it involves cold-calling then you should prepare yourself to have to deal with a few disgruntled refusals. Low response rates are a problem in quantitative research; a 50–60 per cent response rate is barely acceptable and below 50 per cent is generally considered unacceptable as it can seriously bias the findings of a study (Mangione, 1995, p. 61).

Questionnaires can also be administered via the internet although this latter mode of delivery is still somewhat in its infancy compared to other means. While the approach can make large samples possible it is also associated with some significant disadvantages. Not everyone is online for example and those who are may not be representative of the sample under investigation. There is also a poorer response rate where internet services are used (Couper, 2000). If, despite these limitations, you feel that using the internet in some way to disseminate a questionnaire may suit your needs (perhaps you are doing research involving a sample population all of whom have access to internet services) you are advised to follow guidance such as that provided by Dillman and Smyth (2009) and to consult with your dissertation supervisor before proceeding. Whether using paper questionnaires or electronic ones to collect your data, it is advisable to give some thought to how you can improve the response rates.

Points to Think About – Self-administered Questionnaires

Strengths	Limitations
Relatively inexpensive, cost of postage being the main consideration	Risks of bias.
Relatively quick to administer as they tend to be disseminated in large quantities	Poor response rate to postal and internet-administered questionnaires. Bryman (2008, p. 136) outlines ways to improve response rate to postal questionnaires: for example, writing a good covering letter; providing a stamped addressed envelope and following up non-respondents with friendly reminders.
People are generally familiar with questionnaires and therefore tend not to feel apprehensive about filling them in	There is no one present to clarify questions that respondents do not understand which highlights further the need for unambiguous questions and clear instructions.
	Missing data can be a problem, where respondents have, either inadvertently or purposely, skipped a question or questions. It is important, therefore, to highlight to potential respondents the need to answer all the questions, however irrelevant they may seem. This can be done in a covering letter or in an introductory section on the questionnaire.
Less intrusive than interviews as respondents can complete at a time which suits them and at their own pace	With postal or internet questionnaires, you can never be sure that it was completed by the intended respondent, rather than a friend or a member of the intended respondent's family.
No interviewer effects (see disadvantages of structured interviews below)	Respondents whose ability to read and write is limited or those who speak little or no English cannot complete a questionnaire. In the case of the latter, however, you could get the questions and response choices translated, but this could have big financial cost implications.

Constructing a good questionnaire requires great care and attention to detail. An important consideration is the layout and format. It needs to look professional and must be easy to navigate so as to increase the likelihood not only of it being filled in, but of it being filled in correctly. Very importantly, a questionnaire is more likely to be filled in if it is uncluttered and visually pleasing using a variety of print styles in a consistent manner. There are other considerations too such as the reliability of the questionnaire in terms of providing consistent measurement; this is covered at the end of this chapter. A very important consideration in the designing of questionnaires is the formulation and phrasing of the questions and the instructions.

Points to Think About – Designing Questionnaires

Courtesy – always treat questionnaire respondents with courtesy, for example:

- *We would be grateful if you could take 10 minutes to complete this simple questionnaire.*
- *Thank you for taking the time to complete this questionnaire.*

Identification – make sure you start with a brief explanation about the nature of the questionnaire and to end with clear guidance on what respondents should do once they have finished answering the questions, for example:

- *I would be grateful if you could complete this short questionnaire about how you use books and stories at home with your children. The questionnaire is part of a small-scale research project on young children's literacy development.*
- *Please return this questionnaire to your child's class teacher.*
- *Please return this questionnaire to (name) in the stamped addressed envelope provided.*

Length – do not overawe potential respondents by asking too many questions. Piloting your questionnaire will help you to get the number of questions and the overall length right.

Layout and presentation – avoid clutter and overcrowding on the page. Unless your questions are very short and simple a good rule of thumb might be 5 questions maximum per side of A4.

Instructions – put your instructions in a different font or in italics and make certain they are unambiguous to make your intentions clear to respondents, for example:

- *If yes, go to Question 3.*

Question order – think carefully about the order of your questions so as not to prompt, lead or in some other way 'tip off' your respondents. Careful ordering of questions can also help you to test your respondents' consistency and honesty by checking their earlier responses with subsequent related questions.

Points to Think About – Cont'd

Question construction and wording – it is surprising just how much drafting and redrafting a single question may need to get it right. Questions about percentages and time for example can be problematic as people's estimates and recollections can be unreliable. Where you are using scales of various kinds, such as Likert Scales for attitude and priority measurement, do not forget to include an indicator about what 1,2,3,4 or 5 might mean. If you plan to use any open-text questions leave adequate space for the responses, for example:

1. Please indicate (by circling the appropriate number) how often any of the resources below are used with Foundation Stage children in your class where:
   1 = never used
   2 = occasionally used (i.e. once or twice in the year)
   3 = sometimes used (i.e. termly or half-termly)
   4 = regularly used (i.e. most weeks of the year)
   5 = frequently used (i.e. most days of the year)

Pilot – you must try your questionnaire out before administering it for real. Piloting the questionnaire is undoubtedly the best way to test its design and feasibility.

Analysis – Precoded numbers (e.g. in italics below) can speed up your data coding and analysis:

3. How many years experience of primary teaching do you have? Include the current academic year as 1 year, but do not include training or voluntary experience prior to gaining QTS. *Please tick the appropriate box below.*

1 □	**2** □	**3** □	**4** □	**5** □	**6** □	**7** □	**8** □
(1)	(2)	(3)	(4)	(5)	(6)	(7)	(8)

9 □	**10** □	**11–15** □	**16–20** □	**21–25** □
(9)	(10)	(11)	(12)	(13)

26–30 □	**31 or more** □
(14)	(15)

Self-administered questionnaires and young children

It is generally agreed that self-administered questionnaires should not be used with children under 7 years of age (Borgers et al., 2000). This is because children younger than this are unlikely to possess a level of cognitive ability in terms of language, literacy and memory to answer questionnaire-type questions. Where questionnaires are used with children as young as 7 years, then obviously they need to be child friendly and must always be piloted prior to use. According to Shaw, Brady and Davey (2011) most secondary school age children should be able to complete questionnaires (and other data-collection tools) designed for adults; however, they stress the importance of being mindful of differences in cognitive ability and literacy and the potential need therefore to adapt questions in order to ensure inclusivity.

Points to Think About – Self-administered Questionnaires to Use with Young Children

Do ...	Don't ...
• make sure the questions are short, straightforward and written in simple language;	• use hypothetical questions – for example 'What would you do if … ?';
• avoid words that have more than one meaning, even when it is apparent from the context of the question what meaning to apply;	• use questions where a negative response is required to give a positive answer, for example 'Do you find it hard to do your homework on time?';
• direct questions specifically at the child, so instead of asking 'Do children your age …?', ask 'Do you …?';	• ask questions that require children to remember something that happened some time ago, instead concentrate on things that are recent or that they can apply to the here-and-now;
• make scaled responses clear and use verbal categories (e.g. agree, strongly agree, etc.) as opposed to numbered categories (e.g. on a scale of 1–10).	• have too many response options, a general rule of thumb is three to four for children under 11 and four to five for children aged 11 and older.

Structured (or standardized) interviews

In many ways, a structured interview is simply a questionnaire administered verbally by a research interviewer and represents the second most commonly used data-collection method in quantitative research. Indeed, survey research is the main context within which social researchers utilize the structured interview (Bryman, 2016). Interviews can be conducted face-to-face, over the telephone or online, the overall aim being to ensure that all interviewees get asked the same questions in the same way.

As with questionnaires, structured interviews can be used to gather large amounts of information about the distribution and relationships between variables although not usually to the same extent as questionnaires. Just like the questionnaire, the structured interview is generally comprised of fixed response format questions. Open-ended questions can be included but this will complicate data analysis in quantitative research quite substantially. Moreover, the fixed response format, as well as being easier to analyse quantitatively, makes the standardized recording of responses much easier too. The table in the following box sets out some of the advantages and limitations of using structured interviews for data collection.

Points to Think About – Structured Interviews

Strengths	Limitations
The interviewer can clarify questions where necessary, thus reducing the likelihood of answers being based on misunderstood or misinterpreted questions.	'Social desirability' effect is increased. The interviewer's background, that is gender, ethnicity, social class, can influence the answers people give.
Interviews can offer a 'voice' to otherwise disenfranchised groups; for example, they may be useful if respondents have reading difficulties and would not therefore be able to respond effectively to a questionnaire.	Interviewer variability can compromise the validity (see p. 150) of a study. Interviewer variability can occur when there is only one interviewer and consistency in conducting the interviews is not maintained. However, interviewer variability usually applies where there is more than one interviewer and refers to differences in the way that questions are asked and/or the way that responses are recorded by the different interviewers.
The interviewer can make sure all the questions are responded to.	Travel to and from interviews can incur a significant financial cost. Telephone interviewing may be less expensive, although it is still more expensive and time-consuming than postal questionnaires.
Respondents are less likely to become tired of answering questions where interviewing is used.	Where the research sample is relatively large, interviewing can be very time-consuming and this is likely to limit the size of the sample that students completing undergraduate dissertations could realistically manage.
The researcher can be more confident that the right person is answering the questions.	Interviewees may find being asked sensitive questions quite stressful.
Interview surveys tend to get higher response rates than questionnaire surveys.	Interviewers risk influencing responses by inadvertently giving visual and verbal cues.

Prior to embarking on a structured interview, the purpose of both the interview and the study must be clearly stated to the interviewee. It is important, in quantitative research, to ensure that the interview is introduced in the same way to every participant so as to reduce the risk of bias. In the case of face-to-face interviews, whenever possible, you should try to create the right environment for a successful interview. Ideally it should be quiet and private at the very least and preferably warm and comfortable. You should also take whatever steps you can to minimize the social distance between you and the interviewee, for example by ensuring that you are both seated at the same height and not directly opposite each other, showing interest in and being accepting of what the interviewees say and taking care to make people feel at their ease. You should also ensure that you are familiar with your interview schedule so that you are better able to observe the interviewee's non-verbal clues and cues such as any signs of unease (Gubrium and Holstein, 2002).

Telephone and online interviewing have several advantages over face-to-face interviewing, including the fact that such interviews can be cheaper and quicker to administer than face-to-face interviews and may well counter the problem of interviewees' replies being affected by interviewer characteristics such as ethnicity or perceived social class. Moreover, it is harder for interviewers to give inadvertent cues over the telephone. Despite these advantages however, the disadvantages associated with this method of data collection are clear. Relatively recent preference for the use of mobile phones over landlines has complicated the task of getting access to potential respondents as well as increasing the cost of a phone call, while people who do not own a telephone are instantly omitted from a study. People with hearing difficulties can find telephone interviewing very difficult, if not impossible and sometimes sensitive questions are equally difficult to ask and answer over the telephone. Very importantly, some evidence suggests that response rates may be lower in telephone surveys in comparison with the face-to-face approach (Shuy, 2002; Frey, 2004). Despite these and other limitations however, undergraduate researchers employing the structured interview as a method of data collection are sometimes prevented from undertaking a large number of face-to-face interviews mainly on account of their cost in terms of time and money. As a result these approaches to interviewing may offer more manageable alternatives, especially where the research focus is not too sensitive and steps have been taken to enhance the response rate.

Structured (or systematic) observation

Structured observation involves systematically observing individuals' behaviour using predetermined categories to record that behaviour. It entails use by researchers of specific rules as to what constitute behaviours of interest, and how they should be recorded. Structured observation differs therefore from participant observation (a method used in qualitative research), where the researcher is immersed in a social setting for a prolonged period of time, observing behaviour (often without predetermined categories), listening and asking questions (Bryman, 2016). As such, structured observation tends to be non-participant in nature.

The rules applied to structured observation are intended to make explicit to the observer(s) exactly what behaviours they are looking out for, and are articulated in carefully designed observation schedules. These observation schedules contain predetermined categories that 'tap' the behavioural variable under investigation by specifying the types of behaviours that should be recorded within each category. The aim is to ensure that each research participant's behaviour is observed and recorded in the same way.

Although possibly more trustworthy than self-reporting measures of behaviour, structured observation is by no means unproblematic and the table in the following box provides an overview of some of the strengths and limitations of the technique. Two major challenges associated with structured observation are: first, maintaining consistency of observation and second, what is known as the 'reactive effect' (McCall, 1984). Taking care to maintain consistency of observation through endeavouring to ensure inter-observer reliability is unlikely to be an issue for undergraduate students whose dissertations are individual projects and therefore will only involve one observer. Loss of intra-observer reliability can be an issue however and as such if you have opted to use structured observations you need to make sure that you stick to your schedule and that you conduct each observation in the same way. The 'reactive effect' meanwhile refers to people adjusting their behaviour because they know they are being watched. If their behaviour during the observation is different from their usual behaviour the results of the observation could be skewed and unreliable. If you are planning to use structured observation one way around this problem is only to use data from later observations where the participants have become accustomed to you being present and are, therefore, more likely to be behaving normally.

Points to Think About – Structured Observations

Strengths	Limitations
Observations can be carried out 'in context' thus offering greater insight into situational factors that influence human behaviour.	The 'reactive effect' (outlined above); although, this effect can be reduced as research participants become more accustomed to being observed.
Can be very helpful for validating data obtained through other methods.	Inconsistent recording of behaviour can bias the findings of a study (see inter- and intra-observer reliability above).
	To be an effective observer requires training and if you have not had such training you will need to highlight any steps that you took to counter this, that is triangulation of methods or careful attention to written guidance. You will also need to acknowledge any lack of training as a potential limitation of your study when you come to write up your work.
Can counter problems associated with self-reporting by verifying what people actually do as opposed to what they say or think they do.	Observing predetermined behaviours for set periods of time can be extremely tiring. It requires a huge amount of concentration on the part of the researcher, who must exercise control in ignoring interesting behaviours that are not on the observation schedule, this is much easier said than done.

Some of the key considerations to be taken into account when devising questions for use in structured questionnaires and interviews apply equally to developing a schedule for recording structured observations. The variable of interest must be carefully operationalized so as to inform the research focus and to make explicit to the observer who and what is to be observed. It is often useful, as with questionnaires and interview schedules, to have an 'other' category so that unexpected behaviours that might prove relevant later can be noted down at the time. Once again piloting your observation schedule prior to the research proper is essential if you are to gain practice in its use and to iron out any problems with the design. Further reference to research methods literature will furnish you with additional guidance on carrying out structured observations (Bryman, 2016); however, there are several possible approaches to recording behaviour using structured observations that you might wish to consider:

- Time sampling – participants are observed for a set period of time but on separate occasions; for example, you might opt to observe for a total period of 10 minutes noting down behaviour/activity every 30 seconds.
- Event sampling – this involves waiting for the behaviour or behaviours of interest (e.g. an argument) to occur and then recording events for the duration of that behaviour, logging the incidence of predetermined aspects of it, that is raised voices, sighing, facial expressions and/or other behaviours which are likely to arise during the course of an argument.
- Observations over short or long periods of time – for example, the observer could observe and record for 5-minute intervals on separate occasions or continuously for a number of hours respectively.

Content analysis

The fourth common method often used in quantitative research is content analysis which seeks to provide an *objective, systematic and quantitative description of the content of communication* (Berelson, 1952, p. 18). It has been argued that content analysis is first and foremost an approach to the analysis of documents and texts *rather than a means of generating data* (Bryman, 2008, p. 181). However, content analysis carries different meaning in qualitative research (see Chapter 8). In quantitative research, like structured observation, quantitative content analysis is done using pre-specified rules for the allocation of information to predetermined categories so that data is collected and categorized in a consistent manner. The overall aim of this approach is to eliminate, as far as possible, the intrusion of researchers' personal biases. Content analysis often involves several research questions, which determine what sources will be analysed and which content will be noted. Fenton et al. (1998) used content analysis to ascertain the frequency and nature of the reporting of social science research in the mass media over a specified time span. Their sources included national newspapers, magazines, local newspapers and news programmes among others, and their questions focused on issues such as whether some topics received more attention than others, what prompted the reporting of social science research and whether research conducted in prestigious institutions was more likely to be reported. While the work of Berelson (1952) and Fenton et al. (1988) focused on quantifying the content of mass media communications, content analysis can be applied much more widely than this. The sources that could lend themselves to content analysis as part of an undergraduate dissertation are summarized in the following box.

Ideas to Use – Possible Sources for Content Analysis

- Works of reference, for example *Annual Abstract of Statistics*, *The Times Index*
- Statistical records
- Annual and special reports, local and unofficial, including reports by Medical Officers of Health, schools, universities, trade unions
- Parliamentary debates (*Hansard*)
- Documents on foreign policy
- Newspapers
- Cabinet records
- Other government reports and documents, for example green and white papers
- Private papers and letters
- Biographies and autobiographies
- Diaries
- Memoirs
- Social surveys
- Novels, poetry, plays
- Newspapers, journals and other periodicals, including current affairs pieces by journalists as well as social scientists and educational commentators
- Film, television and video materials, for example news broadcasts
- Photographs, maps and pictures
- Radio/audio recordings
- Interviews, tape recorded and other museum artefacts.

Source: Finnegan (2006, pp.140–1) citing Mowatt (1971).

Content analysis can also involve quantifying words that indicate certain dispositions towards a phenomenon of interest. For example, Craig (1992) used content analysis to investigate the effect that the time of day had on gender portrayals in television advertisements. His findings revealed that men and women were portrayed differently at different times of the day such as in weekend afternoon advertisements where men were portrayed as needing escape from home and family. An alternative example of dispositions towards a phenomenon of interest would be the use of pejorative words and phrases used by viewers and listeners groups when complaining about sex, violence or swearing on TV and radio broadcasts (e.g. tabloid television). The decision as to what should be quantified in content analysis is largely dependent on the research question(s) and can include

- the frequency with which certain words appear in a document or documents, for example the use of terms like 'quality' or 'standards' in government education policy documents;
- the use of certain words in preference over alternative words in newspaper reports (e.g. using emotive language to grab the reader's attention, such as the phrase 'shocking revelation' to report something which in reality is quite mundane).

Should you make use of pre-existing data-collection tools or design your own?

Creating a good quality (i.e. user friendly, reliable and valid) data-collection tool, whether a questionnaire, or an interview, observation or content analysis schedule takes considerable time and effort and must be based on sound guidance (see recommended reading list). To give you an idea of how much development work needs to take place the following checklist contains a comprehensive, but by no means exhaustive, list of the elements involved.

Points to Think About – Designing a Quantitative Data-collection Instrument

- Generate questions/items that tap the conceptual variable under investigation. This involves careful scanning of relevant literature for operational definitions and to ascertain how the variable has been tapped by other researchers. It is also helpful to seek opinions from experts in the field such as your supervisor(s).
- If you intend to construct a questionnaire or interview schedule, you need to make decisions related to how to order and group the questions, where to put sensitive questions, what sort of response format to opt for, how to code these and so on. This is why it is essential that you access further research methods literature and take note of guidance on the 'how to' of your chosen method.

Points to Think About – Cont'd

- Where rating scales are to be used, care must be taken in creating the scale values for the response alternatives and the words to use for them. You can inadvertently bias the scale if you do not think these matters through carefully. You will also need to decide whether or not to include a neutral response.
- Once you have operationalized the conceptual variable, you then need to pilot the tool to cover the full range of possible replies (questionnaires, interviews) or behaviours (observation) on which to base response formats (questionnaires, interviews) or behaviour checklists (observation).
- In the case of questionnaires and interview schedules, once your response formats are in place, you then need to pilot the tool again to ensure that questions are interpreted as you intend them to be and that responding is easy.
- You also need to establish, using the relevant procedures, the reliability and validity of your data-collection tool.

Given the significant amount of work involved in designing a suitably robust quantitative data-collection tool you may decide that the best option is to use, wherever possible, existing scales. Not only might this reduce the cost in terms of your time and effort but also because the reliability and validity of externally generated questions will have been previously established. Moreover, using a pre-existing tool puts you in a position of being able to replicate others' work and, in the event of similar findings, being in a position to add to the existing body of knowledge relevant to the area under study. You must make absolutely certain, however, that any tool you select taps the variable of interest to your study in a way that will answer your research questions.

Hundreds of data-collection tools have been developed over the years and your literature review should highlight any potentially appropriate scales. Indeed, some research articles contain copies as appendices of the scales used, which generally means that they are in the public domain and can, therefore, be used without having to obtain permission. However it is best to check this first with your supervisor. If the scales used are not included as appendices, your best course of action is to contact the first in the list of authors in order to enquire about the availability of their scale(s). There may well be an email address included in the article or, alternatively the authors' place of work may be indicated. In the event of the latter, you should be able to ascertain contact details via the World Wide Web.

Email or postal correspondence will probably be preferable to a telephone call, and should be exercised with the utmost politeness. It is important to indicate that you are a student and to identify the institution that you are studying in and to provide a succinct overview of your research focus. Ask if the scale/s is/are available for use and where it/they can be obtained. You may be lucky enough to have them sent to you.

Finally, make sure your supervisor checks any intended correspondence before you send it.

If you are unable to access an existing quantitative data-collection tool, then you will have no option but to construct your own. Although time-consuming, this will provide useful research experience and your dissertation supervisor will be able to offer support and guidance. If you find yourself in this situation a repository of questions used in large scale government and academic social surveys since 1991 may be useful to you. Questions can be selected from a range of 'question banks' (see useful websites) for use in self-constructed questionnaires. These questions will have been extensively tested at the time of their first use in terms of reliability and validity. Given all that is involved in designing your own data-collection tool, a very important consideration is that you start work on this very early in the research process, as none of this can be left to the last minute.

Summary of key points

- It is important to be clear about when quantitative methods are called for. Quantitative methods are generally suited to areas that have already been researched so that established theories can be tested. Quantitative methods can also be used to ascertain the distribution of and relationships between variables.
- Variables represent the cornerstone of quantitative methods. Quantitative researchers are interested in the distribution of and relationships (correlational and/or causal) between variables. Variables can be defined both conceptually and operationally and differ in type and thereby the level of measurement to which they can be subjected.
- Any quantitative data-collection method has advantages and disadvantages and you will need to be able to demonstrate your knowledge and understanding of these and be able to justify your chosen methods when writing up your dissertation.

Reflective task

1 With reference to the following question: *Is there a relationship between gender and food preferences?*
    - What quantitative approach does this question lend itself to?
    - How could the variable of interest be operationalized?
    - Consider how to ensure a good sample size

- Determine data-collection methods that could be used
- Consider what steps could be taken to ensure reliability

2 If the researcher wished to generalize his/her findings, what sampling technique would he/she need to utilize and how else could the option of generalizability be facilitated?

Link to companion website

https://bloomsbury.com/cw/successful-dissertations-second-edition/student-resources/7-data-collection-using-quantitative-methods/

Recommended reading and further sources of information

Bryman, A. (2016, 5th edition), *Social Research Methods*. New York: Oxford University Press.

Denscombe, M. (2014. 5th edition), *The Good Research Guide for Small-Scale Social Research Projects*. Milton Keynes: McGraw Hill Education.

Neuendorf, K. (2017, 2nd edition), *The Content Analysis Guidebook*. Los Angeles: Sage.

Punch, K. and Oancea, A. (2014. 2nd edition), *Introduction to Research Methods in Education*. London: Sage.

Robson, C. and McCartan, K. (2015, 4th edition), *Real World Research*. London: Wiley.

Shaw, C., Brady, L. and Davey, C. (2011), *Guidelines for Research with Children and Young People*. London: NCB Research Centre.

Useful websites

About.Education http://www.about.com/education/

Oxford Bibliographies http://www.oxfordbibliographies.com/obo/page/about;jsessionid=B3C4B61410FF77B8FEDD80AFC974C231

Question Banks https://www.ukdataservice.ac.uk/get-data/other-providers/question-banks

8

Data Analysis

Pam Dewis and Janet Kay

Chapter Aims

By the end of this chapter you will

- know why and how you should plan your data analysis;
- be aware of different approaches to qualitative and quantitative data analysis;
- be able to make an informed choice about an analytical approach that is suitable for your methodology.

Once you have gathered your data your next task is to analyse them to reveal your findings. When your findings have been drawn from the data and recorded, you will then be able to discuss them in relation to the literature and start to draw conclusions and, in some cases, make recommendations. These are the final stages of your project and they need to be well-planned in order to ensure that the project is successful overall. This is often a stage that is left to chance and is not always given enough time or consideration. There have been many projects that start well with a properly researched literature review and well-considered methodology which then do less well because the analysis and the discussion of findings is weak. In this chapter, we explore some of the more common approaches to data analysis in quantitative and qualitative studies and offer advice on how to present and discuss these findings. We do not attempt to cover all possible approaches to data analysis but have focused instead on approaches that you are most likely to use in a small-scale undergraduate dissertation.

Planning ahead

Your data analysis strategy should be an extension of your research methodology which we discussed in Chapter 4. It is very important to make sure that you do this at the planning stage and not as a later 'add-on'. Perhaps the most important point to make is that you need to give plenty of time to the analysis phase of your project, especially in qualitative studies where it can be very time-consuming, often requiring you to revisit the data on numerous occasions. In both qualitative and quantitative research projects, when writing your methodology section you will need to outline the analytical approach before gathering the data. This will give you a chance to ensure that your analytical approach is suitable for your study.

This not only enhances your methodology as it shows you have considered the whole of the research process, but also helps you to plan your time well. Without this pre-planning it is possible to find you have insufficient time to analyse the data properly as this process invariably takes longer than you might think.

There are significant differences in approaches to quantitative analysis and qualitative analysis, which essentially make this a chapter of two halves. While your approach to quantitative analysis is clearly linked to the type of data gathered, in qualitative studies there are more choices about how you can analyse a particular set of data. Whichever type of study you do, these choices and decisions need to be made before the data is gathered.

The analysis of qualitative data can be quite 'messy', with fewer certainties and more choices to be made than when doing quantitative analysis. Qualitative research can be used to explore a wide range of possible social activities using a wide range of methodological approaches. This diversity is a key feature of qualitative research, which is also reflected in an equally diverse range of possible approaches to data analysis. Not only are there many different analytical approaches but in addition data gathered through qualitative research methods can be analysed in more than one way, depending on the focus of the research questions and the subject area (Corbin and Strauss, 2008). Making sure your approach to analysis is compatible with the aims of your study, the data gathered and the overall methodology is a vitally important part of your planning. It also determines whether your study will be 'good' or not as the quality of the qualitative research is measured by the extent to which it is possible to see the thinking behind the data-gathering and analysis approaches chosen and how these fit together. Making sure these choices are well thought through impacts on the validity of any qualitative study. In the first half of the chapter, therefore, various approaches to analysing qualitative data are outlined. Principles underpinning qualitative analysis and issues of validity and reliability are then explored. This discussion is followed by an extended step-by-step example of how to do thematic analysis, drawing out the relevant themes from the data in order to answer your research questions, which is a common approach in undergraduate student dissertations. This example is illustrated by a case study of Vikash's project.

The main feature of quantitative analysis is the use of mathematical and statistical procedures, a feature that makes it somewhat daunting to students who are less mathematically inclined. Thanks to statistical software packages, however, the need for manual calculations has been greatly reduced. Provided you give due consideration to data analysis prior to data collection and follow the relevant 'rules' and procedures for processing quantitative data, there is no reason why you cannot engage in research that requires you to do some quantitative analysis. The second half of the chapter, therefore, outlines approaches to quantitative analysis that are likely to be employed by an undergraduate researcher. It explains how decisions about which approach or approaches to use are largely dependent on the nature of the data collected. It is important to remember that there are a number of crucial steps in the analysis of quantitative data and that these should be tackled before analysis 'proper' begins. This second half of the chapter will outline these steps with reference to examples where appropriate to help clarify some of the processes.

What is involved in qualitative analysis?

The overall aim of analysis is to make sense of the data you have gathered and to draw some conclusions from them that will answer your research questions at least to some extent. Analysing qualitative data is usually a lengthy process and can be daunting in terms of the quantity of data to be considered and the processes that have to be gone through, some of them repeatedly. Writing up findings may be equally lengthy as the work needs to reflect the many perspectives found during data gathering and to justify the findings through exploring and displaying the evidence (Cresswell, 2005). As such, you need to consider this as a major part of your study and to ensure you have plenty of time to analyse and write up.

There is no single or ideal way of doing qualitative analysis. The choices you make about your approach to analysing your data should depend on the sort of data you have, your methodological approach and the research questions you have asked. Analysis is not a single linear process but involves going back and forth between steps or stages to refine and improve the analysis as you complete it. It involves a range of skills and some decision-making and judgements both about how best to approach your data and also about what the data means right from the start. This is where you may really start to understand that you are doing a study within an interpretative paradigm. There are more uncertainties and a greater possibility of making 'wrong' decisions in this type of analysis and losing rigour in terms of a scholarly approach. The very quality of your study depends on making good decisions about how you analyse your data (Coffey and Atkinson, 1996; Thorne, 2000).

As mentioned in the introduction, the language of analysis can be confusing, with interchangeable terms used in different texts. Thorne (2000) suggests that terms like themes 'emerged' from the data can give the impression you left the data out overnight and the analysis fairies did the work! As such, the discussion and examples below will focus on the steps you need to take to analyse qualitative data and terms will be explained throughout.

Common approaches to qualitative data analysis

In this section a small number of qualitative data analysis approaches are outlined. They were chosen because they are the most commonly used in undergraduate student dissertations. The recommended reading section at the end of the chapter includes a range of additional sources that will support you in finding out more about these and other approaches. Refer back to Chapter 4 on methodologies if you need to refresh your memory of the approaches discussed.

Phenomenological analysis

Phenomenological analysis is concerned with participants' subjective views of their experiences of the phenomenon involved and the meaning they place on these experiences. The researcher's role is to try and reveal the essence of the participants' experiences through interpretation of the data (Thorne, 2000). For example, a phenomenological study could explore what it meant to sibling adopters to adopt more than one child at a time. The emphasis is on how the adopters experienced their role – how they thought and felt about it.

In these types of studies there is a strong emphasis on ensuring that the analysis remains true to the 'participants' voices' and that interpretation of the raw data does not lose this. As such, this type of analysis is balanced between a straightforward description of the data and over-conceptualizing the data through higher levels of interpretation. The researcher's role is to interpret the data while preserving the true meanings within it (Shaw, 2001). In order to do this the researcher must 'bracket' or put aside their own views on the research subject to ensure that the participants' interpretations of their experiences are kept central (Moustakas, 1994). There are a number of approaches to phenomenological analysis, although there are common features. Phenomenological analysis could typically follow these steps:

1   The researcher finds pieces of data in the transcripts that express the participants' views and the meanings they place on their experiences.

2   The pieces of data are labelled and organized into thematic groups, that is, groups of pieces of data that have commonalities or make the same point or have a similar meaning.

3   Themes and pieces of data are checked against the transcript to ensure that the analytical process has remained true to the participant's voice.

4   The researcher writes about the themes to further interpret and reflect on their meanings and once again checks against the raw data to ensure that the findings are authentic.

Ethnographic analysis

Ethnographic studies focus on the lifestyles of groups of people in particular contexts and involve collecting data from a range of sources, usually involving extensive fieldwork and participant observations (Hammersley and Atkinson, 1995; Thorne, 2000). The ethnographic researcher writes detailed accounts of their findings, with some description and some interpretation of the findings. Although ethnographic accounts can be descriptive, interpretation is part of the analytical approach. Analysis of ethnographic data should start early in the data-gathering process, using the understandings gained from early analysis to inform further data gathering. This involves moving from descriptions of the group in general to more focused explanations and possibly to theorizing. The data could be analysed as follows:

1   The researcher codes the data and then clusters the coded data (Cohen et al., 2007).

2   Analysis continues as the researcher establishes 'domains' or overarching categories, which can be compared and linked.

3   The researcher then starts to interpret the data by formulating explanations and generating hypotheses about the meanings of that data.

4   The findings are written into a summary, which is also used to identify areas for further data gathering.

5   Negative cases, where the findings contradict the hypothesis, are identified and used to refine or develop the hypothesis further.

Grounded-theory analysis

The analytical approach in grounded theory is focused on generating theory to explain the data as it is gathered. Studies using grounded theory are usually loosely planned in terms of data gathering as data gathering and analysis take place closely together, with early data analysis informing the next stage of data gathering. There are three stages to grounded-theory analysis and at each stage a higher level of abstraction is achieved to support the development of theory:

- Stage 1: Open coding. This involves coding the raw data in terms of conceptual categories. This is different to thematic analysis because the researcher seeks to find abstract concepts in the data from the beginning and not just to describe or interpret it. Data is seen as containing indicators that confirm more abstract concepts. Concepts are developed through identifying a range of indicators and comparing them. The identified concepts are then used to generate theory based on the data.
- Stage 2: Axial coding. This is the process of making connections between the initial conceptual categories identified through the process of open coding. The type of connections made will vary but could include 'causes and consequences' or 'stages of a process' (Punch, 2009, p. 187).
- Stage 3: Selective coding. In this stage of analysis the researcher determines a central category drawn from the analysis so far and this becomes the theoretical aspect of the research, the grounded theory. The other conceptual categories are integrated into this category.

Narrative analysis

Qualitative data is often collected in story or narrative form through semi- and/or unstructured interviews, focus groups and participant observations (Punch, 2009). Oral histories are a good example of this. These narratives are forms of data which involve the unique telling of a story in a particular context. In addition, the narrative does not take place in isolation but is a product of the interaction between the narrator and the researcher. Narrative analysis is different to forms of qualitative analysis that involve breaking data down through coding or labelling sections to abstract particular themes or concepts. In narrative analysis, the focus is on the whole of the narrative or story told by the participant. In this type of analysis, value is not just placed on the content of the story, but also on the form of the story and the context in which the story takes place. In a narrative analysis the *what, how and where* factors are significant to each particular story (Chase, 2005, p. 657).

Skills in qualitative analysis

One of the keys to getting qualitative analysis 'right' is to make sure you know your data well and have understood them through reading and rereading to truly understand what your participants are saying. The process of ordering the data needs to be carefully handled so that there is no bias and all the relevant themes are drawn out and given equal importance. The skills involved are to summarize and interpret the data while retaining the participants' voices and views. As soon as you start to categorize your data you are deciding what they mean and placing your interpretations on them. The researcher's ability to interpret data while remaining faithful to the participant's 'voice' is a key skill in qualitative data analysis. The data need to be interpreted carefully to ensure that the meanings expressed by the participants are not distorted or lost and you will need to avoid over-interpreting the data in the light of your own preconceptions or previous claims in the literature. The analysis must be true to the data and the findings must be drawn only from the data themselves; the data must be allowed to speak for themselves. In the interests of validity your aim is to reflect as accurately as possible the *phenomena under study as perceived by the study population* (Lewis and Ritchie, 2003, p. 274). To do this effectively it is necessary to give some consideration to all your findings and to avoid suppressing those that do not comfortably fit in with other studies or your own expectations.

Case Study – Being Aware of Your Preconceptions

Misha did her study on what makes children happy in nursery. She was interested in the idea that children's happiness was related to their relationships and social interactions, as well as their achievements. She placed her findings in a chart showing how the children had shown that break time and time for play and other potentially social times were causes of happiness. However, Misha told her supervisor that she was concerned that her findings were not what she had expected. She went back and looked at them again seeking new themes, which were there but had not yet emerged. In fact, Misha's findings showed that the children in the study related happiness to activities and parts of the day where they could make their own choices and decisions freely. Misha's findings were not what she expected, but this made them even more interesting and original.

Managing data and transcribing

Whatever qualitative approach you are using there will be some common elements to the analysis, not least the management of your data. The raw data will usually take the form of interview and focus group transcripts, completed observation schedules, questionnaires, notes and other data you have gathered from your participants. They are described as 'raw' because at this stage they have not been processed (analysed) and therefore findings have not been drawn from them. The first step in analysing the data is to transcribe any recordings made in interviews or focus groups. If the data are in the form of questionnaires or observations or if notes have been made instead of recordings then obviously this step is not needed. However, qualitative data usually involve some verbatim recordings to get the depth and quality usually associated with this approach. Make sure that your recording of the data retains the language of the original point. Transcribing may seem to be a mechanistic task but in terms of analysis it can be the first step to really knowing and understanding your data. This familiarization with the data is a crucial step to analysing them and therefore if possible, it is helpful to do your own transcribing. However, transcribing is a very time-consuming process and if you have gathered large amounts of data you may choose to pay for a professional transcriber to do some of this work for you. If this is the case then it is still worth keeping some of the transcribing for yourself to gain a balance between time constraints and the value of familiarization with the data at this stage. Once you have your transcripts the data will need to be summarized or reduced so that the relevant issues can be viewed easily and comprehensively.

Using technology to aid analysis

The arrival of information and communication technologies has made the task of data management and interpretation much easier. You store your transcribed data in Word documents and then use basic computer methods to analyse that data, such as 'copy and paste' and highlighting. For example, you can use a different colour font or highlight for each theme or sub-theme and then change the colour of the text to indicate where that theme arises in each transcript. This makes it easy to find quotes quickly or to check that you have summarized a point correctly. You can then 'copy and paste' any quotes out of the text. You can also write your comments into the text as a theme arises and then 'copy and paste' these comments into your summary charts. There are also a number of data analysis software packages such as NVivo and NUD*IST which can be used for analysing qualitative data. The advantages of these packages are that once you know how to use them they are quick, efficient and consistent, therefore possibly reducing bias. They are particularly good where there are large amounts of raw data to process (Robson, 2002). One of the disadvantages, however, is the time needed at the start of the process to become competent in their use. These packages may also produce some rigidity in categorization and the possibility of the approach to analysis being led by the software rather than the aims of the study. In a study the size of a dissertation it is possible that the disadvantages of using such software packages may outweigh the advantages due to the time needed to become proficient in their use.

Maintaining an audit trail

Ensuring that qualitative analysis is rigorous and valid involves making sure that the processes by which you arrived at your findings based on the raw data are clearly visible to the reader (Burnard et al., 2008). You will need to be able to chart the process of analysis by mapping out how you have travelled from the data to the conclusions in order to support the robustness of the findings. The researcher should demonstrate that there is a clear and logical relationship between data gathering and analysis (Punch, 1998; Thorne, 2000). In studies where transferability is an objective, it can also be argued that reflecting and commenting on your 'audit trail' may improve the reliability of your work (Punch, 2005, p. 200). Through this kind of reflection, you can demonstrate levels of consistency and robustness in your processes and the conduct of your data collection, analysis and interpretation (Lewis and Ritchie, 2003). Each stage of the process of analysis must be recorded to show how analysis has taken place and conclusions reached. This might include an explanation of how themes were identified in the raw data; how these were organized and summarized; how the analytical process was applied to each part of the data and how conclusions were drawn from the analysis. This material showing the stages of analysis needs to be included in the dissertation so that the people marking and examining the work can see how you got from your data to the conclusions you have drawn.

Points to Think About – Audit Trail

An audit trail consists of

- evidence of the consistency and accuracy of each stage of the research process;
- transparency and openness about the way in which the analytical process is presented;
- reflection on that process to highlight any issues that may have affected the outcomes.

Items that may appear as part of the audit trail could include

- annotated transcripts showing where themes have been identified;
- thematic frameworks showing the themes that are being used to analyse the data, including earlier versions as well as the final version;
- charts showing how themes have been identified in each part of the data, including earlier versions as well as the final version;
- descriptions of how the data will be analysed;
- reflection on how the analysis was conducted and any issues arising from that process.

In the next section, thematic analysis of data in qualitative studies is explored in more detail. Thematic analysis has been chosen because it is very common in this type of study and is most likely to be chosen for undergraduate dissertations in the relevant fields. The discussion about steps to take in analysis focuses on inductive approaches to studies, where data is used to generate hypotheses, rather than deductive studies which test hypotheses. This is simply because the majority of qualitative studies use an inductive approach. Deductive studies may follow similar steps during the analysis stage but in these studies the thematic framework is predetermined and the researcher will seek data that conforms with the pre-existing themes (Thorne, 2000; Burnard et al., 2008).

Overview of thematic qualitative analysis

Examining the data and identifying themes

It is helpful to refer to the case study on Vikash's project as you read this overview (see later in this section of the chapter) as it exemplifies each stage of the analytical process discussed here.

The first step in the process of thematic analysis is usually to start to examine the data for significant themes, which can be used to organize or categorize the data into more manageable sections in order to find meanings within it. The data are everything you have gathered through your research, which may include transcripts of interviews, observations, pictures, diaries, stories, documents, drawings, video or audiotape and possibly other textual or visual material. Data that have not yet been analysed is often referred to as raw data, as discussed above. Raw data are a description of what you have seen and/or heard but they do not explain any of the important questions such as why? Or how? Interpretation is needed to give meaning to the data (Burnard et al., 2008).

Examination of the data will involve reading, looking and listening and making notes about any significant points that you notice. These could be annotated transcripts or notes on an audio or video file. You will be looking for patterns, similar points, contradictions and anything that may contribute to answering your research questions (Burnard et al., 2008).

Start with one piece of data (a single transcript or observation or document, for example) and make note of the interesting, relevant themes that emerge from it. Then look for similar themes in other pieces of data while also adding new themes as they emerge. However, if you find data that have no relevance to your research questions then do not waste time analysing them, even if they seem interesting. Make notes, summarize what you are finding and return to earlier transcripts or other pieces of data if you think you have missed anything. It is well worth doing this on a number of occasions with each piece of data so you really know it well and have a good understanding of what it is telling you in terms of your research questions. This repetitive revisiting of the data is sometimes referred to as 'immersing' yourself in the data and is an important feature of qualitative analysis. Start doing this from the first piece of data you gather. Leaving all the analysis until the end of data gathering can mean facing a daunting pile of raw data with deadlines looming.

Labelling or coding

You also need to label pieces of data (a sentence, paragraph, part of a document, a photo and so on) to make it clear which bits of data are linked together as part of the same theme. This is not really a next step or stage as you will probably do this as you examine the data. To find relevant themes you need to read or listen to or look at the data in detail on a number of occasions noting significant points as they arise, as discussed above. A theme refers to an issue, response, idea, concept, attitude, a set of behaviours or opinion that reoccurs in the data making it significant. Themes will be significant because they provide you with an 'answer' to your research questions. Themes are complex in that many are drawn from the data, but because themes have also emerged from the literature review and been used to guide the development of interview or observation schedules some will already be familiar to the researcher.

This process is sometimes called coding as it involves labelling pieces of data (often text in transcripts of interviews or observational data) with a code or other mechanism for identifying it as belonging to a group of similar pieces of data. There are a number of different ways of recording this link between an identified theme and a reference to that theme in the data (coding). One of these is to give a number to the theme or sub-theme and then mark the bit of data with this number. Alternative ways of recording where themes are identified within the data is to underline or highlight and use colour coding or use short phrases that symbolize a particular theme. For example, if you were exploring different sorts of play in a nursery you could highlight each type of play observed in a different colour or give it a number or a short label such as 'imaginative play'.

Creating a thematic framework

At this stage, you will have a lot of themes noted and labelled across all your data and you now have the rather daunting task of reducing these to manageable proportions. As such, the next step is to sort and group the themes into a 'thematic framework' that involves grouping the key themes, placing them in a logical order and dividing them into main and sub- themes (Spencer et al., 2003). A 'thematic framework' is often presented as a list or table and there is an example of the one that Vikash developed as part of his study on page 208, which may be helpful to look at now.

This process may also involve losing or pruning away themes that have only minor significance as they are not added to or developed as exploration of the data has progressed. You will probably find yourself moving backwards and forwards between the processes of finding, grouping and ordering the themes a number of times. As new themes or sub-themes emerge from the data the framework will change and develop. At some point you must decide that you have your final list of themes and sub-themes and then you must go back over all your data to be sure you have noted all the incidents of each theme and sub-theme that are there.

It is important to include copies of earlier thematic frameworks which show the various stages of the analytic process in your submitted work so that your supervisor and examiner can see how the themes have emerged and been sorted, organized and pruned. This is part of the 'audit trail' that validates your work, which is discussed above.

Summarizing your findings

One of the most common ways to do this is to make a chart that records the previously identified bits of data from each piece of raw data that exemplify each theme or sub-theme. This is commonly done in qualitative analysis to reduce the data to a manageable size and to show the processes of analysis. Other ways of summarizing the data includes colour coding each incident of each theme, then cutting out each identified section and pasting together by colour so you have a file on each theme (Burnard et al., 2008). This can be done on hard copy or a computer.

The extract from Vikash's study on page 208 in which he started to chart the themes from his interviews with the school staff offers an illustration of what a summary chart might look like. There is a column for each piece of data (in this case each participant's transcript from the interviews) and rows for each theme/sub-theme. Vikash returned to his annotated transcripts and put each identified piece of information on the chart against the correct theme or sub-theme. He did this for each piece of raw data, leaving gaps where there was no data relevant for a theme or sub-theme.

If you opt for an approach like Vikash's you should not feel compelled to try and fill in all the boxes for each participant. Not all your participants will have made a point on each sub-theme. That said you ought to include a comment where a participant has said that he/she does not know the answer to a question, as this is valuable data in itself. Nor should you be afraid to add themes or sub-themes or get rid of very weak themes (where little has been said) as you go along. The thematic framework you made earlier is a 'live' document and can be altered and tweaked throughout this stage. If this happens though it is a good idea to keep your earlier drafts as this is evidence of the developmental process and could form part of your audit trail as discussed above.

As with the thematic frameworks, when you have completed your analysis it is worth looking over your summary charts again and deciding which are going to be included in your study. You do not need to include every version but just a few to show how the themes have been developed and refined and how the thematic framework has been used to analyse the data. You should take advice from your supervisor about what should go in the body of your study and what should go in your appendices.

Interpreting and presenting your findings

This is the process by which you write up your findings using the summary chart or other summary of themes to guide what you write. It is common to write up your findings theme by theme, explaining what you have found and illustrating your findings with quotes drawn from your transcripts or observational notes (Burnard et al., 2008). Then you should continue by discussing what the findings mean and comparing what you have found to other studies. Each theme can be a subheading in your findings and discussion chapter(s).

The presentation is usually done in one of two ways. You can either write up your findings as a chapter and then in the following chapter discuss your findings in relation to the findings of other similar studies which you have already identified in the literature review. Or you can integrate these two chapters and write up your findings and discuss them all in one. There is no right or wrong way of choosing how to present your findings but take advice from your supervisor before you decide. It is likely that your study will lend itself more readily to one approach or the other (Burnard et al., 2008).

From writing up your findings you can then draw conclusions and recommendations for your final chapter. See the example of Vikash's project write-up on page 208 to better understand how you can draw conclusions from your summary. These may be quite tentative as it is important to remember that your study is quite small and localized, but this should not prevent you from offering some thoughts on what others may learn from your study. Comparing your study to other similar studies may reinforce your findings, where the other researchers draw similar conclusions. In cases where your findings contradict previous studies it is important to look at possible reasons why and discuss these. These may include differences in the sample, the context or the social and cultural values of the time if you are discussing older studies. Drawing out these reasons adds value to your study and shows your understanding of the wider field in which your study has taken place.

Like all the other steps in analysis there are choices to be made about how you present your data. Therefore, one of the key challenges at this point of a dissertation is to ensure that the findings are presented in a way that is true and *faithful* to the raw data but that also provides *clarity about the interpretative process that has taken place* (White et al., 2003, p. 288). This simply means that in the methodology section you need to carefully describe how you analysed your data, the steps you took and the decisions you made. You will also need to refer to the formative work you put into your study as discussed above so the examiner or supervisor can see how you went from your raw data to your written up chapters on findings and discussion. This is part of the audit trail as discussed above.

Your summary needs to be examined and explored further to interpret what it means and to use the data to answer your research questions. In qualitative research projects the presentation is part of the analysis because the interpretative process is ongoing. This means that you find yourself considering and interpreting your summarized data at this stage and discussing and comparing and commenting on your themes. It is now that there may be the most danger of losing your participants' 'voices' as you place your own interpretations on the data as you discuss the findings. It may be valuable, therefore, to return to the raw data at times to check that you have not made 'leaps' in your interpretation that the data cannot support by placing meanings on them that do not exist.

The following case study is an example of the analysis of a study, showing the stages that Vik goes through to transform his raw data into findings. It is useful to read this in conjunction with the discussion on how to do a thematic analysis above.

Vikash's project

The rest of this chapter will follow through the stages of a thematic analytical approach as a means of illustrating qualitative data analysis in practice. Vikash's project was an exploratory case study designed to explore the ways in which children with EAL were supported in a Year 1 class in a school. His overall research question was 'What strategies are used to support children with EAL in accessing the curriculum?' As part of this project he gathered data through interviewing teaching staff and through observations of staff working with children with EAL. Vik planned to analyse the data by seeking themes that related to strategies and activities that were used to support children with EAL. He also intended to compare his interview data with his observational data to see if the rhetoric and the reality matched up or in other words to discover to what extent the strategies described in the interviews were found in practice by observing. In discussing his findings Vik set out to critically analyse the strategies that were used by the school in comparison to the 'best practice' approaches he had identified in his literature review.

Vik interviewed the teacher and two teaching assistants, one of whom was bilingual and he observed a number of teaching sessions focusing on activities to support the children with EAL.

At the end of his data collection Vik had three interview transcripts and ten observation records. Vik started by reading all his interview transcripts through to get an overview of their content. He then took one of the transcripts and went through it making notes on the margin where relevant issues arose. For example, he noted that the participant stated that she used signs and gestures to help the children with EAL to understand instructions. Vik made a list of the issues that arose from this interview. He then read the other two transcripts and where they introduced anything new to the themes identified in the first interview he added this to his list. This process was repeated, revisiting the transcripts several times to check if all the relevant themes had been identified.

Vik drew his themes from the interview data, grouped them into themes and sub-themes and then refined them by getting rid of weak themes. He could then use this framework to analyse all his data including the observations.

Case Study – Vik's Thematic Framework

- **Theme: Structure of support**
  - Sub-theme: Policy
  - Sub-theme: Classroom organization
  - Sub-theme: Deployment of teaching assistants/bilingual teaching assistants
  - Sub-theme: Curriculum differentiation
- **Theme: Pedagogical practices**
  - Sub-theme: Gestures and signs to convey instructions
  - Sub-theme: Using words from the child's home language
  - Sub-theme: Correcting language use
  - Sub-theme: Working in small groups/pairs
- **Theme: Partnership with parents**
  - Sub-theme: Regular feedback
  - Sub-theme: Formal meetings
  - Sub-theme: Using interpreters
  - Sub-theme: Communication problems

Next Vik had to systematically go through all of his data and apply the identified themes to it. This meant reading and rereading all the data carefully and noting where the identified themes arose within it. He had to ensure that all references to the themes had been captured and recorded. Therefore, having drawn up his 'thematic framework' Vik worked his way through each piece of data, recording where the themes are identified within that data. He decided to give each theme a number and each sub-theme a letter as in the example above. For example, the theme on 'Pedagogical practices' was number 2 and the sub-theme 'Gestures and signs to convey instructions' was 2(a). Whenever there was reference within the data to using gestures or signs with the children to give instructions, then this passage or sentence was marked with the label 2(a). The same principle applied to the allocation of the other theme and sub-theme labels.

Having applied his themes Vik needed to summarize all the data he had identified as relevant. He did this by creating a table (see below) which summarizes each participant's comments on the theme or sub-theme identified. The numbers such as 5.4 just before the summary are the page and line number on which the reference to the theme was found in the relevant participant's transcript. This was a very useful way for Vik to return to his data to find a quote or to clarify the meaning of something where it had become obscured during the analytical process. Vik wrote enough in the box to be sure he had captured what the participant was saying and their meaning, without inserting large chunks of text. The aim was to summarize thereby providing an effective referencing system so that he could revisit his data quickly and accurately.

Case Study – Extract from Vik's Data Summary Chart

Theme: Structure of support	Participant 1	Participant 2	Participant 3
(a) Policy	5.4 Not seen any EAL policy	7.11 Policy seen but contents not remembered	4.32 Policy discussed on INSET day but not seen recently
(b) Classroom organization	9.20 Children with EAL seated together	10.17 Children with EAL seated together with teaching assistant	
(c) Deployment of teaching assistants/ bilingual teaching assistants (BLTA)	10.5 BLTA sit with small group of children with EAL	10.20 BLTA works with small group or sometimes with individual children	8.29 No BLTA in this class

This chart was Vik's final summary chart but he had several drafts before completing this one. At this stage, Vik was still refining his themes, creating sub-themes and deleting weak themes. It is also worth noting that where a particular participant did not comment on a theme, then the box is left blank. Vik now started to write up the findings and discussion chapters. Writing up the findings is the last stage of analysis as Vik now needed to interpret what meanings he could find from his summarized data. So far, his summary chart describes what the participants have said, and it is at this next stage that he draws out what the data implies or means. As an example, Vik looked at theme 1(a) from his data summary chart above and noted that one of the participants had never seen an EAL policy, another respondent had seen one but could not remember what was in it and the third was aware that the policy had been discussed on an In-service Training of Teachers (INSET) day but not recently. From these findings, Vik concluded that there was an EAL policy in the school but that it was not readily available to staff and that they were not aware of its contents. This was his interpretation of the data he had gathered. He suggested that there may not have been any recent training involving this policy and that if the policy had been updated recently, that process had not included the teaching staff he interviewed.

Vik decided to have separate findings and discussion chapters. As part of these chapters, he wrote up his interpretation of theme 1(a) in the findings chapter and then in his discussion section he commented that his conclusions were similar to another study which found that there was little policy-development and training in supporting children with EAL in schools. However, he also referred to a further study, which found that where there were large numbers of children with EAL in a school there was more training for staff. He compared the concept of 'large numbers' between the sample in that study and the school he did his data gathering in. Both studies which Vik referred to had already been discussed in the literature review. Vik went on to write up all his other findings theme by theme in a similar way and to discuss them in relation to existing studies.

Vik concluded his study by making a few recommendations to the setting about their work with children with EAL, drawn from his findings. He was confident about doing this because his findings clearly emerged from the raw data gained from staff in the school and his own observations. One of Vik's recommendations was that the school should consider steps to make sure that the EAL policy was available to all staff and that new staff were introduced to it as part of their induction. He also suggested that the policy should be revisited annually as part of staff training to refresh staff members' understanding of the requirements for their work with children with EAL.

Reflective task on Vik's project

1   Vik's data-gathering methods are interviews and observations – what do you think are the reasons behind his approach to analysis?

2   When Vik wrote up his findings and discussion chapters he returned to his raw data and used quotes to illustrate his main points. What is the value of using direct quotes in qualitative analysis?

3   Vik makes several recommendations based on his findings. Who would benefit from these recommendations? Why should he be cautious with them?

What is involved in quantitative analysis?

Quantitative analysis in education is the process of presenting and interpreting, in numerical fashion, research participants' attitudes, views, opinions and/or behaviours. In other words, to examine the distribution of and/or relationships between the variables under investigation: how they are distributed and to what extent and in what ways they are related in a given context (Punch and Oancea, 2014). The primary aim is to identify patterns and regularities in the data (Fielding and Gilbert, 2006).

A key issue in quantitative analysis is that the analysis can be undertaken at two distinct levels. The first, and the one that you are most likely to be engaged in as an undergraduate student, is descriptive analysis, or descriptive statistics as it is commonly known. Put simply, this involves the use of appropriate statistical techniques to transform potentially large amounts of numerical data into a form such as tables and/or charts that 'describe' your findings in such a way as to make them easy to understand and interpret (Crossman, 2016). The second-level of analysis is what is known as inferential statistics. This is more complex than descriptive statistics and is aimed at drawing conclusions from the data and establishing the extent to which the findings from a sample can be applied to the reference population from which that sample was drawn (Crossman, 2016). Thus descriptive statistics stop at presenting and interpreting data obtained from a sample (a sample of university students, for example), whereas inferential statistics goes a step further: it uses the findings from a sample to make predictions about the reference population (e.g. all the students in a university). Given that it is unlikely that you will be using inferential statistics for your project this chapter will focus primarily on descriptive-level analysis. If, on the other hand, you do intend to attempt to generalize your findings to a reference population, a useful starting point would be the latest edition in the SPSS Made Simple series (Gray and Kinnear, 2012)

You will know from Chapters 4 and 7 that in order to examine the extent to which findings from a sample apply to the research population as a whole (the reference population) a representative sample is required, which of necessity should be fairly large (in absolute not relative terms) and selected at random. It is because of the time, expertise and resources involved in generating a representative sample that undergraduate research rarely involves attempts at generalization and the associated use of inferential statistics. It is worth checking with your research supervisor, however, whether or not attempted generalization of your research findings is indeed an expectation. Even where this is not the case, however, a well-prepared undergraduate researcher will be able to demonstrate that a limitation of her/his research is that the findings can only be said to apply to the sample and will be able to explain, with reference to the size and nature of the sample and why this is the case.

Steps in the analysis of quantitative data

There are several stages involved in the analysis of quantitative data. The first step is taken even before the data-collection phase of the research process begins. This is because the types of data collected such as nominal, ordinal and/or interval/ratio, coupled with the size and nature of the sample have implications for the level and types of analysis that can be undertaken and the statistical techniques that can be used (see Chapter 7). This means that when using quantitative methods of data collection, you must be clear from the outset what it is that you want your data to demonstrate, for example:

- the distribution of variables;
- the relationships between two or more variables or;
- findings that can be generalized from a sample to a reference population.

As quantitative data in its raw form cannot be subjected to statistical analysis the data gathered needs to be organized and coded first. Finally you will need to decide on which statistical tests are to be used, if any. There are several statistical techniques that can be used to analyse quantitative data, so it is important that you know how to choose the most effective and appropriate one for your purposes. Once decisions have been finalized as to which statistical tests will be used, these are often done using software packages such as Excel and SPSS.

What do you want your data to demonstrate?

Quantitative data are generated more often than not by means of surveys and experiments using fixed choice format questions and scales and/or structured observations (see Chapter 7). Thus the data takes the form of numbers, such as the frequency of an activity, or categories that can easily be translated into numbers, such as strongly disagree, disagree, agree, strongly agree scales. There are also different levels of measurement affecting variables and these have implications for both the types of analyses that can be undertaken and the techniques that can be used. Therefore, prior to the data-collection phase of your project, careful consideration needs to be given to what sorts of statistical techniques you want to use.

If you were conducting a study into children's television viewing habits for example, one of your research questions might be 'What types of TV programmes do children watch?' Thus your questionnaire or structured interview would include a list of possibilities for children and or their parents to choose from. Using some fairly basic data analysis techniques, you would be able to present an easy to understand and interpret overview of the TV programmes watched by the children making up the sample. Showing the distribution of a variable (in this case the programmes watched) requires relatively little sophistication in terms of statistical analysis and nominal-level data will suffice. However, simply showing the distribution of variables alone may be too simplistic at degree level and might show little of any interest or note. It is only when a sample is viewed in terms of commonalities and differences (i.e. the relationships between variables) that findings become more interesting and throw up more opportunity for theorizing about possible explanations for any relationships found.

There are a number of statistical techniques that can be used to look for relationships between variables but the more sophisticated of these demand that variables be measured at ordinal and where possible, interval/ratio level. Indeed, a lack of attention to data analysis at and before the data-collection phase of your project could leave you with data in a form that limits the level of analysis that can be carried out. There is nothing worse than finding yourself with data that do not allow for a level of analysis you were hoping for, so you need to take great care to ensure this does not happen. Indeed, this would be a useful point in the research process to utilize the support of your supervisor. Alternatively, a rule of thumb might be to avoid too many yes/no and either/or categories wherever possible and to opt instead for the use of Likert-type scaled responses or to ask for a specific number where appropriate; for example, if you were doing a lifestyle survey of sixth formers, those who answered yes to a question asking whether or not they drink alcohol could then be asked, 'How many units of alcohol do you drink during an average week?'

All of the above said, however, about levels of data measurement, you will remember from Chapter 7 that some variables quite simply can only be measured at a nominal level (e.g. social class, religious affiliation, eye colour and so on) because such variables cannot be quantified in terms of one being numerically less or more than the other.

Organizing and coding the data

This stage in the process is best explained by means of an illustration. Cara is a final year education studies student whose research project is an exploration of the use of Information and Communications Technology (ICT) for the purposes of doing school homework by children in Key Stage 3. Her approach to the research is a survey and her data-collection tool is a self-administered questionnaire. The following questions show some of the questions in Cara's questionnaire as completed by one of the research participants and coded by Cara.

Case Study – Cara's Questionnaire

Questions from Cara's questionnaire and codes assigned on completion

1. How old are you?   *Code*
   13 years   (13)
2. Are you male or female? ***(please tick)***
   Male   Female   (1) 2

3. How often do you use ICT to do homework? ***(please tick)***

   Always   (4)
   Usually   3
   Rarely   2
   Never   1
   (if you ticked never – please go to question 7)

Case Study – Cont'd

4. How frequently do you use ICT to do homework? *(please tick)*

Every day	5
4–6 days per week	(4)
2 or 3 days per week	3
Once per week	2
Less than once per week	1

5. When you use ICT to do homework, how often do you use the internet? *(please tick)*

Always	(4)
Usually	3
Rarely	2
Never	1

6. When using ICT to do your homework, how many minutes do you spend on each occasion on average? *(please round up to the nearest 5 or 10)*
   20 *Minutes*   (40)

7. Do you use other sources to assist you in completing your homework (e.g. the library, help from parents)? *(please tick)*
   Yes   No   (1) 2

This is an abridged version of the questionnaire that Cara designed which as well as helping to illustrate the coding process shows how she was careful to collect data that could be used to look for relationships between variables (such as a possible relationship between gender and the amount of time spent using ICT). As you can see, Cara has assigned a numerical value to each answer. In addition, the values increase in line with the frequency of the activity so as to reflect the increase in frequency so in Question 3 'Always' is signified by 4 and 'Never' is coded 1. The table below goes on to show the coded data for 20 (labelled A–T for the purpose of preserving participants' anonymity) out of Cara's 87 respondents as they relate to questions 1–7.

Case Study – An Abridged Version of Cara's Survey Data

	Q 1	Q2	Q3	Q4	Q5	Q6	Q7
A	13	1	4	4	4	20	2
B	12	2	3	4	2	25	1
C	12	1	3	4	3	30	1
D	11	1	4	3	4	20	1
E	11	1	3	3	4	20	1
F	11	1	3	3	4	45	1
G	14	2	3	3	4	10	1
H	12	1	3	3	4	10	1
I	13	0	4	3	4	30	1
J	13	2	2	0	0	0	1
K	11	2	3	3	4	15	1
L	12	2	3	3	3	20	1
M	12	1	3	3	4	35	1
N	13	2	4	3	3	20	1
O	12	1	4	3	4	15	2
P	14	2	2	4	4	10	1
Q	14	1	3	3	3	0	1
R	13	1	4	4	4	10	1
S	12	1	3	3	2	15	1
T	11	1	3	4	4	20	2

The use of data array tables like this make the data easier to handle when it comes to inputting it into Excel or SPSS; however, they do not usually form part of the data analysis section of your dissertation (see Chapter 9). This is because data when presented in this way are extremely difficult to interpret. Moreover, such tables do not provide the full picture because the data have not been statistically processed. They can be included as part of the appendices, however. You will notice in the table, that a zero has been assigned as a code in some of the cells: this is done to denote missing data, where a respondent omitted, for whatever reason, to answer the relevant question(s). It is important when entering data into SPSS to highlight codes that denote missing data and to only use codes that do not represent a possible value.

It is easily apparent from Cara's table that rows in her data array table are dedicated to respondents and the columns to the questions/variables. Once a data array table is complete, the data is ready to be subjected to statistical analysis using SPSS or other statistical software packages such as Minitab or Info Centricity Xeno. Note that when using SPSS the question number reflects the variable number so that when you input the data codes in the Q1 column these would be inputted against var00001, the data in the Q2 column would be inputted against var00002 and so on. It is unlikely that you will have to purchase such software because most universities' IT services provide statistical software for students' use. For guidance on the use of SPSS see the recommended reading list at the end of the chapter. Your supervisor and/or your university's IT support team may also be able to help you to master the software.

Deciding which statistical tests to use

Approaches to quantitative analysis are generally categorized as univariate analysis, bivariate analysis or multivariate analysis. You can probably guess that univariate analysis is concerned with the analysis of one variable at a time, bivariate analysis with two and multivariate with the analysis of three or more variables at a time. This section focuses on the first two categories. This is due to the fact that they are the most frequently used and most suitable for undergraduate research students. However should you need guidance on multivariate analysis, the Oxford Bibliographies website highlights a range of sources you could draw upon.

Although the main purpose of univariate analysis is to describe one characteristic of the sample at a time (e.g. age, sex, religious affiliation), it is also an important prerequisite to bivariate analysis. The commonest approaches to univariate analysis are frequency tables, graphical displays, measures of central tendency (e.g. median) and measures of dispersion, each of which can be produced using Microsoft Excel.

Frequency tables show the number of participants in a sample and the percentage belonging to each of the categories of a particular variable. Percentages are usually rounded up or down and when using interval-/ratio-level variables such as age, they may need to be grouped, being careful not to create any overlap (e.g. 21–30, 31–40 and so on). Grouping of variables is only necessary where there are likely to be several categories, thus making the frequency table large and thereby difficult to interpret.

Example – Frequency Table

Time spent travelling to school – to the nearest 5 minutes (Sample of Y7s)					
Time		Frequency	Per cent	Valid per cent	Cumulative per cent
Valid	5.00	4	7.4	7.4	7.4
	10.00	10	18.5	18.5	25.9
	15.00	20	37.0	37.0	63.0
	20.00	15	27.8	27.8	90.7
	25.00	3	5.6	5.6	96.3
	35.00	2	3.7	3.7	100.0
	Total	54	100.0	100.0	

Graphical displays such as pie charts, bar charts and histograms, are among the most commonly used means of summarizing quantitative data. They are sometimes easier to interpret than frequency charts and present marked differences between the categories of a variable more strikingly. However, where interval variables such as age are involved, information can be lost and decisions have to be made about what is most important, how best to achieve clarity and ease of interpretation as well as making sure that all the information about the variable is included (Robson and McCartan, 2015).

Pie charts can either be used to show the relationship of parts to a whole or to show how parts of a whole relate to each other. To illustrate this point, if you were researching children's food preferences and found that 72 per cent of your sample chose chips as their favourite food, you could show this in relation to the sample, for example 72 per cent of the 100 per cent. Alternatively, you could show it in relation to the other categories making up the sample, for example 72 per cent – chips, 10 per cent – pizza, 11 per cent – pasta, 3 per cent – biscuits, 2 per cent – ice cream and 2 per cent – fruit = 100 per cent (see examples below).

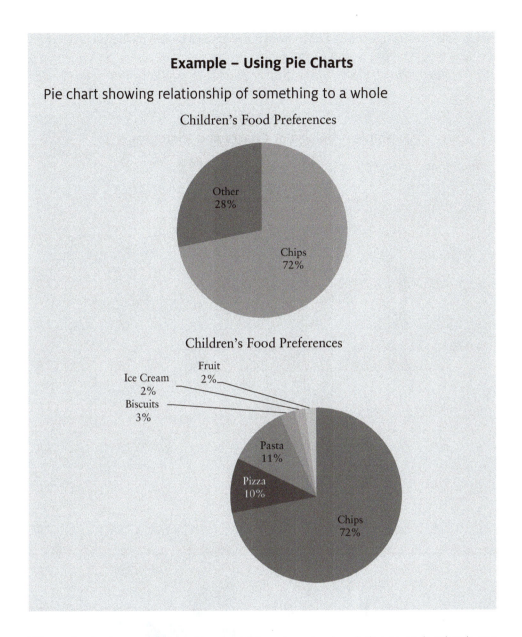

Example – Using Pie Charts

Pie chart showing relationship of something to a whole

Children's Food Preferences

Other
28%

Chips
72%

Children's Food Preferences

Ice Cream
2%

Fruit
2%

Biscuits
3%

Pasta
11%

Pizza
10%

Chips
72%

When pie charts are used to show variable categories in relation to each other it can be difficult to determine at first glance the extent to which some of the 'slices' differ in size. Bar charts and histograms sometimes do this much better. Bar charts are used to plot frequencies (absolute magnitudes) or percentages (relative magnitudes) against categories. Generally, the categorical scale is on the horizontal axis (χ) and frequencies, as expressed either in absolute or relative terms, on the vertical axis (γ). The axes are usefully reversed however, creating a horizontal bar chart, when the category labels are long. There is very little difference between the appearance of bar charts and histograms. Basically, as can be seen from the examples below, the bars in a bar chart are separated from one another, whereas in a histogram, they are joined. Histograms are the preferred method for displaying findings relating to interval-level data.

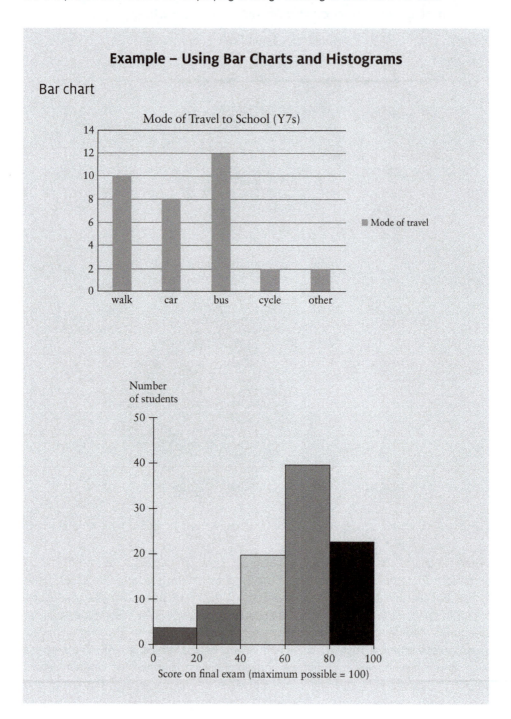

Example – Using Bar Charts and Histograms

Bar chart

Mode of Travel to School (Y7s)

Measures of central tendency (i.e. mean, median and mode) result in a single figure or value that is typical of a distribution of values and thereby provide another means of summarizing the distribution of variables (Bryman, 2015). The mean is basically another word for average and is calculated in exactly the same way: by totalling the values in a distribution and then dividing them by the number of values present. The median meanwhile is the middle value of a distribution when the values are arranged in order of magnitude. There should be as many values above as below the midpoint when calculating the median, which in the event of there being an even number of values will involve calculating the average of the middle two values to reach a single value. The mode represents the value that occurs most frequently in a distribution, for example the commonest age in a sample. The table below provides further information about measures of central tendency.

Points to Think About – Central Tendency

Measure of central tendency	When should it be used?
Mean (arithmetic average)	To summarize interval/ratio data
Median	Used primarily in relation to ordinal data but also appropriate for interval/ratio
Mode	Can be used when summarizing any type of variable

Whereas measures of central tendency provide estimates of typical numerical values in a sample, measures of dispersion are concerned with the extent of variation (or spread) of the data. Measures of central tendency when used on their own provide only part of the picture and should, therefore, be used together with measures of dispersion. Dispersion is most commonly measured in terms of standard deviation, which provides a measure of the average amount of variation around the mean value. As before all the approaches to analysis mentioned in this section can be calculated using software such as excel.

Example – Median and Mean

The median and mean of these two sets of numbers is clearly 50, but the spread can be seen to differ markedly

48 49 **50** 51 52
30 40 **50** 60 70

Bivariate analysis is used to look for a relationship or association between two variables. This occurs when the distribution of numerical values relevant to one variable (e.g. age) is in some way related to the distribution of values on another variable (e.g. preferred leisure activity). It might be, therefore, that in a study looking at people's leisure activity habits, the younger end of the sample preferred activities such as going to clubs at night while the older end of the sample preferred less noisy pursuits. It is important to be aware that relationships which are established through survey/questionnaire research are not viewed as causal; that is, a relationship where the independent variable affects another dependent variable in some way (see Chapter 7). However, some relationships may be found through questionnaires that lend themselves to the possibility of a causal relationship. For instance, a survey may throw up the existence of an apparent relationship between students' attendance at seminars (independent variable) and good coursework marks (dependent variable). However, without conducting an experiment it cannot definitely be stated that higher levels of attendance cause students to do better in their coursework. Below are some of the techniques open to you when looking for relationships between pairs of variables in a sample. Each of the techniques outlined below serves to reduce raw quantitative data into a form that is easier to interpret, be this through a single figure and/or in tables or charts. Which techniques you choose will depend on the nature of the variables being analysed.

Example – Contingency Tables

These are simple and commonly used methods for showing relationships between pairs of variables and are very similar to frequency tables in that they include percentage values, making for easy interpretation of the information conveyed.

They can be used to show relationships between any types of variables, but are more usefully employed for the following combinations:

Two nominal variable categories
Nominal and ordinal variable categories
Nominal and interval/ratio variable categories

Contingency table showing relationship between gender and reported number of times per week engaged in walking to keep fit

			Walking frequency						Total
			zero	x1/wk	x2/wk	x3/wk	x4/wk	x5/wk	
Gender	Male	Count	15	11	7	1	1	0	35
		% within gender	42.9%	31.4%	20.0%	2.9%	2.9%	.0%	100.0%
	Female	Count	0	0	8	9	4	8	29
		% within gender	.0%	.0%	27.6%	31.0%	13.8%	27.6%	100.0%
Total		Count	15	11	15	10	5	8	64
		%	23.4	17.2	23.4	15.6	7.8	12.5	100.0

Example – Cont'd

This table shows a relationship between gender and walking for the purposes of exercise. It can be seen that in this hypothetical sample, females use walking as a method of exercise more often per week than males. Note that this relationship includes nominal (gender) and interval- (equidistant frequency) level variables.

Example – Measuring the Strength of a Linear Relationship between Two Variables

Pearson's Correlation Coefficient (Pearson's *r*)

Correlation is method of investigating linear relationships between pairs of interval/ratio variables, for example age and time spent reading. Pearson's Correlation Coefficient (Pearson's *r*) is a measure of the strength of the association, if any, between two interval/ratio variables and takes on a value between +1 and −1, with 0 indicating no relationship. A correlation coefficient of +1 (positive correlation) indicates a perfect positive linear relationship between two variables: as one variable increases in value, so does the other, following an exact linear rule. In the case of age and reading a correlation coefficient of +1 would indicate that time spent reading increases with age. A correlation coefficient of −1 (negative correlation) on the other hand would denote the opposite, that is that time spent reading decreases with age. The closer the coefficient is to one (in both directions) the stronger the correlation so that the nearer to zero the coefficient, the weaker the relationship. Correlations are often presented using scatter diagrams.

Table showing Pearson Correlation Coefficient of +1			
		Age	Walking frequency
Age	**Pearson Correlation**	1	**.969****
	Sig. (2-tailed)		.000
	N	64	64
Walking frequency	**Pearson Correlation**	**.969****	1
	Sig. (2-tailed)	.000	
	N	64	64
**. Correlation is significant at the 0.01 level (2-tailed).			

The footnote indicates that the linear relationship between the two variables in questions is statistically significant: that is, it is unlikely to have occurred by chance. When using SPSS to calculate correlation coefficients using Pearson's *r* and other similar statistical tests (see below) statistical significance is automatically calculated.

Example – Cont'd

Spearman's Rank Correlation Coefficient (Spearman's rho)

Spearman's rho is almost exactly the same as Pearson's *r* in that it is used to denote the strength of a linear relationship between two variables taking on a value between +1 and –1. Spearman's rho, however, is used where the pairs of variables are either both ordinal or where one variable is ordinal and the other interval/ratio. The strength of the relationship appears in a table like the Pearson's *r* table above.

Phi (*Φ*)

The phi coefficient is a measure of the degree of a relationship between two dichotomous variables (e.g. gender and a yes response where the possibilities were simply a yes or a no). Like Pearson's *r* and Spearman's rho, phi takes on a value between +1 and –1 and is also displayed in a table like the previous two examples.

* SPSS can be used to produce scatter diagrams to give a graphical display of these linear relationships alongside the tables.

Cramér's *V*

Cramér's *V* differs slightly to the tests above in that it is used to analyse the relationship between pairs of nominal variables and is only capable of a positive value. Thus it can only indicate the strength of an association between two variables and not the direction (i.e. it does not show a positive or negative association). The value of Cramér's *V* is usually indicated on a contingency table (see above) rather than being presented on its own.

Findings from a small-scale quantitative study can be used to make recommendations to a setting from which a sample was drawn. However, quantitative researchers also often make suggestions for further research as part of their recommendations. This is largely on account of the fact that quantitative studies often identify areas that need additional study. As a result of undertaking some bivariate analysis, Cara found that in her sample, boys are markedly more likely to use IT to do their homework than girls. This finding mirrored the findings of two of the studies discussed in her literature review, so she highlighted this common finding in her discussion section. Interestingly, 82 per cent of Cara's sample had access to IT at home, compared to much smaller proportions of others' samples. Thus, Cara raised this difference in her discussion section and put forward some possible explanations for it.

Content analysis

Quantitative content analysis was introduced in Chapter 7 as a means of asking questions of secondary data, and discussion ensued as to what this should entail, focusing especially on considerations on which to base data selection. The emphasis in this chapter, however, is on how to analyse the secondary data gathered. You will remember that the first step in analysing primary quantitative data is to make it more manageable by means of coding; likewise, secondary data also requires a coding scheme to make it more manageable, which in quantitative analysis involves developing small units (categories) of information each of which can be assigned a number. This thereby allows for data to be transferred from a coding schedule to a software programme for more sophisticated analysis.

The success of quantitative content analysis relies on the development of effective coding categories for use in a coding schedule. This demands you follow relevant guidance (see, for example, Neuendorf's, 2017 content analysis guidebook) and undertake careful piloting of the coding schedule before it is used proper.

Summary of key points

- Plan ahead, include your analytical approach in your methodology.
- Leave enough time to analyse, write up your findings and discuss them.
- A good literature review will stand you in good stead when you start to analyse your data.
- Conclusions and recommendations should be in line with the size of the study. You should avoid making too many generalizations beyond the context of the study.

Reflective task

Consider the question, Do you watch TV often?

This will most likely generate an answer of yes or no – which is nominal-level data and thereby only lends itself to a very basic level of analysis.

Now consider the questions, How often do you watch TV? or When do you watch TV?

Such questions allow the researcher to provide a list of categories from which participants can choose; for example, every day, every two to three days, once per week, etc. This would generate ordinal-level data that lend themselves to more sophisticated techniques than nominal data simply because once the categories are coded there will be a difference in amount (see Chapter 7 to recap)

Now consider how you could go a step further and asking, how many minutes per day on average do you watch TV?

This would generate ratio-level data that have a higher level of sophistication because there are now equal distances between possible answers (e.g. the distance between 30 minutes and 31 minutes is the same as the distance between 40 minutes and 41 minutes). This allows for more mathematical activity and more sophisticated tests (again, you can refer back to Chapter 7 to recap your knowledge and understanding of different levels of data sophistication).

Link to companion website

https://bloomsbury.com/cw/successful-dissertations-second-edition/student-resources/8-data-analysis/

Recommended reading and further sources of information

Flick, U. (2014, 5th edition), *An Introduction to Qualitative Research*. London: Sage.

Marshall, C. and Rossman, G. R. (2015, 6th ediiton), *Designing Qualitative Research*. London: Sage.

Miles, M. B., Huberman, A. M. and Saldana, J. (2014, 3rd edition), *Qualitative Data Analysis: A Methods Sourcebook*. London: Sage.

Neuendorf, K. (2017, 2nd edition), *The Content Analysis Guidebook*. Los Angeles, Sage.

Punch, K. and Oancea, A. (2014, 2nd edition), *Introduction to Research Methods in Education*. London: Sage.

Robson, C. and McCartan, K. (2015, 4th edition), *Real World Research*. London: Wiley.

Useful websites

About.Education http://www.about.com/education/

Analyse this http://archive.learnhigher.ac.uk/analysethis/index.html

Oxford Bibliographies http://www.oxfordbibliographies.com/obo/page/about;jsessionid=B3C4B61410FF77B8FEDD80AFC974C231

9

Writing Your Dissertation

Mark O'Hara

Chapter Outline

Chapter Aims

By the end of this chapter you will

- be aware of how techniques such as 'frame and fill' can help you to structure your dissertation;
- understand what it means to write academically in relation to
  – presentation and standards of written English;
  – being critical, reflective and analytical;
- be familiar with the likely structure and contents of the different sections and chapters of a dissertation.

Academic writing is not an inherited talent that emerges naturally in a few fortunate individuals. It is instead a skill that has to be learnt, honed and developed by every student willing to put the work in and using the right techniques. Seeking to acquire knowledge of the expectations and protocols associated with academic writing through an unfocused process of osmosis will not work very well. It needs to be taught not caught and your university will have made provision for this either during your previous studies or using academic guidance teams. However, you can also teach yourself to write well. This chapter introduces you to some useful techniques to help you to get going with writing your dissertation and to understand what it is expected of you when your tutors talk about academic writing and being critical and reflective in your approach. Writing a dissertation could be likened to making a film in so far as both are rarely done in a single take. By planning, drafting, editing, redrafting, checking and double-checking you can make real progress in your academic writing skills (Bell, 2014). The chapter concludes with a step-by-step guide to the likely contents of the various sections that feature in most undergraduate dissertations.

Getting going and developing a structure

Being faced with an extensive and extended project often of anything between 8,000 and 15,000 words in length depending on the academic credit weighting associated with the module is a daunting prospect. However by breaking it down into more manageable components the challenge can come to seem less insurmountable than you first thought. Education and social science dissertations are all individual pieces of work and certainly those that are predominantly interpretative or qualitative in nature may not always follow conventional formats (Punch, 2005, p. 260); this said, certain key sections will usually be present in the final dissertation even if not necessarily in the precise order outlined below.

Points to Think About – Common Components of an Undergraduate Dissertation

- The 'preliminaries' – for example, your title page, contents pages, acknowledgements, abstract and introduction – setting out the focus of your study, its rationale and any necessary background information.
- A balanced, non-partisan review of the literature highlighting key and relevant debates, controversies, any accepted 'facts' and positioning your study within this context.
- Methodology and methods section(s) setting out the rationale for approaching your research question in the way that you have and articulating some of the issues and dilemmas that you had to work through when weighing up the relative strengths and weaknesses of different approaches.
- Your data; what you did and what your findings were. You will need to provide the reader with information on the context, the sample selected, any data-collection tools used and any ethical issues raised.

Points to Think About – Cont'd

- Analysis and discussion of the data including your interpretations of the evidence gleaned coupled with discussion of any emerging themes with references back to the literature review.
- Conclusions, recommendations, suggestions for further research and reflections on your own study.
- The 'postscripts', for example, references/bibliography and appendices.

Once you have worked out the focus for your dissertation you will be able to divide the available word length up among the different elements to make a rough estimate of how much space you can devote to each. Although in the final version you may find that these relative weightings have altered during the process of researching and writing the dissertation, it does not necessarily matter at this early stage as this is primarily a device to help you to get started and also to avoid overshooting the word limit. Below is an example of what mapping out the relative weightings of the different sections of your dissertation might look like at this early stage.

Example – Distributing the Available Word Length of a Dissertation

Dissertation involving primary data collection – word limit 10,000

Introduction/problem/research question: 500–1,000 words
Literature review: 2,500–3,000 words
Methodology/Methods: 1,500–2,000 words
Data/Discussion and analysis: 3,000–4,000 words
Conclusions/Recommendations: 1,000–1,500 words
References/Appendices: Not counted against the word limit

Literature-based dissertation using secondary data – word limit 8,000

Introduction/problem/research question: 500–1,000 words
Methodology/Methods/Theoretical perspective: 1,000–1,500 words
Literature review, discussion and analysis: 4,000–6,000 words
Conclusions: 1,000–1,500 words
References/Appendices: Not counted against the word limit

Pay attention to your assessment criteria

Every dissertation module will have its own accompanying assessment criteria and your dissertation will have to meet these criteria if you are to be successful. In spite of the unique nature of every university's assessment criteria there will be some generally identifiable features associated with good quality pieces of work at this level. The best undergraduate dissertations tend to

- have a clearly stated and purposeful focus;
- make well-referenced and effective use of the literature in the field not just offering a critical evaluation of the strengths and weaknesses of previous research but also using this familiarity and understanding to inform decision-making and interpretation throughout the dissertation as a whole from the introduction to the conclusions;
- feature a well-designed and efficiently executed programme of research, characterized by an intelligent methodology;
- employ data-collection tools that are sensitive to the context and acknowledge the costs as well as the benefits associated with their use;
- consider potential alternative explanations and interpretations of any findings during analysis; all data, even those which may be contradictory, discrepant or inconvenient in some way are considered rather than being omitted or quietly disposed of;
- avoid making misleading or unsubstantiated conclusions and include reflection on the implications of any conclusions that are made for the author, the reader(s) and/ or any others;
- be integrated with links and connections made between the different sections offering the reader a clearly signposted route through the approaches used, the findings, the decision-making and actions taken and contain reflection on, critical analysis of and provide insight into the process of research itself;
- have a coherent and logical overall structure as well as being well written and argued with clear prose that adheres to the conventions of standard English and academic writing.

Writing well

Writing a dissertation is not simply a summative activity to be completed at the end of the process once all the reading, data collection and analysis have taken place. It is instead a continuous process that ought to start when the dissertation does. Anyone who has ever had to write an essay, let alone a dissertation, will recognize the sense of despair and hopelessness on occasions caused by staring at that first blank screen or piece of paper. Mowing the lawn may take on a sudden urgency or perhaps you experience an inexplicable desire to file your entire music collection in date order but what you probably do not feel like doing is writing. Your reluctance may stem from a lack of confidence or perhaps you are worried and want to 'get it right' but as you are at such an early stage of your dissertation 'getting it right' is probably an unrealistic and unhelpful expectation that can result in paralysis rather than action (Kirton and McMillan, 2007). However as you have been through the experience before you will also be familiar with the sense of release and new optimism that can be brought about when you do, finally, start to write. Practice makes perfect so start writing early and keep writing often.

One technique for getting started is sometimes referred to as *frame and fill* (Walliman, 2014). Having broken your dissertation down into sections with rough weightings, then break each of these down further into subsections and use these to help you to begin to write. Remember, while your audience will most likely begin reading your dissertation at the beginning that does not mean that you have to start writing it at the beginning. Writing the different sections and subsections is unlikely to follow the linear, sequential process involved in reading them. It may be much better to get writing knowing that you will want to return to this early material at a later stage in order to undertake revision and editing. You can think of your plan as made out of clay rather than granite, you may wish to remould it as your dissertation progresses (Greetham 2009).

At least once you have started writing, the fact that you *are* writing is likely to boost your morale and with luck generate some momentum. There are many strategies for keeping this momentum going and you will need to experiment a little to find which ones work best for you. For example, some students like to set themselves deadlines or targets such as 'a thousand words a week'. For others the answer lies in blocking out regular periods of time in each week dedicated to writing and rewriting the different sections of the dissertation. The aim is to stick to deadlines and to avoid too much drift or slippage. Most dissertations are now largely, if not completely, word processed and you should try to get into the habit of properly word processing your dissertation rather than writing sections by hand and then copying them into your PC or laptop (Kirton and McMillan, 2007). The latter approach is enormously wasteful of time and time is something you can ill-afford to squander.

Critical friends and supervisors can offer another means of keeping up the momentum of writing by providing you with ongoing, formative feedback. Remember that if you are acting as, or seeking support from a critical friend at any point during your dissertation you must keep the boundaries between peer tutoring and collusion clearly in mind; if in doubt, talk to your dissertation supervisor. Your supervisor meanwhile may also offer you formative feedback on your written material while it is still in draft form. Such feedback may present you with some challenges. To begin with you may be urged to cut parts of your work which may have taken you a considerable amount of time to write and so you could have a good deal of emotional and temporal capital invested in them. However, the best dissertations avoid padding out the text with irrelevant or at best peripheral content and concern themselves with quality as well as quantity (Hamp-Lyons and Heasley, 2006). Be prepared to cut where and when it is necessary and if you are unable to bring yourself to scrap something completely you can always store it as a separate document by way of insurance just in case you need to change your mind at a later date.

A second challenge centres on the need for you to respond promptly to your supervisor's advice. Planning ahead and clearing some time in your diary for the days immediately following the receipt of formative feedback is an effective way of reducing the risk that you will forget or omit anything important. Not only does such a strategy ensure that things are fresh in your mind, it is also an effective technique for preventing your workload from backing up. Your supervisor is there to help you so make sure you seek that help. Here is an example of the kind of formative feedback supervisors can provide.

Case Study – Tutor Feedback

Sam (student)

Draft interview schedule for use with teachers in my placement school:

Q1. How would you define 'creativity'?
Q2. How is 'creativity' planned for and used in this classroom?
Q3. Do you think the changes to the role play area have affected the children's creativity?
Q3a. If yes, why and how?
Q3b. If no, why and how?
Q4. What suggestions do you have on how the role play area could have been made better to enhance the children's creativity?
Q5. Has the project made you think about different ways in which you can try and enhance the children's creativity within the role play area?
Q5a. If yes, what are your ideas?
Q6. Overall, how do you think the project has gone in the classroom?

* Some questions may be elaborated on or I may create new ones as I hear the answers given to Q1–6.

Janet (tutor)

Given the limited time available for these interviews and the busy nature of the school why not reduce the number of questions being asked. For example:

Q1. *What does creativity mean to you?/How would you define it?*
     * This could be a tricky question to answer at short notice. One way round this though, Sam, if your respondents are struggling is to ask them for examples of creativity and then use these to tease out what they think it is that makes them creative.

Case Study – Cont'd

Q2. *How do you provide opportunities for the children to be creative in the classroom/curriculum?*
* Ask respondents about drama and/or role play specifically if they omit to mention it. You might also explore practical challenges, that is setting up areas, integrating provision into the rest of curriculum, adult involvement, etc.

Q3. *What examples of the children being creative have you seen?*
* You could seek information on events prior to your research as well as events during/as a result of it. Play it by ear and depending on what response you get try to explore whether the new role play themes you have introduced as part of your project have created new/different opportunities for creative activity by the children. If appropriate ask for suggestions on how the teachers would have improved the role play area in terms of its creative potential.

A consequence of revising, editing and possibly having more than one version of the various sections of your dissertation is the need for careful version control and backup copies. Mistakes can easily be made so make sure you indicate clearly on the different documents and their respective file names which is which. A simple code can involve putting 'v' for version and the number at the end of file names. For example, the third draft of your methods section or chapter might be filed as 'Ch.3.v3'. Alternatively, you may opt to describe the content of files rather than number the different sections in which case the second version of your literature review might be filed as 'Lit. Review. v2'. Whichever system you decide to adopt it is important to remember that even the best filing system is not immune to human error and sometimes in the heat of the moment when you are tired and under pressure it is all too easy to overwrite or delete the wrong file. While there are ways of retrieving such data electronically for those who are sufficiently IT-literate, for the rest of us it is a good idea to get into the habit of saving often and backing up our files whenever we finish writing (Walliman, 2014).

Writing 'academically': Presentation and standards of written English

Presentation

Your institution will have a house style when it comes to the presentation of dissertations. There will be a series of university and/or course expectations relating to a whole range of things, including

- title pages, coversheets and binding;
- preliminaries and postscripts (e.g. contents pages, acknowledgements, glossaries and appendices);

- page layout (numbering, margins, figures and tables);
- text (e.g. use of bold, italic and underlining; font types and sizes; line spacing; headings and subheadings; paragraphing);
- citation (e.g. quotations, referencing).

It is a good idea therefore to familiarize yourself with these requirements early on so that you can set your work out accordingly right from the start. If you decide to ignore the requirements until later in the process of completing your dissertation you may find that you are faced with having to carry out a large and potentially time-consuming conversion activity at a point when time is likely to be in very short supply.

Written English

In addition to the institutional protocols relating to the layout and appearance of your dissertation you must also consider the clarity, flow and lucidity of your writing. You are aiming to produce a cogently argued piece of work with a logical overall structure, featuring intelligently sequenced paragraphs constructed from clear and unambiguous sentences. Writing academically has both technical and intellectual dimensions to it. Highlighted below are some of the technical aspects of academic writing that you will need to consider.

Example – A Word-and Sentence-Level Checklist

- grammar;
- sentence structure;
- repetition;
- word order;
- punctuation;
- vocabulary;
- flow/style;
- citation protocols.

It is certainly the case that academic writing carries with it some formal expectations. For example contractions (e.g. 'wasn't') and colloquialisms (e.g. 'kids') are normally frowned upon unless in reported speech. Students are also often advised to avoid the use of the first person (e.g. 'I') when writing although this may sometimes be deemed unavoidable in certain circumstances, for example when reporting on action research projects (Walliman, 2014). These protocols should be made clear to you early on when writing your dissertation if you have not already been introduced to them earlier on in your studies. If you are uncertain you should consult your supervisor.

Example – Avoiding the Use of 'I' and 'one'

Version 1 – It was only when I collated the responses on parental involvement and intervention relating to ICT that I noticed consistent differences began to appear more widely between schools, age ranges and genders.

Version 2 – It was only when one collated the responses on parental involvement and intervention relating to ICT that consistent and noticeable differences began to appear more widely between schools, age ranges and genders.

Version 3 – Only when the responses on parental involvement and intervention with ICT were collated, did repeated and noticeable differences begin to appear more widely between the schools, age ranges and genders.

It is essential to come to terms with the conventions associated with academic writing and it does take time. At first, trying to adopt or emulate a more academic style of writing can result in some clunky, overly complicated and sometimes very awkward prose. A good example is the replacement of 'I' with the use of terms such as 'the researcher' in an effort to avoid the use of the first person.

Example – Avoid Replacing 'I' with 'the researcher'

Version 1 – The researcher chose to focus on the therapeutic benefits of play and art therapy and how features of each of these can be used in schools. From the literature the researcher learnt that art therapy is a form of psychotherapy in which art therapists use people's interactions with art materials in order to help them express emotions that they might not be able to express verbally (Green and Drewes, 2013). Play meanwhile is an innate activity that children engage in in order to make sense of the world around them. It also offers another means of expressing and processing feelings and emotions in familiar and safe surroundings that may be difficult to put into words. The researcher realized that although schools appear at first to be ideal environments in which to utilize art and play therapy techniques there are in fact a number of challenges which practitioners need to overcome.

Version 2 – This research focused on the therapeutic benefits of play and art therapy and how features of each of these can be used in schools. From the literature it was apparent that art therapy is a form of psychotherapy in which art therapists use people's interactions with art materials in order to help them express emotions that they might not be able to express verbally (Green and Drewes, 2013). Play meanwhile

Example – Cont'd

is an innate activity that children engage in in order to make sense of the world around them. It also offers another means of expressing and processing feelings and emotions in familiar and safe surroundings that may be difficult to put into words. These observations have shown that although schools appear at first to be ideal environments in which to utilize art and play therapy techniques there are in fact a number of challenges which practitioners need to overcome.

Not only does a dense and convoluted writing style use up valuable space, it can also leave the reader perplexed as to your meaning, particularly when vocabulary is used in a discordant, slightly off-key fashion as shown below. As stated earlier at the beginning of the chapter, starting to write early, writing often and getting plenty of practice are some of the keys to improving your mastery of the technical aspects of academic writing.

Example – Choosing Your Words Carefully to Ensure Clarity

Version 1 – Imaginative play can help children to overcome trauma as they can reinforce scenes they have experienced in order for them to become someone else, also superhero play is important to a child as it will help them express and regulate their emotions enabling children to learn right and wrong, being a good guy or a bad guy, feeling emotions as if they were a victim, feeling power as the bad person and lastly as the hero saving the day as children act out their fantasies of danger, good and evil (Hoffman, 2014).

Version 2 – Imaginative play can help children to overcome trauma as they can reinforce scenes they have experienced in order for them to become someone else. Superhero play for example is important to a child as it will help them express and regulate their emotions enabling children to learn right and wrong (Hoffman, 2014). Children can act out their fantasies of danger, good and evil as they play at being a good guy or a bad guy, feeling emotions as if they were a victim, feeling power as the bad person and lastly as the hero saving the day.

Individual words and sentences are the basic building blocks of any essay or dissertation and you should aim to use them accurately, clearly and succinctly (Osmond, 2016). Avoid long sentences incorporating multiple and sometimes tortuously complex clauses. It is also a good idea to watch out for sentences that run-on or are overly verbose and 'wordy'. Resist the temptation to use 20 words when you can see that 10 would be sufficient and be prepared to break up an overly convoluted sentence into two or more concise and coherent ones. Sometimes bloated sentences are written in the hope that they will 'soak up' more of the word limit but more often than not they are the result of poor editing or the misguided assumption that the longer and more convoluted a sentence is, the more 'academic' it is.

Example – Breaking Up Unnecessarily Long and Complicated Sentences

Version 1 – The Reggio Emilia approach is a creative system of education that is built around an intellectual fusion of the consideration of the community users of a setting (teachers, children, families and other stake holders), inspirational research from international countries, curriculum foundations and the rights of the child in the belief that this will ensure the best future for children by helping them to become responsible citizens.

Version 2 – The Reggio Emilia approach is a creative system of education that brings together a number of factors in an effort to ensure the best future for children by helping them to become responsible citizens. The approach seeks to bring together a consideration of the needs of children, families, teachers and other stake holders, along with inspirational research into best practice from around the world.

Given the nature of education and other social science disciplines it is highly likely that you will need to include examples of specialist, professional and/or methodological vocabulary throughout the dissertation so make sure these terms are properly introduced. Take care not to overdo the use of jargon and make sure you understand it yourself before sprinkling your writing with it. If you are not secure in your understanding of key terms, phrases and concepts then using them inappropriately will simply serve to highlight the fact that you are confused (Smith et al., 2009). Inappropriately used terminology is a good way to simultaneously obscure your meaning and baffle your readers. It also acts as a 'red flag' to examiners by suggesting that your knowledge of the subject may not be as sound and secure as it should be.

One issue that often causes problems for undergraduate students who are grappling with sentence structure centres on punctuation. The problems can be neatly grouped into two broad categories; punctuation that is missing and punctuation that is there when it should not be. Below lists three of the most common punctuation marks that often trip students up (commas, colons/semicolons, apostrophe) and provides guidance on how they should be used.

Points to Think About – Common Punctuation Problems

1. Indiscriminate use of commas rather than using them to

    ● separate items in lists, for example: You have a duty to abide by
      ethical principles and practices such as doing good, avoiding harm,
      confidentiality, anonymity, obtaining informed consent and ensuring
      participant autonomy.
    ● separate clauses in sentences, for example: Some researchers adopt a
      positivist approach to their enquiries, others are more interpretivist.
    ● bracket words, for example: Facing a dissertation for the first time
      is a daunting prospect, however, and partly by breaking it down into
      more manageable components, the challenge will come to seem less
      insurmountable.

2. Uncertain and inaccurate use of colons and semicolons instead of using:

    ● colons to introduce lists or quotations, for example:

      ○ In this assignment I will critically appraise three key areas related
        to inclusive practice, these include the standards versus inclusion
        agenda; the extent to which special schools can be viewed as
        inclusive; the challenges faced by mainstream schools in meeting the
        needs of disabled students.
      ○ When asked about her pretend use of the mobile phone by the
        nursery nurse, Helen (aged 4) answered: 'I'm phoning Sarah to see if
        she can pick me up from nursery.'

    ● semicolons to separate parts of a sentence that are linked but not
      sufficiently closely to warrant the use of a comma, for example:

      ○ Good dissertations consider potential alternative explanations and
        interpretations of any findings during analysis; all data, even that
        which may be contradictory, discrepant or inconvenient is considered
        rather than being omitted or quietly disposed of.

3. Erratic and inconsistent use of apostrophes when in fact the apostrophe
    should be used to

    ● indicate missing letters, for example: we'll (we will), you're (you are),
      it's (it is/has). Remember, these contractions are normally avoided in
      academic writing unless you are reporting speech or quoting.
    ● denote the possessive, for example: Piaget's theories, the reader's
      perspective, the dissertation's central theme. Remember 'its' is an
      exception to this use of the apostrophe in that it is never used to denote
      the possessive, for example: 'The policy had failed to achieve its primary
      objective.'

At the level of paragraphs you need to remember that a paragraph is a collection of sentences that are supposed to coalesce around a particular theme, issue or idea (Osmond, 2016). Usually the opening sentence in a paragraph introduces the theme of the paragraph. This theme is then discussed further and elaborated on in the subsequent sentences while the final sentence is sometimes used to link the paragraph to the rest of your dissertation and/or the next paragraph. If you find yourself moving on to discuss a new idea or theme therefore, perhaps it is time for a new paragraph (Kirton and McMillan, 2007). Although paragraphs are bound to vary in length you should edit and redraft material to avoid micro or macro versions. Individual and paired sentences masquerading as paragraphs will simply serve to give an atomized and fragmented feel to your writing. At the other extreme vast, densely packed paragraphs covering whole pages threaten to intimidate and demoralize your readers while simultaneously making it harder for them to understand your meaning. It is important to signal clearly where your paragraphs start and finish and this could be done in a number of ways – for example, by indenting the first line or by inserting a line space between paragraphs. You should consult your dissertation handbook to find out what conventions, if any, your tutors expect you to follow.

Points to Think About – Sentences Masquerading as Paragraphs

Practitioners can work with parents to support children's physical development, for example by requesting that children practice dressing and undressing unaided to help develop their fine motor skills or by giving additional opportunities for outdoor play to increase confidence, balance and control to develop locomotor skills.

Because paragraphs are thematic it is not uncommon for certain words, phrases or concepts to crop up repeatedly in quick succession. For example, look at the number of times the word 'paragraph' appeared in the previous paragraph. Inevitably on occasions this repetition is unavoidable but in other instances there will be opportunities to vary the terms you use to improve the flow and reduce the sense of tedium. You do, however, need to be careful not to overcompensate as there are also times when in the interests of precision only that particular word or phrase will do. This said, a thesaurus can be an invaluable aid when writing a dissertation (Bell, 2014).

At the level of sections or chapters, meanwhile, there also needs to be a logical sense of progression through the dissertation and you need to signal your intentions to your readers (Greetham, 2009). Headings and subheadings may help you to signpost in this way but if your dissertation makes use of subheadings below the level of chapter titles make sure you check for consistency in font type and size across the various sections. Each section will also need introducing and summarizing. This does not have to take up a large amount of space but an introduction helps the reader to understand the purpose of the section within the dissertation as a whole while a summary allows you to reinforce, reiterate and recap on the key points you wish to get across. Signposting like this helps your readers to make explicit links and build bridges between the different sections of your dissertation.

Examples – Signposting in the Text

- As the previous paragraph demonstrated …
- In summary therefore …
- Put another way …
- Turning now to …
- The following chapter …

A further issue to look out for with a dissertation that has been written in sections over an extended period of time is that of tense. Methodology and methods sections are often begun prior to conducting data collection and so early drafts may be in the future tense; however, analysing the data will inevitably involve the use of the past tense. The dissertation should be integrated rather than appearing as a collection of discrete and unrelated chapters; the different sections ought to refer to and inform one another. Prior to handing your work in, therefore, you may need to check that the tense employed is consistent and/or appropriate and this will usually mean that the final version of the work adopts the past tense as standard. Your supervisors will be aware of the pitfalls and will be able to alert you to any inconsistencies if and when they are asked to feedback on draft material.

Proofreading, drafting, redrafting and editing will all help you to become increasingly effective in getting to the point clearly and succinctly (Greetham, 2009). These activities are also vital if you are to spot problems such as simple spelling and grammatical errors which, if allowed to mount up, will cost you dearly in marks but which are easily rectified, provided you take the time to check before handing your work in (Osmond, 2016). Below is a list of some of the more common errors.

Points to Think About – Common Errors

Watch out for some of the more common errors such as:

- writing the same word twice, for example: … the the … Or … they they …;
- using the wrong version of similar sounding words, for example:
  - its and it's
  - there, they're and their

Points to Think About – Cont'd

- o   to, too and two
- o   right and write
- o   your and you're
- o   practice and practise
- o   effect and affect
- o   where and were

- misspelling simple words, for example:
  - o   swop instead of swap
  - o   emphasize instead of emphasise
- giving incorrect or misspelled names for key authors, ideas and terms associated with your research, for example:
  - o   discussing the work of Harold instead of Howard Gardner in a dissertation about multiple intelligences; or
  - o   referring to a Language Attainment Device instead of Language Acquisition Device (LAD) in a literature review focusing on Chomsky and the development of young children's spoken language.

Having said previously that when writing you should try to become true word processors the reverse may be true when it comes to proofreading and editing. Many people find this activity quite difficult to do on screen and prefer instead to be able to lay a printout on the table in front of them before annotating it manually. Whichever approach you adopt it is advisable to allow for the passage of time before proofreading. When you are working on draft text for any length of time you can sometimes come to see what you believe to be there rather than what is actually there. The phrase 'I can't see the wood for the trees' sums it up quite nicely. Spending a day or two on another task therefore can give you a valuable breathing space or 'time out' so that you can return to the draft material refreshed and better able to spot the problems (Bell, 2014).

Ideas to Use – Proofreading

Proofread the following sentence:

Planning ahead and clearing some time in you're dairy for the day's imediately following the reciept of formative feedback is an affective way reducing the risk that you will forget or omit any thing important.

A corrected version can be found at the end of this chapter (p. 255).

Writing 'academically': Being critical, reflective and analytical

The technical academic expectations and protocols are important but there is another equally important intellectual dimension to academic writing. Of the two dimensions this latter one is probably harder to master. Academic writing is not just defined by whether you deftly avoid the use of the first person or type 'were not' instead of 'weren't'. Adopting an academic style of writing also requires you to become more thoughtful, analytical, measured and critically reflective when you write. When writing your dissertation you will be expected not only to adhere to the technical protocols associated with academic writing, but also to

- comment on, as well as describe, key works, concepts and ideas in your literature review, acknowledging any disputes and alternative, contrasting or competing viewpoints that may exist;
- weigh up the pros and cons, strengths and weaknesses, costs and benefits of alternative methodological approaches and data-collection tools and to provide a coherent and convincing rationale for your final decisions;
- reflect on your solutions to any ethical dilemmas or practical problems associated with sample selection and/or data collection;
- remain open to alternative interpretations of the data even when you are clear about your own position on something;
- base any conclusions on the literature and/or the data collected and avoid 'over-claiming'.

Example – Being More Thoughtful and Reflective in Your Writing

First draft

Rainbow (1996) supports the notion that there are problems in the music training of primary teachers. Kelly (2002) commented that some head teachers are forced to rely on their own classroom teachers to teach music and that it is wrong to assume that all these teachers are musically orientated and can easily teach the subject. Spodek et al. (1987, p. 220) state, 'Just as teachers can have a good art education program without being artists themselves, they can also plan and implement good music experiences with young children even though they are not good musicians themselves.' Hennessey (1998) describes the isolation of music lessons when they are taught by visiting specialists as the specialists are often unable to discuss their work with teachers and be involved in planning. Hennessey (1998) continues by saying that there is a place for specialists to teach music, but improving the knowledge and skills of the full-time teachers would be more beneficial. Hallam (2002) suggests that one method of developing teachers' skills is by allowing peripatetic teachers to teach some classes, in turn giving the teachers some valuable in-service training with minimal costs.

Example – Cont'd

Second draft

Kelly (2002) commented that some head teachers are forced to rely on their own class teachers to teach music and that it is wrong to assume that all these teachers are musically orientated and can easily teach the subject. However, perhaps as Rainbow suggests the problem lies more in training rather than orientation (Rainbow, 1996). With the correct training teachers should be able to teach the basic skills needed for music education. Spodek et al. state:

> Just as teachers can have a good art education program without being artists themselves, they can also plan and implement good music experiences with young children even though they are not good musicians themselves. (Spodek et al., 1987, p. 220)

This statement reflects the importance of good quality teacher training to enable teachers to become as competent in teaching music as they are in teaching art. Having said this, specialist music teachers may be a necessity when music education has advanced beyond the basic skills which are required in the early years for teaching music. Specialist music teachers might raise standards of music education and improve the musical abilities of children from a young age.

However, while initially the idea of using specialist music teachers seems a sound one, there are counter arguments; segregating music from other lessons by having specialist teachers, for example, may encourage the idea that music is somehow different from and unrelated to other subjects. Hennessey describes the isolation of music lessons when they are taught by visiting specialists and how this approach may not contribute to musical development across a school as a result of the specialists having little or no opportunity to discuss their work with teachers and be involved in wider planning (Hennessey, 1998). For Hennessey there may be a place for specialists to teach music, but improving the knowledge and skills of the full-time teachers would be more beneficial (Hennessey, 1998). That said, the two things are not necessarily mutually exclusive as one method of developing teachers' music skills and knowledge could involve peripatetic music experts co-teaching classes as a means of providing the regular teachers with some valuable in-service training at minimal cost (Hallam, 2002).

The authority and power of the printed, published word can make it hard at times for undergraduate students to find a way of expressing their own thoughts and ideas with confidence. Many are left feeling unworthy or at least unequal to the task of passing comment on the work of influential and authoritative bodies or eminent and experienced scholars. For others the notion of what it means to be academically critical becomes confused with common sense, everyday uses of the term which are largely concerned with identifying only the negative aspects of something. However, students critiquing research publications and data collection as part of their dissertations are as concerned with the strengths and positive aspects of the different studies they encounter as they are with any weaknesses or shortcomings associated with them.

Examples – Useful Phrases When Analysing and Thinking Critically

According to …
… concluded that …
… found that …
… claimed by …
… asserted that …
… suggests that …
… indicate that …

Source: Walliman, 2006.

Writing the different sections of your dissertation

Writing the 'preliminaries'

The 'preliminaries' in this instance refer to those early sections of your dissertation such as the title page, the contents page, any acknowledgements and the abstract. Ironically some of these elements may be both the earliest things you write and some of the last. It is not uncommon, for example, for students' dissertation titles to 'evolve' during the course of the dissertation itself. Similarly, contents pages too are likely to develop over time. Projects that involve numerous versions as a result of editing mean that the sequencing and location of different sections and passages will alter from version to version and so inevitably contents pages are best left until quite late in the process of writing. Contents pages need to include details of any tables, figures or appendices. Tables usually contain lists or numerical data of some kind while figures usually involve exemplar and other non-numerical data; it must be said though that these are not hard and fast rules and you should consult your supervisor about precisely what approach to adopt (Bell, 2014).

In addition to the obvious need for title and contents pages, dissertations will usually need to make space for an acknowledgements page particularly those involving primary data collection where there is a need to thank research participants or any gatekeepers of one kind or another without whose cooperation your whole project would have ground to halt even before it had started (Bell, 2014). These acknowledgements should not undermine your efforts to give anonymity to participants elsewhere in the main body of the dissertation. It is also customary to mention the support and guidance from your supervisor at this stage.

Some universities and courses also require the inclusion of an abstract as part of the final submission. An abstract is a short paragraph of the kind you will have seen in refereed journals that provides the reader with an 'at-a-glance' overview or thumbnail sketch of the dissertation's contents. It needs to set out the purpose or focus of your research; the methodological tradition within which the work is located; information on the data-collection tools used and finally a brief synopsis of the main findings and conclusions. Abstracts do not usually exceed 150–250 words.

The introduction normally accounts for between 5 and 10 per cent of the total word count and in it you will set the scene by identifying your chosen theme, topic, theory or question. You need to outline the underlying motivation or rationale behind this choice of theme and will briefly highlight some of the salient issues, debates and arguments involved (Smith et al., 2009). This rationale may cite prior or current personal experience or it may draw on existing literature and research in the field; alternatively, your theme may originate from events and activities in the national or global contexts. As with the rest of the preliminaries your introduction may well be one of the last as well as one of the first pieces of your dissertation to be written and for the same reasons. The final version should whet the readers' appetites, get them interested in the topic and prepare them for what is to come before leading (usually) into the subsequent literature review.

Checklist – The Sequence of Your Preliminaries

- Title page: full title, name of author, month and year of completion
- Contents: page numbers for each chapter/section, heading and subheading as well as lists of tables, figures and appendices
- Acknowledgements page
- Abstract page
- Introduction

Writing your literature review

Your review of the literature is your chance to demonstrate your familiarity with, and understanding of, previous and contemporary thinking about your topic and this often accounts for 25–30 per cent of the word limit of an undergraduate dissertation. In the case of literature-based projects this percentage figure may be much larger as the literature, analysis and discussion elements of the dissertation may run 'long and thin' through much of the thesis. Drafting the literature review is often one of the first tasks you will undertake when completing your dissertation but it continues for a long time. Those of you engaged in primary data collection, for example, will still find yourselves referring back to, updating and amending your literature review even while engaged in field work. On the one hand, you are trying to locate your project within the wider context; however, you will simply not have the space to include everything, even assuming that would be desirable. You need to ensure that any general literature review leads on to a more tightly focused review centred on your research question or theory and you must not allow yourself to be sidetracked or distracted by some of the more tangential or peripheral issues associated with your chosen topic. The first part of the literature review should map out the key elements that you are going to discuss, explain the logic of the order that you have chosen to discuss these in and make clear the links between the literature and the topic of your own research.

The main body of the literature review involves much more than simply reporting or listing a string of findings from various authors and organizations. It is sometimes a good idea to step back from the detail to rough out which key ideas, issues or sources you want to prioritize and in what order; you need a plan. Using the 'literature map' technique (see Chapter 3) is one way of doing this and the ubiquity of information technology in contemporary education means that there are an increasing number of mind-mapping software packages (e.g. Inspiration, MindGenius) that will enable you to structure, plot and manipulate your ideas and thoughts on a given topic electronically. If you fail to plan there is a danger that your literature review becomes little more than a large annotated bibliography in carousel form as you summarize first the work of one author/source then another (see Chapter 1). Working out a plan, therefore, can help you to spot overreliance on particular sources both within the literature review as a whole and at particular points within the review. There is likely to be a bewildering array of sources, ideas and concepts to get to grips with and so it is important to be discriminating about which ones you include (Walliman, 2014). Although you will be expected to draw on a wide range of pertinent and reputable material you need to exercise your critical faculties in the literature review. Not all authors and organizations will be equally believable, reliable or authoritative. Your aim is not simply to repeat a set of different viewpoints; you also need to demonstrate your understanding of the reasons behind these arguments and to give your assessment and evaluation of the relative merits of them too (Booth et al., 2013).

The main part of the literature review is likely to be broken down into sections and subsections according to the themes, theories and issues in your literature map or plan. The order in which these are presented may have to be experimented with as you write; it may not be immediately obvious what the best sequence is. There needs to be a logical argument throughout to bind the review together as a whole and this may only emerge fully as you write. Within each element there should be a summary and possibly a critique of the different sources referred to, including any critical or controversial aspects. Compare and contrast what each study tells you and make sure you discuss similarities and differences between the findings from the different studies. Links need to be made between the various aspects of your review to demonstrate how they fit together and the logic of the order you have put them in. Explain the significance of the studies you are discussing in terms of your own study and others in the review. Give your view on the value of certain sources in informing the body of knowledge in the area and comment on the quality of any claims made or refer to other articles or items that critique the study. At the end of each section, summarize the main points made and link them to the next section. Where you draw conclusions such claims should be supported by some of the studies that you have chosen and you must be fair and even-handed in presenting contrasting opinions even if you have concluded that you do not share them. Finally, there needs to be a summary of the key issues and links to your own research, including a rationale for where your enquiry fits into the body of knowledge discussed and what your work will contribute to knowledge in the field.

A key consideration when writing a literature review is whether or not to use quotes. The printed word carries a certain authority which leaves some undergraduates wondering how they could possibly say something any better. However, academic writing is not simply a matter of stitching together a patchwork quilt of phrases and paragraphs lifted verbatim from other sources and tied together using a few of your own linking sentences, no matter how competently referenced. Quoting can use up a large amount of space with other people's words thus reducing the space available for you to set out your own understanding and thoughts. As a result you may decide it is more efficient to synthesize, paraphrase or précis some ideas drawn from the literature by putting things into your own words while all the time clearly referencing your sources (Pears and Shields, 2016).

Case Study – The Dangers of Over-quoting

Pete's latest sociology essay was being marked. When his tutor checked the word length she discovered that around 1,500 of the 2,000 words were quotations loosely strung together with a few of Pete's own words. There was little or no commentary or discussion by Pete. It was all referenced properly but it did not pass because only around 25 per cent of the work was Pete's and what there was did little more than provide a series of links between quotes.

However, there will be times where it does make perfect sense to quote directly and when you decide to do so there are certain conventions that you will need to adhere to (Pears and Shields, 2016). Quotations are there to support your arguments not to replace them. To begin with you must make sure that you lay out your quotes according to your course guidance or as advised by your supervisor. For example, quotes over a certain length such as anything over three lines or 30 words may have to be indented and single line spaced. Shorter quotes, words and phrases may be better incorporated into the main body of the text so as not to unduly interrupt the flow of your argument. Below are some examples of both approaches. Secondly, you will need to demonstrate that you understand the meaning or significance of any quotes or the problems and issues that they throw up. To do this you will be expected to introduce and/or follow up on any quotes used. It is also worth remembering that you may need to tinker with the original material in order to get to the heart of what it is that you need. If this happens you must make sure that any cuts or alterations are clearly shown (Pears and Shields, 2016). If you

- leave out any words you should use ellipsis (…) to indicate the missing content, for example: 'You do get more able children helping the others and sometimes it's not necessarily those that are more able generally. … That's good for their self-esteem.'
- add or substitute words in the interests of clarity you must insert the words into the quote using square brackets [], for example: 'He used to be on it [Xbox 360] everyday, but at the minute he just wants to play out as soon as he comes home.'

Example – Setting Out Your Quotes: Indenting and Embedding

Support for writing development can be seen by some first-year students as irrelevant as they prioritize learning new subject knowledge over induction into more advanced writing practices (as do some of their lecturers). Similarly, the ubiquitous institutional response of creating free-standing, discrete academic writing support services has been shown to be far from unproblematic in terms of its impact:

'Students seek help when they get positive information about help opportunities, for example, how attending a review session will benefit their performance on an exam. First experiences getting help are predictive of follow-up requests for help. Sometimes cultural background and gender are factors, for example, students not part of a majority group may be less likely to seek help, especially if they feel isolated and "different." Men sometimes find it more difficult than women do to admit needing help. And, sometimes the students most in need of help are the least likely to request it' (Faculty Focus, 2017).

Support for academic writing in this form can often appear as an essentially remedial resource suitable only for the less able or the less well-prepared students. Even when referred to existing academic writing support services by their subject tutors the onus is on the students concerned to take the next step and this they do not always do.

Plagiarism is something that everyone must guard against throughout their dissertation (Neville, 2016). Although not confined to the literature review, this section of a dissertation holds dangers for the unwary as well as temptations for more knowing students. At its simplest plagiarism means deceiving your audience. It may be an intentional, conscious attempt to fool the person(s) marking your dissertation perhaps by trying to pass work off as your own when in fact you have copied it word for word from somewhere else, for example a book, a website or another student's assignment. Alternatively plagiarism could be unintentional and unconscious perhaps as a result of not properly referencing your sources in the text thereby giving the impression that you are trying to deceive when in fact it is a case of carelessness (Neville, 2016). It is worth noting that lack of intent may not protect you from censure or sanction. University authorities may well feel unable to make an accurate assessment about the reasons why plagiarism has occurred and as a result they are likely to focus simply on the fact that it has. A student claiming that an incident of plagiarism has happened due to poor study skills may discover therefore that this does not constitute a defence. Keeping meticulous records of your sources and mastering your institution's preferred referencing system when writing, making it clear when you are quoting and/or drawing on the work of others can do much to protect the unwary (Booth et al., 2013).

Another good habit to get into when trying to avoid charges of plagiarism is to exercise extreme caution about cutting and pasting large chunks of text from electronic sources directly into your draft dissertation; ideally, do not do it. Nor should you share or swap electronic files of draft material with your fellow students. Your supervisors are likely to know the literature as well as and often better than you, they will also have marked dissertations and other extended essays before and so will be sensitized as to what to expect and will often be quick to spot any sections of a dissertation that seem to originate elsewhere but which do not include any acknowledgements. It also worth noting that the technology that makes cutting and pasting so easy also makes tracking these sources much easier too.

Turnitin

Increasingly in many universities the software package Turnitin is being used to assist academics to spot plagiarism. In some institutions Turnitin is also being used formatively by students as a means of improving their use of sources when engaged in academic writing. Although very helpful the use of Turnitin is by no means unproblematic. To begin with Turnitin is not a plagiarism detection tool, it is a text matching tool. The judgement about plagiarism has to be an academic one. A student's assignment may have a Turnitin score of 25-30 per cent which could appear to indicate that large parts of the work have been plagiarized. However if it is not set up correctly beforehand the software may have included cover sheets and references in the score which would boost it misleadingly. Many of the other matches may be no larger than 1 per cent or 2 per cent as well as being perfectly referenced. In such cases it is hard to allege plagiarism. Equally a script with 10 per cent of copied and unreferenced text in a solid block might be. For this reason most institutions using Turnitin will provide training for both staff and students to learn how to interpret the scores.

Matches That Should NOT Get You into Trouble

- **Quotations**: properly referenced quotations can be ignored (although using too many quotes could result in your writing being regarded as too derivative);
- **References/Bibliographies**;
- **Matching formats**: for example assignment cover sheets;
- **Tables/charts/graphs**: as long as the source is properly referenced;
- **Small matches**: common phrases in a sentence or subject terminology will be detected but often there are no other words you could use;
- **Paraphrased text**: this will be highlighted even where words in the phrase have been changed. However provided your source has been properly cited and provided you don't overdo it, this would not normally be seen as plagiarism.

Writing the methodology and methods sections

At some point in your dissertation you will be expected to set out your methodological standpoint and to outline and justify your methods in the light of a clear statement, or restatement, of your research question. This is likely to take up between 10 and 20 per cent of the available word limit and in this section you will need to explain to the reader whether your work is rooted in positivist, interpretivist, critical, pragmatic or some other research tradition and to include a rationale for the thinking behind this particular methodological approach. For those of you undertaking a literature-based study you will need to set clear parameters on the scope of your project and to set out what theoretical perspective will underpin and inform your analysis and assessment of the data. Other important issues arising from and feeding into your methodological considerations that may well emerge in this section include your positionality and any ethical dimensions to your proposed project (Greetham, 2009; Walliman, 2014).

As well as reflecting on your methodology you will also need to include a similar commentary and rationale on your sources of data and the thinking behind your choice of data-collection methods. The discussion will acknowledge the advantages and disadvantages of any methods chosen, any dilemmas raised and the reasons for resolving them in the way that you did. You may have decided, for example, to use more than one means of data collection as a way of checking and verifying your results. Where your dissertation involves primary data collection of any kind you will also need to explain your decisions concerning sample selection and access.

Setting out, analysing and discussing your findings

In a dissertation the findings of the research may be reported separately and are then subsequently analysed but it is also possible to adopt a parallel rather than sequential approach to reporting and analysing your data. In total the various sections are likely to amount to between 35 and 40 per cent of your dissertation. Your supervisor will be able to advise you on the most appropriate approach to adopt for your work. Whichever approach is adopted your discussion will need to explain the process by which the data were analysed and to include some comment on the practicalities associated with data collection where they have resulted in any changes to your original intent. Perhaps, for example, you had planned some interviews which subsequently could not take place thus forcing you to alter your plans in response. You need to make sure that you report your findings honestly and that includes those findings that might be inconvenient or discrepant in some way.

Your data, suitably anonymized, may appear in a variety of forms. You may wish to include tables of various kinds to present numerical or quantitative data, such as charts, graphs or percentages. You may need to use figures which present the reader with text or images. Alternatively, you might be drawing on reported speech and interview transcripts. Irrespective of the findings that you are presenting clarity is essential; make sure any tables or figures are numbered properly and have headings or titles to explain what they are about and what any values represent. Graphical displays should also be accompanied by clear axes and column labels or, where column labels are not used, a legend.

In quantitative studies, discussion usually occurs in a separate section. This does not preclude you from presenting your discussion with your findings; however, if this suits you better, but do check this out with your module tutor or supervisor. The results-findings section of a quantitative dissertation should include information about your sample such as the size, number of males/females, age and so on. You can then proceed to convey your univariate or bivariate findings (and multivariate if you entered into this level of analysis) as they relate to your research questions (see Chapter 8). It is important not to present tables and graphs without accompanying these with some commentary. You should provide a brief summary that points out the more salient aspects of the visual displays used as they relate to your research questions. Remember, you should not include any findings that do not relate to your research questions. In a quantitative study the findings are discussed in relation to the literature but are not reinterpreted at this stage. The discussion in a quantitative study should

- compare your findings with the literature you reviewed, making links between your study and others or identifying differences in findings and commenting why there may be such differences;
- discuss the strengths and limitations of the methodology and methods;
- make recommendations for further research.

In qualitative studies one of the first decisions to make is whether to present the findings and then discuss them in relation to the literature or whether to combine these processes into one written account. It is common to separate these processes but some studies work better if the two processes are blended. You will need to ask your supervisor for advice on this if you are unsure. Any literature discussed in this section should already have been referred to in the literature review. When making comparisons between your findings and others you need to take into account differences in methodology, size of sample and recency of the studies you are comparing with and to comment on this. One of the simplest ways to write up your findings is to discuss them in terms of each theme using the themes and sub-themes as headings and stating what you have found in each section drawing on and interpreting the summarized data in the final version of your data summary chart (see Chapter 8). By this stage the themes should appear in a logical progression on the chart, but if this is not the case then now is the time to reorder them. There may be benefits in using direct quotes from your participants to illustrate particular issues. Qualitative studies are often written in some detail and the discussion and explanations illustrated with quotes and comments on the data. These should be included but should not overwhelm the discussion. In a qualitative study interpretation continues into the discussion stage as you seek to make meanings from your findings in relation to the literature. The discussion in a qualitative study should, therefore,

- focus on your key themes, explaining and interpreting the meanings of your findings;
- compare and contrast themes where applicable;
- compare your findings with the literature you reviewed, making links between your study and others or identifying differences in findings and commenting why there may be such differences.

Having set out your findings and explained the process of analysis you then need to discuss your findings. This will require you to use your data to illustrate any emerging themes to articulate what you think is important and why. You may also need to set out what you regard as the implications of your research for any research participants or for your subject discipline, your profession, your own learning and practice, society or indeed future research projects. Your interpretations and claims need to be justified and supported and so at this point you will find yourself referring back to your literature review and the findings of previous research in your chosen area.

Writing your conclusions

The final 10–15 per cent of your dissertation is your chance to succinctly sum up your conclusions, claims and thoughts about the process of research itself. In this section you will be expected to summarize, synthesize and recap on the main points and to state or restate your own position (Walliman, 2014). Most undergraduate dissertations will be small in scale and you will need, therefore, to premise any claims with an acknowledgement of the limitations of your work in terms of its scale and the implications this might have for drawing more generalizable conclusions (Bell, 2014). You may also decide that any claims you are making need to be qualified with some remarks about any compromises that had to be reached concerning things such as your data-collection methods or sample selection. In addition, you will need to acknowledge the presence of any findings that were unusual, unexpected, inconvenient or somehow out of line with the rest of your findings and to offer some thoughts on the possible reasons for this. In spite of such limitations you should still be able to provide thoughtful and reflective conclusions in response to your original research question. Below are some tips to help you pull this part of your dissertation together.

It may also be appropriate to make recommendations, albeit limited, including identifying areas for further study. Not all studies lead to recommendations but some will. It is important when considering this stage to think about the audience for your recommendations. It may be the setting you have completed your study in or the participants or even a wider audience. However, you have to bear in mind that you are recommending in the context of a small-scale study and as such you are making some suggestions for improvements or changes in that context. The recommendations need to be on a scale in keeping with the size of the study and must not be either too grandiose or too generalized. You cannot be absolute in terms of what your findings mean. Yours is a small study and while your findings are hopefully very interesting and relevant they do not constitute absolute 'proof' of anything. Therefore the language of your writing up should be tentative and acknowledge that your findings show possibilities but not certainties.

Checklist – Bringing Together Your Conclusions

- Start this section with a reminder to the reader about the original purpose of your research.
- When summarizing your findings and claims start with the strongest/most significant and work down towards the most tenuous/least important.
- Link your conclusions back to your original literature review and/or your underlying theoretical perspective.
- Where appropriate explain the significance of your findings for existing policy and practice (this will probably be at a local rather than a national level).
- Acknowledge any shortcomings or limitations to your work, including any relevant commentary on the process of carrying out your research.
- Do not introduce new literature and ideas (unless in the context of the final point below).
- Where appropriate set out what further research in the area might be useful.

Appendices

The purpose of your appendices is to illustrate the narrative contained in the main body of your dissertation using examples or supporting information but without breaking the flow of your writing. You need to take care not to use them as a dumping ground or to see them as a means of padding out your thesis. Nor should they be viewed as a cunning means of circumventing any word limits. It's worth noting that appendices are often not marked so there is no marks advantage to packing them out with material that is peripheral to your main arguments. In short, appendices should only include material that is important or relevant to your dissertation and you will not necessarily include everything. For example, if you have a dozen interview transcripts you might decide to include one as an example rather than all twelve. Alternatively if you have 50 questionnaire returns you are very unlikely to include all 50, one will suffice. Finally, don't forget that all the ethical issues considered when designing your research apply throughout your project. It is very easy to let something slip past you at this stage which could inadvertently identify a location or an individual so make sure you proofread these parts of your dissertation carefully to ensure that confidentiality and/or anonymity are not compromised

Setting out your 'postscripts'

At the back of your dissertation you will need to set out the sources that you have consulted in the completion of your project. It is important to get this right as your references help to demonstrate the extent of your knowledge and help you to guard against accusations of plagiarism (Neville, 2016). In addition, they provide a trail that would enable others to follow and build on your work (Pears and Shields, 2016). References can also provide examiners and other markers with an indicator of levelness and experienced markers will often turn to your references first to get a 'feel' for this before starting to read the dissertation itself. You should, therefore, refer to your course handbook and consult your research supervisor if you are unclear about referencing as the conventions about citation differ from course to course and from institution to institution. Some institutions or courses will, for example, expect you to adhere to a particular referencing style such as Harvard. Some institutions require a bibliography which includes every source you have looked at irrespective of whether you referred to them in the text or not; others are only interested in seeing a list of references, that is those sources that are cited in your dissertation. Irrespective of your institution's preferred approach to referencing your sources should be itemized in a single list and ordered alphabetically unless you are instructed to do otherwise in your course handbook or by your research supervisor.

Many dissertations also feature appendices, particularly if they are based on primary data collection of any kind. Appendices are a useful device for providing your readers with access to material such as data-collection tools, letters and other correspondence and samples of raw data without cluttering up and interrupting the flow of the main text. Appendices are also useful because frequently their contents do not count towards your overall word limit. This said there are some important points to bear in mind when putting your appendices together. To begin with they must not become a dumping ground for irrelevant information included simply to pad the dissertation out.

If you do not make reference to something in your dissertation it should not appear in your appendices. A second point to bear in mind is that it may not be necessary to include all your data in your appendices. You should consult with your research supervisor about what to include and/or leave out but if, for example, you have ten interview transcripts it may be acceptable to include a single transcript as an example of one of your data-collection methods rather than inserting all ten. If this is acceptable you should still retain the other data in a safe place until such time as you have successfully passed the dissertation. After that you should follow your institution's ethical procedures for dealing with such data. In some cases the expectation is that it must be destroyed; in others, the expectation is that it will be kept secure for a period of time first.

Summary of key points

- Bite the bullet and start writing early. Do not worry if your early sections are not perfect, they will improve as time goes on and you will feel much better because you have begun.
- Draw up a rough schedule showing the different sections of your dissertation, when you propose to do them and how many words you expect to allocate to each section.
- The technical aspects of academic writing (e.g. spelling, punctuation, signposting, referencing) can be mastered with practice so get into good habits such as spellchecking draft material and regular proofreading.
- Your writing will need to be analytical as well as grammatically correct. The two best ways to improve your critical thinking skills are to read widely and to discuss your thinking with your supervisor.

Ideas to Use – Proofreading (Corrected Version)

Planning ahead and clearing some time in your diary for the days immediately following the receipt of formative feedback is an effective way of reducing the risk that you will forget or omit anything important.

Reflective task

Here is a Turnitin report. Look carefully at this and reflect on whether or not you feel this is plagiarism and why / why not.

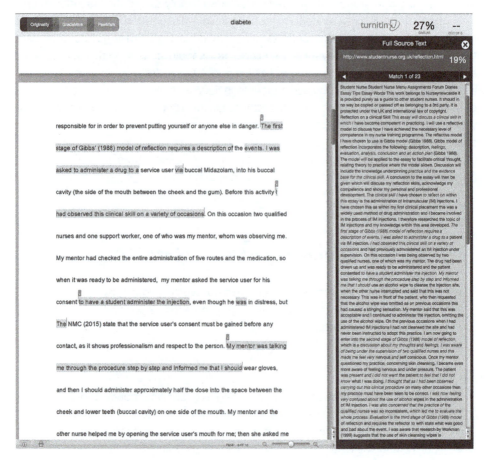

Link to companion website

https://bloomsbury.com/cw/successful-dissertations-second-edition/student-resources/9-writing-your-dissertation/

Recommended reading and further sources of information

Bell, J. (2014, 6th edition), *Doing Your Research Project: A Guide for First-time Researchers in Education, Health and Social Science*. Maidenhead: Open University Press.

Greetham, B. (2009), *How to Write Your Undergraduate Dissertation*. Basingstoke: Palgrave Macmillan.

Kirton, B. and McMillan, K. (2007), *Just Write: An Easy-to-use Guide to Writing at University*. Abingdon: Routledge.

Neville, C. (2016, 3rd edition), *The Complete Guide to Referencing and Avoiding Plagiarism*. London: Open University Press.

Osmond, A. (2016, 2nd edition), *Academic Writing and Grammar for Students*. London: SAGE Publications Ltd.

Pears, R. and Shields, G. (2016, 10th edition), *Cite Them Right: The Essential Guide to Referencing and Plagiarism*. London: SAGE Publications.

Walliman, N. (2014, 2nd edition), *Your Undergraduate Dissertation: The Essential Guide for Success*. London: Palgrave.

Glossary

Acquiescence effect refers to respondents consistently responding to items in the same way regardless of the appropriateness of that response. For example, opting for one or other of the extreme response ends of a rating scale in a consistent way throughout a battery of such scales; opting for the 'strongly agree' option across a battery of Likert Scales for instance

Bivariate analysis The analysis of two variables at a time

Causal relationship When a variable (the independent variable) causes a change in another (the dependent variable). This is otherwise referred to as a cause and effect relationship

Cause and effect relationship When a variable (the independent variable) causes a change in another (the dependent variable). This is otherwise referred to as a causal relationship

Conceptual definition of variables A conceptual definition of a variable tells you what that variable is; it defines it

Contingency tables Simple and commonly used methods for showing relationships between pairs of variables

Continuous variables Variables that vary in degree. Unlike discrete variables, they have possible values in between them. This allows for ranking or measurement to take place

Control group A group of research participants closely resembling an intervention group but not receiving the active medication or dependent variable under study, thus serving as a comparison group in the evaluation of result. If the dependent variables in the control and the group receiving the intervention are the same, it is something else that is causing the change and not the independent variable

Correlation A relationship between two or more variables where their values increase or decrease in conjunction with each other, sometimes in opposite directions

Cramér's V analysis of the relationship between pairs of nominal variables, only capable of a positive value

Dependent variable In experiments, these are the variables of interest to the researcher in terms of how, if at all, they are affected by an independent variable

Descriptive statistics The use of appropriate statistical techniques to transform potentially large amounts of numerical data into a form such as tables and/or charts, making the findings of the research easier to understand

Discrete variables Discrete (also known as categorical) variables vary in kind only in that they have no possible values in between them; they are only meaningful as whole numbers

Fixed response refers to questions where there are a set of predetermined answers for the respondent to choose from

Frequency tables show the number of participants in a sample and the percentage belonging to each of the categories of a particular variable

Independent variable In experiments, the independent variable is the one (there is only ever one independent variable) that is manipulated in some way (e.g. introduced, decreased, increased, etc.)

in order to see the effect this has on the dependent variable

Inferential statistics draws conclusions from data and establishes the extent to which the findings from a sample can be applied to the reference population from which that sample was drawn (Crossman 2016)

Interval-level variables Similar in nature to ordinal variables except that the distance between each value is equal. Temperature is a good example; the difference between 12 and 13 degrees centigrade is the same as the difference between 22 and 23 degrees centigrade, thus they are continuous

Journaling This refers to the process of keeping a written record (on paper or electronically) of the research process

Mean Another word for average and calculated in exactly the same way

Measures of central tendency A means of summarizing the distribution of variables by calculating mean, median and mode as a single figure or value that is typical of a distribution of values

Measures of dispersion Concerned with the extent of variation (or spread) of the data. Dispersion is most commonly measured in terms of standard deviation, which provides a measure of the average amount of variation around the mean value

Median The middle value of a distribution when the values are arranged in order of magnitude. There should be as many values above as below the midpoint when calculating the median

Mode The value that occurs most frequently in a distribution – for example, the commonest age in a sample

Multivariate analysis Analysis of three or more variables at a time

Nominal-level variables (e.g. gender, marital status) have no evaluative distinction in that they cannot be measured in terms of one being greater or lesser than the other. Their difference is therefore in kind as opposed to being quantitative

Non-probability sampling Used as an umbrella term to refer to sampling methods that do not require random selection

Operational definition of variables An operational definition of variables translates them into something that can be counted in some way (this is called operationalization)

Ordinal-level variables do have evaluative distinction. Although, like nominal variables, they can fall into distinct categories and so are discrete in nature, unlike nominal variables, they can be ordered or ranked in some order of importance within that category. For example, individuals can perceive their state of health as excellent, good or poor. Similarly, classifications of socio-economic status are good examples of ordinal-level variables

Pearson's Correlation Coefficient (Pearson's r) A measure of the strength of the association, if any, between two interval/ratio variables and takes on a value between +1 and –1, with 0 indicating no relationship

Phi coefficient A measure of the degree of a relationship between two dichotomous variables (e.g. gender and a yes response where the possibilities were simply a yes or a no)

Positionality This refers to your own position – for example, your beliefs, experiences and values in relation to your research

Probability sampling Sampling methods that do rely on random selection

Ratio-level variables have the same properties as interval variables but differ in that they have an absolute zero point

Reflexivity This calls for the researcher to be aware of their own positionality and how this might influence their research

Reliability in quantitative research, reliability refers to the strength of a measure to measure in the same way across time, situation and researcher

Research proposal This is usually a form that provides a brief summary of the research you intend to do. It will include the literature you intend to focus on, the methodology and methods you will use, the participants, the ethical issues, an outline of how you will analyse the data

Response style Associated with rating scales and refers to how strongly opinionated people tend to opt for extreme responses, while more cautious individuals consistently opt for the more moderate responses

Social desirability effect refers to a tendency on the part of some respondents to respond according to the option that they perceive as being the most socially desirable

Spearman's rank correlation coefficient (Spearman's rho) denotes the strength of a linear relationship between two variables taking on a value between +1 and −1. Spearman's rho is used where the pairs of variables are either both ordinal or where one variable is ordinal and the other interval/ratio

Standard deviation A measure of the average amount of variation around the mean value

Univariate analysis The analysis of one variable at a time

Validity Concerned with the truthfulness of the conclusions generated by a piece of research. In other words, has the research been conducted in such a way that we can believe its findings to be true

Variable Anything that can differ between people, places and situations

References

Albon, D. and Mukherji, P. (2014). *Research Methods in Early Childhood: An Introductory Guide*. London, United Kingdom: SAGE Publications.

Alderson, P. and Morrow, V. (2011, 2nd edition). *The Ethics of Research with Children and Young People*. London: SAGE.

Bell, A. (2007). 'Designing and testing questionnaires for children', *Journal of Research in Nursing*, 12 (5): 460–9.

Bell, J. (2014, 6th edition). *Doing Your Research Project: A Guide for First-time Researchers in Education, Health and Social Science*. Maidenhead: Open University Press

Bell, J. and Waters, S. (2014, 6th edition). *Doing your Research Project: A Guide for First-time Researchers*. Maidenhead: Open University Press.

Berelson, B. (1952). *Content Analysis in Communication Research*. New York: Free Press.

Booth A., Papaioannou D. and Sutton A (2013, reprinted). *Systematic Approaches to a Successful Literature Review*. London: SAGE Publications.

Borgers, N., De Leeuw, E. and Hox, J. (2000). 'Children as respondents in survey research: Cognitive development and response quality', in Bell, A. (ed.), 'Designing and testing questionnaires for children'. *Journal of Research in Nursing*, 12 (5): 460–9.

Bryman, A. (2008, 3rd edition). *Social Research Methods*. Oxford: Oxford University Press.

Bryman, A. (2015, 5th edition). *Social Research Methods*. Oxford: Oxford University Press.

Bryman, A. (2016, 5th edition). *Social Research Methods*. New York: Oxford University Press.

Bryman, A. (2016, 5th edition). *Social Research Methods*. Oxford: Oxford University Press.

Burnard, P., Gill, P., Treasure, E. and Chadwick, B. (2008). Analysing and presenting qualitative data *British Dental Journal* 204: 429–32.

Calder, J. and Sapsford, R. (2006, 2nd edition). 'Statistical techniques', in Sapsford, R. and Jupp, V. (eds), *Data Collection and Analysis*. London: Sage.

Clark, R. (2013). *Childhood in Society for the Early Years*. London: Sage.

Clough, P and Nutbrown, C. (2012, 3rd edition). *A Students Guide to Methodology*. London: Sage.

Cohen, L., Manion, L. and Morrison, K. (2011, 7th edition). *Research Methods in Education*. London: Routledge.

Couper, M. P. (2000), 'Web surveys: A review of issues and approaches'. *Public Opinion Quarterly*, 64 (4): 464–94.

Craig, S. (1992). 'The effect of day part on gender portrayals in television commercials: A content analysis'. *Sex Roles: A Journal of Research*, 26 (5): 197–213.

Cresswell, J. (2013, (3rd edition). *Qualitative Inquiry and Research Design: Choosing among Five Approaches*. ThousandOaks, CA: Sage.

Cresswell, J. W. (2014, 4th edition). *Research Design- Qualitative, Quantitative, and Mixed Methods Approaches*. London: Sage.

Crossman A. (2016). *Understanding Descriptive vs. Inferential Statistics*. Retrieved from http://sociology.about.com/od/Statistics/a/Descriptive-inferential-statistics.htm.

Davidson, C., Neale, J. and Hindman, D. (2000). *Abnormal Psychology*. Chichester: John Wiley and Sons.

Davies, M. and Hughes N. (2014, 2nd edition). *Doing a Successful Research Project Using Qualitative and Quantitative Methods*. Basingstoke: Palgrave Macmillan.

Denscombe, M. (2009, edition). *Ground Rules for Social Research Guidelines for Good Practice*. Maidenhead, England: Open University Press/McGraw-Hill.

Denscombe, M. (2012, 4th edition). *The Good Research Guide: For Small-Scale Social Research Projects*. Maidenhead: Open University Press.

Denscombe, M. (2014). *The Good Research Guide: For Small-Scale Research Projects*. Maidenhead, United Kingdom: Open University Press.

Denscombe, M. (2014, 5th edition) *The Good Research Guide for Small-Scale Social Research Projects*. Milton Keynes: McGraw Hill Education.

Denzin, N. K. and Lincoln, Y. S. (2011, 4th edition). *The Sage Handbook of Qualitative Research*. London: Sage.

Dillman, D. A. and Smyth, J. D. (2009). *Internet, Mail and Mixed Mode Surveys*. New York: John Wiley and Sons.

Divyadeepa, E. (2015). *Sampling Techniques in Educational Research*. Raleigh, USA: Lulu Publications.

Edwards, R. and Holland, J. (2013) *What is Qualitative Interviewing?* London: Bloomsbury.

Fenton, N., Bryman, A. and Deacon, D. (1998). *Mediating Social Science*. London: Sage.

Fielding, J. and Gilbert, N. (2006). *Understanding Social Statistics*. London: Sage.

Finnegan, R. (2006, 2nd edition). 'Using documents', in Sapsford, R. and Jupp, V. (eds), *Data Collection and Analysis*. London: Sage.

Fontana, A. and Frey, J. H. (1998). 'Interviewing: the art of science', in Denzin, N. K. and Lincoln, Y. S. (eds), *Collecting and Interpreting Qualitative Materials*, 361–7. London: Sage.

Frey, J. H. (2004). 'Telephone surveys', in Lewis-Beck, M. S., Bryman, A. and Liao, T. F. (eds), *The Sage Encyclopaedia of Social Science Research Methods*. London: Sage.

Gauntlett, D (2015), 'The LEGO System as a tool for thinking, creativity, and changing the world', in *Making Media Studies: The Creativity Turn in Media and Communications Studies*. New York: Peter Lang.

Giddens, A. 1987. *Sociology and Modern Social Theory*. Cambridge: Polity.

Gra, C. and Kinnear, P. (2012). *IBM SPSS Statistics 19 Made Simple*. Hove: Psychology Press.

Green and Stoneman, (2015, 4th edition), 'Formulating research questions', in Gilbert, G. and Stoneman, P. (eds), *Researching Social Life*. London: Sage.

Greetham B. (2009) *How to Write Your Undergraduate Dissertation*. Basingstoke: Palgrave Macmillan

Greig., A., Taylor, J. and Mackay, T. (2012, 2nd edition). *Doing Research with Children* London: Sage.

Grix, J. and Watkins, G. (2010). *Information Skills: Finding and using the Right Resources*.

Grover, S. (2004). 'Why won't they listen to us? On giving power and voice to children participating in social research', *Childhood*, 11 (1): 81–93.

Gubrium, J. F. and Holstein, J. A. (eds) (2002). *Handbook of Interview Research: Context and Method*. Thousand Oaks, CA: Sage.

Hamp-Lyons, L. and Heasley, B. (2006, 2nd edition). *Study Writing: A Course in Writing Skills for Academic Purposes*. Cambridge: Cambridge University Press

Homan, R. (1992). *The Ethics of Social Research*. New York: Longman.

Horkheimer (1937) Traditional and Critical Theory, tr. Jeremy J. Shapiro, (1972) in *Max Horkheimer, Critical Theory*. New York: Herder & Herder.

King, N. and Horrocks, C. (2010). *Interviews in Qualitative Research*. London: SAGE.

Kirton, B. and McMillan, K. (2007). *Just Write: An Easy-to-use Guide to Writing at University*. Abingdon: Routledge

Kodish, E. (2005). *Ethics and Research with Children: A Case-based Approach*. New York: Oxford University Press.

Kvale, S. and Brinkmann, S. (2015, 3rd edition). *InterViews Learn Craft of Qualitative Research Interviewing*. London: Sage.

Lea, M. and Creme, P. (2003, 2nd edition). *Writing at University: [a guide for students]*. Philadelphia: Open University Press.

Liamputtong, P. (2007). *Researching the Vulnerable: A Guide to Sensitive Research Methods*. London: Sage Publications.

Lincoln, Y. and Denzin, N. (2011, 4th edition). *The Sage Handbook of Qualitative Research*. London: Sage.

MacKay, T., Taylor, J. and Greig, A. (2012, 2nd edition). *Doing Research with Children: A Practical Guide*. Los Angeles: Sage Publications.

MacNaughton, G., Rolfe, S. and Siraj-Blatchford, I. (2001). *Doing Early Childhood Research – International Perspectives on Theory and Practice*. Maidenhead, Berkshire: Open University Press.

Malcolm, T., Waldman, J., Todd, M. and Smith, K. (2009). *Doing Your Social Science Dissertation: A Practical Guide for Undergraduates*. New York, NY: Taylor & Francis.

Malim, T. and Birch, A. (1997). *Research Methods and Statistics*. Basingstoke: Palgrave Macmillan.

Mangione, T. (1995). *Mail Surveys: Improving the Quality*. Applied Social Research Methods Series,

Marshall C. and Rossman, G. B. (2006, 4th edition). *Designing Qualitative Research*. Thousand Oaks, CA: Sage.

Marvasti, A. (2004). *Qualitative Research in Sociology: An Introduction*. Thousand Oaks, CA: SAGE Publications.

McCall, M. J. (1984). 'Structured field observation'. *Annual Review of Sociology*, 10: 263–82.

McCartan, K. and Robson, C. (2013, 4th edition). *Real World Research*. United Kingdom: Wiley-Blackwell (an imprint of John Wiley & Sons Ltd).

Miles, M. and Huberman, A. (1994, 2nd edition). *Qualitative Data Analysis: An Expanded Sourcebook*. London: Sage.

Moon, J. (2004). *A Handbook of Reflective and Experiential Learning: Theory and Practice*. New York: Routledge Falmer.

Morrow, A., Morrow, V., and Alderson, P. (2011, 2nd edition). *Ethics, Social Research and Consulting with Children and Young People*. London, United Kingdom: Barnardo's.

Mrug, S. and Windle, M. (2010). Prospective effects of violence exposure across multiple contexts on early adolescents' internalizing and externalizing problems. *Journal of Child Psychology and Psychiatry*, 51: 953–61. doi:10.1111/j.1469-7610.2010.02222.x.

Mukherji, P. and Albom, D. (2010). *Research Methods in Early Childhood*. London: Sage.

Neville C. (2016, 3rd edition). *The Complete Guide to Referencing and Avoiding Plagiarism*. London: Open University Press.

Nutbrown, C. and Clough, P. (2012, 3rd edition). *A Student's Guide to Methodology: Justifying Enquiry*. London: SAGE Publications.

Oliver, P. (2010, 2nd edition). *The Student's Guide to Research Ethics*. Maidenhead, England: McGraw-Hill/Open University Press.

Pears, R. and Shields, G. (2016, 10th edition). *Cite Them Right: The Essential Referencing Guide*. London: Palgrave.

Punch, K. F. (1998). *An Introduction to Social Research: Quantitative and Qualitative Approaches*. London: Sage.

Punch, K. (2014, 2nd edition). *Introduction to Social Research*. London: SAGE.

Ridley, D (2012). *The Literature Review: A Step-By-Step Guide For Students* (Sage Study Skills Series). London: Sage.

Roberts-Holmes, G. (2014, 3rd edition). *Doing your Early Years Research Project: A Step by Step Guide*. London, United Kingdom: SAGE Publications.

Robson, C. (2009, 1st edition). *Real World Research*. Oxford: Blackwell.

Robson, C. and McCartan, K. (2015, 4th edition). *Real World Research*. London: Wiley.

Robson, C. and McCartan, K. (2016, 4th edition). *Real World Research*. Chichester, West Sussex, UK: Wiley.

Rose, G. (2016, 4th edition). *Visual Methodologies: An Introduction to Researching with Visual Materials*. Maidenhead: Oxford University Press.

Rosenberg, M. (1968). *The Logic of Survey Analysis*. New York: Basic Books.

Sallant, P. and Dillman, D. A. (1994). *How to Conduct Your Own Survey*. Chichester: Wiley and Sons.

Sargeant, J. and Harcourt, D. (2012). *Doing Ethical Research with Children*. Maidenhead: Open University Press.

Seale, C. (2011, 3rd edition). *Researching Society and Culture*. London: Sage Publications.

Shaw, C., Brady, L. and Davey, C. (2011). *Guidelines for Research with Children and Young People*. London: NCB Research Centre

Shuy, R. W. (2002). 'In-person versus telephone interviewing', in Gubrium J. F. and Holstein J. A. (eds), *Handbook of Interview Research: Context and Method*, 537–55. London: Sage.

Silverman, D. (2011, 1st edition). *Interpreting Qualitative Data*. London: SAGE.

Silverman, D. (2015, 5th edition). *Interpreting Qualitative Data: A Guide to the Principles of Qualitative Research*. Los Angeles: SAGE Publications.

Smith, K., Todd, M. and Waldman, J. (2009), *Doing Your Undergraduate Social Science Dissertation*.

Smith, P. (2002, 5th edition). *Writing an Assignment: Proven Techniques from a Chief Examiner that Really Gets Results*. Oxford: How To Books.

Stevens, S. S. (1951). 'Mathematics, measurement and psycho-physics', in Stevens S. S. (ed.) *Handbook of Experimental Psychology*, 1–49. New York: John Wiley and Sons.

Sumsion, J. (2000). Negotiating Otherness: A male early childhood educator's gender positioning. *International Journal of Early Years Education*, 8(2): 129–40.

Swetnam, D. (2004, 3rd edition). *Writing Your Dissertation*. How To Books Ltd.

Thorne, S. (2000). Data analysis in qualitative research *Evidence-based nursing Vol 3 Issue 3 pp68-60*. University College London. Research Ethics at UCL. https://ethics.grad.ucl.ac.uk/. Last accessed 20-4-17

Walliman, N. (2014, 2nd edition). *Your Undergraduate Dissertation: The Essential Guide for Success*. London: SAGE Publications.

Walliman, N. (2015, 2nd edition). *Social Research Methods (SAGE Course companions)*. London: SAGE Publications.

Webb, E. J., Campbell, D. T., Schwartz, R. D. and Sechrest, L. (1966). *Unobtrusive Measures in the Social Sciences*. Chicago: Rand McNally.

Wevers, J. and McMillan, K. (2011, 2nd edition). *How to Write Dissertations and Project Reports* (Smarter Study Skills) Essex, England: Pearson Education Ltd.

Woodhead, M. and Maybin, J. (2003). *Childhoods in Context*. Chichester, United Kingdom: John Wiley, in association with the Open University.

Yin, R. (2014, 5th edition). *Case Study Research Design and Methods*. Thousand Oaks, CA: Sage.

Index